DUQUESNE STUDIES

Philosophical Series

20

FROM PHENOMENOLOGY
TO METAPHYSICS

REMY C. KWANT is Professor
of Philosophy at the University of
Utrecht. He is the author of numerous
books and articles about Marxism, existentialism, phenomenology and other
contemporary issues. In 1959 and 1965
he was Visiting Professor of Philosophy
at Duquesne University, where he has
been invited to return.

FROM PHENOMENOLOGY
TO METAPHYSICS

An Inquiry into the Last Period of Merleau-Ponty's Philosophical Life

by

Remy C. Kwant, Ph.D.

Duquesne University Press, Pittsburgh, Pa.
Editions E. Nauwelaerts, Louvain

DUQUESNE STUDIES

Philosophical Series

Andrew G. van Melsen, D.Sc., D.Ed., and Henry J. Koren, C.S. Sp. S.T.D., editors.

Library of Congress Catalog Card Number: 66-18452

©1966, by DUQUESNE UNIVERSITY

Volume Nine—*Maxwell J. Charlesworth,* PHILOSOPHY AND LINGUISTIC ANALYSIS. Pp. XIII and 234. Second impression. Price: paper $4.75, cloth $5.50.

Volume Ten—*Remy C. Kwant,* PHILOSOPHY OF LABOR. Pp. XI and 163. Price: paper $4.50, cloth $5.25. Italian and Spanish editions in preparation.

Volume Eleven—*Remy C. Kwant,* ENCOUNTER. Pp. VIII and 85. Second impression. Price: cloth $3.25. Published also in Dutch.

Volume Twelve—*William A. Luijpen,* EXISTENTIAL PHENOMENOLOGY. Pp. XIII and 355. Fourth impression. Price: cloth $6.25. Published also in Dutch. German and Spanish edition in preparation.

Volume Thirteen—*Andrew G. van Melsen,* SCIENCE AND TECHNOLOGY. Pp. X and 373. Price: paper $6.20, cloth $6.95. Published also in Dutch and German.

Volume Fourteen—*P. Henry van Laer,* PHILOSOPHY OF SCIENCE. PART TWO: A STUDY OF THE DIVISION AND NATURE OF VARIOUS GROUPS OF SCIENCES. Pp. XIII and 342. Price: paper $5.75, cloth, $6.50.

Volume Fifteen—*Remy C. Kwant,* THE PHENOMENOLOGICAL PHILOSOPHY OF MERLEAU-PONTY. Pp. IX and 257. Price: paper $4.50, cloth $5.25.

Volume Sixteen—*John A. Peters,* METAPHYSICS: A SYSTEMATIC SURVEY. Pp. XVIII and 529. Price: paper $9.00, cloth $9.75.

Volume Seventeen—*William A. Luijpen,* PHENOMENOLOGY AND ATHEISM. Pp. XIV and 342. Price: paper $5.75, cloth $6.50.

Volume Eighteen—*Martin G. Plattel,* SOCIAL PHILOSOPHY. Pp. XI and 346. Price: paper $7.20, cloth $7.95. Published also in Dutch and German.

Volume Nineteen—*Andrew G. van Melsen,* EVOLUTION AND PHILOSOPHY. Pp. 208. Price: paper $4.75, cloth $5.50. Published also in Dutch.

Volume Twenty—*Remy C. Kwant,* FROM PHENOMENOLOGY TO METAPHYSICS. Pp. 247. Price: paper $7.20, cloth $7.95.

In preparation
William A. Luijpen, PHENOMENOLOGY OF NATURAL LAW
Joseph J. Kockelmans, PHENOMENOLOGY AND PHYSICAL SCIENCE

TABLE OF CONTENTS

Contents

CHAPTER FOUR—LANGUAGE, PHILOSOPHY, BEING

Contents

INTRODUCTION

The author of this work in 1962 published a book on the philosophy of Merleau-Ponty,[1] whose English edition, *The Phenomenological Philosophy of Merleau-Ponty,* appeared in 1963 in the DUQUESNE STUDIES, *Philosophical Series.*[2] As the subject of the present work is again the philosophy of Merleau-Ponty, the reader will naturally expect an explanation of the relationship between this book and the preceding one.

The first book was a provisional synthesis of Merleau-Ponty's philosophy. It was a synthesis because, before writing the book, I had published about ten articles on the subject, and these had an analytical character. After having analyzed several aspects of Merleau-Ponty's philosophy, I felt the need to bring them together into a synthetic view. The synthesis had to be provisional because Merleau-Ponty was still living then. I knew that he was preparing a new book, and rumors were spreading of important changes in his philosophical thinking.

Merleau-Ponty died on May 3, 1961. Before his death he published one important article, "The Eye and the Mind."[3] Since his death a new book has been published, *The Visible and the Invisible,*[4] the character and composition of which I will explain later on in this introduction.

No Radical Break

There are indeed important changes in Merleau-Ponty's philosophy. In several notes, published in his last book, he explicitly criticizes some of his former points of view. The changes, however, do not have the

---

[1] R. C. Kwant, *De Fenomenologie van Merleau-Ponty,* Het Spectrum, Utrecht, 1962.

[2] Remy C. Kwant, *The Phenomenological Philosophy of Merleau-Ponty,* (DUQUESNE STUDIES, *Philosophical Series,* no. 15), Pittsburgh, 1963.

[3] Maurice Merleau-Ponty, "L'Oeil et l'Esprit." It was published in *Art de France,* 1961, no. 1, and reprinted in *Les Temps Modernes,* vol. 17, nos. 184-185, October 1961, pp. 193-227. When quoting this article, we use the reprint in *Les Temps Modernes.* It has also been published in the form of a book, Gallimard, Paris, 1964.

[4] Merleau-Ponty, *Le Visible et l'Invisible,* Gallimard, Paris, 1964. Hereafter quoted as *V.I.*

character of a radical break. He continues the fundamental direction of his former thought; but some central points of view, which formerly were presented as conclusions, have now become the starting point of a deeper reflection.[5] I will try to explain the changes of Merleau-Ponty's philosophy in this book.

This work is based primarily on two books and one article by Merleau-Ponty. The main source is, of course, the book published after his death. The article on the relationship between the eye and the mind, which I mentioned already, was written in the period in which Merleau-Ponty was working on this book; both are, therefore, closely connected. One other book of Merleau-Ponty, which was published in 1960, one year before his death, also is very important for our subject, viz., *Signs*.[6] It is a collection of articles. Some of them which were written as early as 1950[7] are not important for us here. Other articles, however, were composed when Merleau-Ponty was already preparing *The Visible and the Invisible*. We find there the questions, the terminology and the approach of Merleau-Ponty's last book.[8] *Signs*, consequently, partially belongs to our subject. It has an ambiguous character; in some of its parts it belongs to the former period, in others it announces the new one. Its real importance has become manifest by the publication of the later works.

When I published my first book on Merleau-Ponty's philosophy, I did not yet understand the importance of *Signs*. I noted the use of new terms, "the flesh of the world," "the invisible in the visible," etc.; but I was not aware that they were the announcement of a significant change in Merleau-Ponty's philosophy.[9] This is quite understandable. Merleau-Ponty's main work, *Phenomenology of Perception*, undoubtedly was the most important of his publications. *The Structure of Behavior* was a preparation for it; and the books which followed contained elaborations of points of view which had been implicit in Merleau-

---

[5] The dialectic relationship between man and world is, according to Merleau-Ponty, no longer the final source of all meaning, and contingency is no longer Merleau-Ponty's final philosophical perspective. These changes are the main reason why Merleau-Ponty's philosophy could become a metaphysics.

[6] Merleau-Ponty, *Signes*, Gallimard, Paris, 1960. English translation by Richard C. McCleary, *Signs*, Northwestern University Press, 1964.

[7] E.g., the article "On the Phenomenology of Language," *Signs* pp. 84-97.

[8] E.g., the article "The Philosopher and His Shadow," *Signs* pp. 159-181.

[9] Richard C. McCleary wrote an excellent preface to his English translation of *Signes*. He does not emphasize, however, the important changes which begin to reveal themselves in this book.

Ponty's earlier writings, or applications of his fundamental perspective in the practical field, or confrontations of his own thought with the views of other philosophers.[10] Although Merleau-Ponty's main work did not offer a system—insiders know that he was an enemy of any philosophical system[11]—it certainly contained a synthesis in which the deepest points of view were worked out systematically. None of the other works could be compared with the main one, and the other books, therefore, had to be read in the light of *Phenomenology of Perception.* Moreover, Merleau-Ponty did not explicitly criticize his former points of view. I was aware that there were new accents in *Signs,* but I was inclined to integrate them in the fundamental perspective of the principal work.

A New Perspective

The Visible and the Invisible, on the contrary, has a different character. It is quite clear that Merleau-Ponty intended to write a new synthesis of his fundamental points of view. The former one no longer satisfied him. The real meaning of several articles in *Signs* becomes clear in the light of Merleau-Ponty's last book. These articles, therefore, belong to the subject of the present work.

Merleau-Ponty did not finish his new book, he had only started it. The part he has written contains mainly a new confrontation with currents of philosophical thought with which he did not agree, viz., scientism, rationalism, Sartrian philosophy, and the essentialistic aspects of Husserl's thought. Merleau-Ponty had already confronted these currents of thought; but because he himself had come to new points of view, a new confrontation became unavoidable. This confrontation would evidently have been the introductory part of the new book. He finished this introduction, and also one brief chapter in which he started to work out his new philosophical position. Moreover, there are a number of notes. Merleau-Ponty often made short notes when thoughts came to his mind, and he usually dated them. In some of these notes we find an explicit criticism of his former points of view. A large number of these notes have been published, and they help us to understand

---

[10] I gave a brief description of Merleau-Ponty's works and of their coherence in my first book on Merleau-Ponty's philosophy. See *The Phenomenological Philosophy of Merleau-Ponty,* Introduction, pp. 2-6.

[11] "Metaphysics is the opposite of system." Merleau-Ponty, *Sense and Non-Sense,* English translation by Hubert L. Dreyfus and Patricia Allen Dreyfus, Northwestern University Press, 1964, p. 94.

something more of Merleau-Ponty's development. Still his new vision has not been elaborated.

We must even say that his new vision does not "exist" in the full sense of the word. The philosopher is, according to Merleau-Ponty himself, a writer.[12] Philosophical thought does not exist prior to being expressed.[13] It comes into existence by the expression. While writing, Merleau-Ponty is in search of truth, in search of his own thought. His thought is born in the expression. There is no guarantee that the book would have been published had Merleau-Ponty lived longer. The possibility that he would not have succeeded in his attempt to rebuild his philosophy cannot be excluded. The deepest meaning of the parts which have been written would have become manifest only by the later chapters which do not exist. I became aware of this when reading the first part of the book. The first reading was somewhat disappointing. The criticism of scientism, of reflexive analysis, of Sartre's philosophy was already present in *Phenomenology of Perception;* and, therefore, I got the impression that Merleau-Ponty was repeating himself. I noted, it is true, that there were new accents in his criticism but did not understand the importance of the new critical approach until I read his positive exposition of the new viewpoints. I had to read the critical chapters again in the light of the positive one, and then I understood the really new character of Merleau-Ponty's criticism. The positive part of the book is very small; he had hardly started it. The full meaning of the book is not evident because the book is not completed. Several people who are interested in Merleau-Ponty's philosophy told me that the new book had disappointed them. They probably read the book only once and perhaps not deeply enough. I understand their reaction because I had exactly the same impression after a first superficial reading.

The task of capturing the new perspectives of Merleau-Ponty's philosophy is, therefore, not an easy one. I must try to explain a philosophy which does not fully exist, which is there only in embryonic form. Even the author of *The Visible and the Invisible* did not fully know the perspectives he was developing. I will have to draw conclusions which are only implicit in the text of Merleau-Ponty. The publication of the notes, however, has been helpful to me. In them

---

[12] "Le sensible est au contraire, comme la vie, trésor toujours plein de choses à dire pour celui qui est philosophe (c'est-à-dire écrivain)." *V.I.,* p. 305.

[13] "En principe, c'est ensuite seulement que je serais en mésure de définir une ontologie et de définir la philosophie." *V.I.,* p. 221.

Merleau-Ponty sometimes anticipated the implications of his new vision. Since the notes are often brief and very condensed, it is usually difficult to understand them. The meaning of several notes remains to a high degree obscure. Still we find them helpful in understanding the meaning and the importance of the text completed by Merleau-Ponty.

The question could be raised whether it is useful to write a book which concerns only the new points of view of Merleau-Ponty. This practically means writing a book about one unfinished work and some articles. Would it not be better to write about the whole philosophical outlook of Merleau-Ponty in such a manner that the new points of view are integrated in the whole? Both the life and the works of Merleau-Ponty form a real unity, and, since he is dead, his works should be treated as a unity. It would be desirable, indeed, to present the total philosophical view of Merleau-Ponty; but such a comprehensive work must be prepared by preliminary specialized studies. This work is such a specialized study. There are hidden treasures in the last book of Merleau-Ponty, views which have remained implicit, hidden conclusions which have not been drawn. It is useful, therefore, to make a study of the last work of Merleau-Ponty and of the articles related to it. Only when this is accomplished, can the question of the integration of the new viewpoints into the earlier works be treated. Then the total and final perspective of Merleau-Ponty will appear.

The fact, however, that the period of *The Visible and the Invisible* has been made the proper theme of this book, does not at all mean that we will abstract from the preceding periods of Merleau-Ponty's life. That would be impossible and ridiculous. One who does not thoroughly know the *Phenomenology of Perception* cannot write about *The Visible and the Invisible*. He cannot even read the latter correctly. There may be important changes in Merleau-Ponty's philosophy, but continuity prevails. We will, therefore, examine the last period of Merleau-Ponty's life in the light of the preceding ones. We will concentrate our attention on the period of *The Visible and the Invisible,* considering, however, this period as a part of an undivided philosophical life.

Three Periods in Merleau-Ponty's Philosophical Life

We can roughly distinguish three periods of Merleau-Ponty's philosophical life. The first period is the one in which he wrote *The Structure of Behavior* and *Phenomenology of Perception*. Merleau-

Ponty was then inquiring into the deepest foundations of philosophical thought. There are two movements in philosophical reflection, one into depth, into the final base of human knowledge, and another of a synthetical character, which can be called a movement into breadth. Man wants to ground his knowledge, but he also wants to know something about the whole field of his existence. In the first period Merleau-Ponty's thought was moving into depth.

In the second period of his life, the period of *Sense and Non-Sense, Humanism and Terror* and *The Ventures of Dialectic Thought,* we find more the movement into breadth. He manifests the fertility of his fundamental perspective, applying it to widely divergent subjects. During that period he wrote about several of the arts, movies, communism and christianity, and political topics. In the third period, which this book treats, Merleau-Ponty returns to depth. He had understood that his former search for the base of philosophical thought was insufficient. He asks again the questions of the first period, looking for a new, or rather, a deeper answer.

This third period has been called the period of *The Visible and the Invisible*. A few remarks must be made about this work's composition. Merleau-Ponty was writing the book during his final years, although its outline was not yet fixed. In his notes we find many schemes, yet there is no indication that any had been definitely decided upon. The present outline was made by Merleau-Ponty's friend, Claude Lefort, who explains in a preface why he edited the book as he did.[14] He also chose the title, which aptly characterizes the development of Merleau-Ponty's thought. In the beginning Merleau-Ponty had in mind the title *The Origin of Truth,* more or less announced in *Sense and Non-Sense*.[15] Because of the development of his views the new title became more obvious, as we will see later on.

Structure of Merleau-Ponty's Latest Book

The Visible and the Invisible has two main parts. Merleau-Ponty has more or less prepared the first part for publication. More or less, because it seems quite certain that he intended to revise the text after

---

[14] Claude Leford summarized the most important schemes in his Introduction, *V.I.,* pp. 10-11.

[15] "It would obviously be in order to give a precise description of the passage of perceptual faith into explicit truth as we encounter it on the level of language. We intend to do so in a work devoted to 'The Origin of Truth'." *Sense and Non-Sense,* p. 94, note 13.

finishing the whole book.[16] It seems clear that some sections would not have been published.[17] The second part contains a large number of notes which never would have been published by Merleau-Ponty.[18]

In the first chapter, "Reflection and Interrogation,"[19] Merleau-Ponty establishes his starting point. In our perceptive life we find three fundamental certainties: that we perceive the real world, that the same world I perceive is also perceived by others, that the real world is a coherent unity. When we pass from perceptive evidence to reflection, it appears extremely difficult to maintain and to defend the three original certainties of perception. Hence the question: what is the final basis of philosophical knowledge? Merleau-Ponty demonstrates that science supposes, but does not explain, this base. Then he criticizes the reflective, rationalistic philosophy which, flying away from the ambiguity of perception, tries to establish a final basis in the interiority of the human mind itself.

In the second chapter, "Interrogation and Dialectics,"[20] Merleau-Ponty examines the solution given by Jean-Paul Sartre. It is one of the best expositions, and one of the most severe criticisms, of Sartre's doctrine that I have ever read.

The third chapter, "Interrogation and Intuition,"[21] is a criticism of Edmund Husserl's essentialistic way of thinking. This chapter is very important in order to grasp Merleau-Ponty's attitude toward phenomenological thought.

The fourth chapter, *"L'Entrelacs—le Chiasme,"*[22] begins the positive elaboration of Merleau-Ponty's thought. He analyzes our vision and touching, discovering in the human body itself a real beginning of reflection. In our body the world comes to awareness of itself. The text ends with two short pieces[23] which are relatively unimportant. Then follow more than one hundred pages of notes, all of which are dated.[24]

---

[16] There are repetitions, says Claude Lefort, which indicate that Merleau-Ponty had yet to revise the text. *V.I.*, p. 161, note.

[17] The two short pieces printed in *V.I.*, pp. 207-216, would certainly not have been published by Merleau-Ponty.

[18] In a note Merleau-Ponty speaks of the queer custom of publishing even *"notes de travails."* *V.I.*, p. 293.

[19] *V.I.*, pp. 17-74.

[20] *V.I.*, pp. 75-141.

[21] *V.I.*, pp. 142-171.

[22] *V.I.*, pp. 172-204.

[23] *V.I.*, pp. 207-216.

[24] *V.I.*, pp. 219-328.

I will first examine here Merleau-Ponty's self-criticism in order to establish the new points of view at which he has arrived. Then I will try to explain the new fundamental problems and the new light implied there. After that I will speak about Merleau-Ponty's criticism of other ways of philosophical thinking. Finally, I will try to show the conclusions of Merleau-Ponty's new trend of thought.

I want to express my gratitude to Father Nicholas Senecal, O.S.B., for having corrected the text.

Remy C. Kwant

Duquesne University
Pittsburgh, Pennsylvania

CHAPTER ONE

THE SELF-CRITICISM
OF MERLEAU-PONTY

In the text which Merleau-Ponty prepared for publication we do not
find any explicit self-criticism. He evidently did not like to write about
himself. In his preceding works we find only one passage in which he
explicitly changes a former point of view. In *Humanism and Terror* he
had defended what he called his *attentisme Marxiste,* viz., his neutral
attitude in the conflict between East and West.[1] Marxism had,
according to him, the right idea about the future of mankind, but it tried
to realize this future in the wrong way. He could not, therefore, choose
the Western position because of his sympathy for the Marxist vision; but
neither could he choose the Marxist position because of its wrong praxis.
He felt obliged, consequently, to take a neutral attitude. When
Marxism, however, started an aggressive war in Korea, when it tried to
impose its ideas upon the West by force, the neutral and awaiting
attitude became impossible for him. In a period of armed conflict it is
impossible to maintain a neutral attitude because the very existence of
the group in which one lives is threatened. In these circumstances
Merleau-Ponty changed his *attentisme Marxiste,* and chose the side of
the West.[2] In this instance he changed his attitude and explicitly said
so. This did not imply a change in his fundamental ideas, however, but
was a change only of his practical attitude in the mobile realm of
political reality.

1. First Critical Note of January, 1959[3]

In his notes, however, Merleau-Ponty sometimes formulates critical
remarks about his own philosophy, and it is very useful to study them
thoroughly. We find a first critical remark in a note dated January,

---

[1] Merleau-Ponty described this attitude in *Humanisme et Terreur,* Gallimard,
Paris, 1947, pp. 195-206.
[2] Merleau-Ponty, *Les Aventures de la Dialectique,* Gallimard, Paris, 1955, p.
308.
[3] *V.I.,* pp. 221-223.

1959. He starts from a text of Husserl in which Husserl says that the human body has an "other side," a "spiritual side."[4] Merleau-Ponty takes up this point of view in his new program. The note says that, after having written chapters about physical nature and about living beings, he plans to write a third one about the human body insofar as it has a "spiritual side." The life of the human body cannot be described, according to Merleau-Ponty, unless it is viewed as a psycho-physical reality. Descartes described it in this manner but did not maintain its real unity. Descartes was forced into dualism because of his concept of nature. As if he could sovereignly dispose of the whole matter, Descartes reduced nature to quantity and movement; the human soul, therefore, had to be conceived as a substance separated from nature. For Merleau-Ponty this Cartesian notion of nature had to be overcome. This will give birth to a new conception of the senses, of time, of the soul; these notions will come closer to the concepts of Husserl. All of this will have an ontological character, viz., it will reveal the *Being* of the appearing world.

Merleau-Ponty intended to start with a *description* of the perceived world, but its deeper reality will be revealed by the ontological reflection. Perception will appear to be not only a possession of perceived reality, but also a gliding away from it;[5] it will be clear that the so-called "object" transcends perception, that not the whole of reality is apprehended by perception. And, above all, the question of a radical philosophical reflection will be posed, viz., whether we will have to arrive at the transcendental immanence of Husserl.[6] By posing these questions Merleau-Ponty hopes to arrive at what he calls "savage Being,"[7] Being which precedes the order of reason. He hopes to penetrate into the real unity of life which precedes the serial multiplicity of acts. While doing so, Merleau-Ponty hopes to *take up in a new and deeper manner and to correct* the perspectives of his first two books.[8]

---

[4] In his notes Merleau-Ponty often refers to texts of other writers, without mentioning the book and the page, and even without quoting literally. It is not easy, therefore, to find the passages he speaks of.

[5] "Perception comme écart." *V.I.,* p. 222.

[6] "Et surtout: le problème est posé du rapport entre ces "vérités" et la philosophie comme réflection radicale, comme réduction à l'immanence transcendantale." *Ibid.*

[7] "L'être 'sauvage' ou 'brut' est introduit." *Ibid.*

[8] "Mais tout cela, -qui reprend, approfondit et rectifie mes deux premiers livres. . . ." *Ibid.*

It is remarkable that he mentions only his first two books. This means that he returns to his first period, during which he tried to penetrate into the fundaments of philosophy; the second period of his philosophical life is evidently not so important for him. He returns to the fundamental questions of the beginning, for he feels that he has not solved them. He wants to elaborate them in a deeper manner, for he thinks that he remained to a certain extent superficial. According to him a rectification is necessary; there must have been some wrong solutions.

How does Merleau-Ponty want to correct his vision? The central point seems to be a new conception of man which recognizes both the material and the spiritual aspect of man without falling into dualism. He plans to achieve this by seeing the spiritual aspect as the "other side" of the body, so that both sides, the material and the spiritual, are two sides of one and the same reality.[9] The human body itself cannot be conceived without the spiritual side. This notion should be founded on a new notion of nature and of living beings. This makes us understand the theme of the book expressed in the title: *The Visible and the Invisible*. The invisible is evidently conceived by Merleau-Ponty as the "other side" of the visible. We must see now whether this obvious interpretation is confirmed by the other texts.

2. *Second Critical Note of January, 1959*[10]

In the same month, January, 1959, Merleau-Ponty wrote a note in which his self-criticism becomes more explicit. Again he confronts Descartes. It is most remarkable that during his whole life Merleau-Ponty continued to face the founder of modern philosophy. The cogito of Descartes, he says, operates on meanings and tries to establish relationships between different meanings. These meanings have come into existence by expressive acts. Merleau-Ponty does not say that Descartes has been aware of this. There is no guarantee that a writer really does what he thinks he does; he may be wrong in his interpretation of his own activity. In his *Phenomenology of Perception*, Merleau-Ponty had already said that Descartes intended to indicate the most original data, but that as a matter of fact the so-called original data had

---

[9] "Le corps humain sera décrit comme ayant un côté 'spirituel'." *Ibid.*
[10] *V.I.*, pp. 224-225.

been constituted by speech.[11]   Descartes considered human consciousness to be the most fundamental and original reality; but in fact, our consciousness, as it reveals itself now, has come into existence by speaking.   Human consciousness is not there like a tree is there; it has developed itself in the course of history.   Descartes considered his fundamental concepts, e.g., the concept of quantity and of thought, as absolutely original; he even called them innate.   These concepts, however, have been developed during the history of human language and human thought.   When Merleau-Ponty says that Descartes operated on concepts and that he established relationships between them, he does not say what Descartes intended to do, but what he really has done.

If human consciousness operates on meanings, we must make a distinction between consciousness itself and the meanings with which it is confronted.   The meanings have the character of an object, and the object presupposes a subject.   Hence it becomes necessary to accept a contact of human consciousness with itself; consciousness must be an awareness of itself which precedes all reflective acts.[12]   It is a contact of the self with itself within a perfect identity.   Sartre also presupposes this contact within an identity; he speaks about a consciousness (of) ourselves.   He puts the word "of" in parentheses in order to indicate the identity between the self which is aware of itself and the self which is the quasi-object of this awareness.   There is no real object in this case because there is identity.

In the second note of January, 1959, Merleau-Ponty says of himself that, although he had opposed the Cartesian trend of thought, he had still remained within it.   In the chapter about the cogito in the *Phenomenology of Perception,* he rejected the clear Cartesian self-awareness of man.   But then he posed the objection that, if man is not aware of himself from the beginning, he must be a thing which is lost in complete unawareness of itself.   If this is true then it is unthinkable that a thing can ever become a conscious being.[13]   Man, however, is a conscious being.   Hence ever since he began to exist he must have been

---

[11] "Descartes, and *a fortiori* his reader, begin their meditation in what is already a universe of discourse." *Phenomenology of Perception,* translated from the French by Colin Smith, The Humanities Press, New York, 1962, p. 401.

[12] "Il présuppose donc un contact pré-réflexif de soi avec soi." *V.I.,* p. 224.

[13] "If ultimate subjectivity cannot think of itself the moment it exists, how can it ever do so?   How can that which does not think take to doing so?" *Phenomenology of Perception,* p. 404.

aware of himself. Man, therefore, is, and has always been, a being aware of itself. While Merleau-Ponty rejected the clear awareness which manifests itself in speaking, he accepted an obscure awareness which must be there from the beginning. He called it the *cogito tacite,* the "silent cogito," i.e., the obscure self-awareness of man which does not yet express itself but which is there, notwithstanding its obscurity.[14] Although he opposed the Cartesian view, Merleau-Ponty had tacitly admitted its fundamental principle.

There remains, indeed, a fundamental ambiguity in *Phenomenology of Perception.* Merleau-Ponty repeatedly calls perceptive life preconscious. He says that the subject of perception is unconscious, that it has the character of the anonymous *on,*[15] that it is pre-personal.[16] He speaks of the "logic of the world" which is well-known to the body but which remains unknown to our conscious life.[17] My body, he says, knows more about the world than I do as a conscious subject. The deepest level of our life seems to be, therefore, preconscious; and what is preconscious must be unconscious. Merleau-Ponty refuses to identify intentional and conscious life. On its deepest level our life is intentional, but not yet conscious. However, Merleau-Ponty then proceeds to accuse himself of reducing the subject to a thing. His answer to this accusation seems to withdraw what he said in the preceding chapters: he replies that man never can become conscious if he is not conscious from the beginning; so there must be a kind of consciousness even on the level where human life is called preconscious.[18] In the *Phenomenology of Perception* Merleau-Ponty has tried to transcend the absolute Cartesian opposition between thing and consciousness; but in the end he falls back into it, admitting that man, because he never is a thing, must be a conscious being from the beginning.

Rejection of the "Silent Cogito." He has given a name to the lowest level of human consciousness. He has called it a *cogito tacite,* a "silent

---

[14] The English translation of Colin Smith uses the expression "tacit cogito." *Phenomenology of Perception,* pp. 403-404.

[15] "Perception is always in the mode of the impersonal 'one'." *Phenomenology of Perception,* p. 240.

[16] "But we have seen that primary perception is a non-thetic, pre-objective and pre-conscious experience." *Phenomenology of Perception,* p. 242.

[17] "Expressed in more general terms, there is a logic of the world to which my body in its entirety conforms." *Phenomenology of Perception,* p. 326.

[18] "We do not mean that the primordial I completely overlooks itself. If it did, it would indeed be a thing, and nothing could cause it subsequently to become consciousness." *Phenomenology of Perception,* p. 404.

cogito." The expression is to a certain extent understandable. On the higher level of human awareness man speaks about himself. There he becomes a "verbal cogito," viz., a cogito which expresses itself in words. On the lower level there is a kind of awareness, but there it is not yet expressed in words. Hence the term "silent cogito."

In his note Merleau-Ponty rejects the "silent cogito" as an impossibility.[19] The reason he gives is most remarkable: words, language, are strictly necessary for a real cogito.[20] There is a real cogito when man *knows* that he sees and that he feels, when there is a kind of "reduction," a certain immanence, a consciousness to which something appears. When Merleau-Ponty on this level speaks of "reduction," he evidently does not speak of the famous phenomenological method. He cannot mean that there is a cogito only when philosophical methods are developed. By the term "reduction" here, Merleau-Ponty probably means immanent life: when man is aware of the existence of objects, he reduces himself to a subject, to a consciousness to which objects appear. We must admit, however, that it is confusing to use the term "reduction" here. But we must not forget that we are reading now a note which was never prepared for publication. But Merleau-Ponty does say that language is necessary for a real cogito.

This sentence, however, is not at all clear. It sounds very strange in the whole context of the works of Merleau-Ponty. For one of the merits of this philosopher is that he considered language to be just one of many human expressions. He emphasized that man also expresses himself in work, in art, in his behavior. How, then, can he say now that man becomes a cogito by speaking?

Language and Cogito. In the note Merleau-Ponty explains his point of view. By combining words we constitute meaning. Merleau-Ponty has always rejected the view that isolated words have a completed meaning. Within different contexts the same word gets a different meaning. This implies that words determine one another and that the combination of words constitutes the completed, the real meaning. The same combinations of words are regularly repeated. There are, therefore, meanings which continue to exist. This leads to the hypothesis that meanings precede the verbal expression. This is not true, however, for the existence of meanings depends on verbal expression.

---

[19] "Ce que j'appelle le cogito tacite est impossible." *V.I.,* p. 224.

[20] "Pour avoir l'idée de 'penser' (dans le sens de la 'pensée de voir et de sentir'), pour faire la 'réduction', pour revenir à l'immanence et à la conscience de . . . il est nécessaire d'avoir les mots." *V.I.,* pp. 224-225.

Because the same words which have a certain meaning within one context, can have another meaning within a different context, the speaking person enjoys some freedom in relation to the field of meanings.

This freedom is not a ready-made gift of nature, but it has been conquered by man who learned to speak. By learning to combine words, man *causes* the transcendental attitude, he *constitutes the constituting consciousness*.[21] Our words, or rather, our combinations of words are not related to meanings which are there as positive data; they do not refer to the stream of experiences as a final datum.[22] In the last sentence Merleau-Ponty criticizes Husserl, who in the beginning viewed the "essences" as the final term of "eidetic reduction" and who in a later period referred to the so-called "stream of experiences." Husserl always accepted a datum to which human speaking refers. Merleau-Ponty rejects such a datum, since it denies the constituting character of human speaking. He also rejects the myth of a given consciousness to which our term "consciousness" refers,[23] because consciousness too is constituted by speaking. For Merleau-Ponty there are only different meanings which are constituted by human speaking.[24]

Until now we followed closely the condensed text of Merleau-Ponty. We must try now to understand it better, for it confronts us with many difficulties. The function of language seems to be exaggerated. Language constitutes meanings which, therefore, do not precede language. Language moreover constitutes human consciousness; it is a myth to think that the term "consciousness" refers to a real consciousness which would precede our words. Finally language constitutes the transcendental attitude and the constituting consciousness. We must understand language, of course, not as the "spoken word" (*parole parlée*), but as the "speaking word" (*parole parlante*) because the "spoken word" has been constituted by the "speaking word."[25] Expressive, creative language is, therefore, the origin of meaning, of con-

[21] "C'est par la combinaison de mots (avec leur import de significations sédimentées, et capables par principe d'entrer dans d'autres rapports que les rapports qui ont servi à les former) que je *fais* l'attitude transcendantale, que je *constitue* la conscience constituante." *V.I.*, p. 225.

[22] "Les mots ne renvoient pas à des significations positives et finalement au flux des *Erlebnisse* comme *Selbstgegeben*." *V.I.*, p. 225.

[23] "Mythologie d'une conscience de soi à laquelle renverrait le mot 'conscience'." *Ibid.*

[24] "Il n'y a que des différences de significations." *Ibid.*

[25] See Kwant, *The Phenomenological Philosophy of Merleau-Ponty*, pp. 53-54.

sciousness, of the transcendental attitude, of constituting consciousness.

We should not think that language is the cause and that the other realities are its effects. Merleau-Ponty is now further removed from causal thinking than ever before. We must understand it in this way: by speaking, man makes himself a constituting consciousness which is confronted with meanings. In this way the transcendental attitude comes into existence. The act of speaking implies a development, a promotion of human existence. It is by this act that man makes himself the bearer of meanings, a constituting, transcendental consciousness. In speaking not only does all of this become manifest, but it comes into existence. Language is not only a self-manifestation, but a self-realization of man.

A Difficulty. Does this imply that language is the only self-realization of man? Merleau-Ponty's text could make us think that this is the case. But this is certainly not true. During the same period in which he composed this text, he also wrote the article, "The Eye and the Mind." Here he says that language does not sufficiently manifest our contact with reality and, therefore, he pays attention to painting in which he can learn important things about human life which remain concealed to one who attends only to language.[26] Merleau-Ponty tries to regain contact with *l'être sauvage,* with "savage Being," and on this point the painter has a privileged position.

Science, according to Merleau-Ponty, is too activistic, too interested in building up our orderly world; it has no concern, therefore, for "savage Being" which is the origin of our neat and orderly world. The writer and philosopher are not completely free to suspend the well-ordered world for the purpose of reflecting upon its basis, because they are expected to take a position in the human field of action; they cannot avoid the responsibility of the man who speaks. The musician is far too removed from the common world and from indicating real, concrete things; music only expresses the fundamental rhythm of Being without pointing at concrete things. The painter, on the contrary, directly faces real things, and the great painters face them in their original "savageness."[27]

Accordingly, Merleau-Ponty recognizes the original role of the musician and of the painter. He especially studies the expression of the

---

[26] Maurice Merleau-Ponty, "L'Oeil et l'Esprit," *Les Temps Modernes,* October 1961, p. 195.

[27] "Le peintre est seul à avoir droit de regard sur toutes choses sans aucun devoir d'appréciation." *Ibid.*

painter in which he can learn things which verbal expression does not teach him. But how can Merleau-Ponty write, in the same period, a note in which he says that language is at the origin of consciousness, that man by speaking constitutes the constituting consciousness?

Possible Solutions. There are two possible solutions. In the first place, it is possible that Merleau-Ponty takes verbal expression in a very broad sense, so that music, painting, etc., are conceived as human words. In the second place, it is possible that the term "constituting consciousness" must be understood in a rather strict sense.

It seems to me that the first interpretation is excluded by the text. Merleau-Ponty speaks of the combination of words, of the possibility that the same words take on a different meaning within a different context. It is evident that he speaks about language in the strict sense.

Hence the second interpretation is the only acceptable one. In this text Merleau-Ponty speaks of reflective thought, of thought which constitutes the objects. He speaks of reflective consciousness which transforms appearing reality into an object, into a quasi-object. We must not forget that the note starts with the cogito of Descartes, placing us in the realm of intellectual, objective knowledge. We must understand the whole note in this sense. Merleau-Ponty says that objective, intellectual knowledge, which places itself at a distance from its object, is realized by language. Language constitutes the consciousness which constitutes meanings. Language is possible, not because man is an objectifying consciousness, but man is an objectifying consciousness because he is speaking.[28]

---

[28] The question of the original character of consciousness has always been extremely difficult for Merleau-Ponty, and he did not arrive at a final solution. He knew very well that the clear consciousness of the adult who speaks and reflects is not original, but constituted. He denied that the consciousness of the adult who speaks and reflects would be completely clear. Clarity refers to the figure which appears in a frontal manner, and not to the field which co-appears, which appears in a lateral manner. Since Merleau-Ponty, as a philosopher, was more interested in what co-appears in a lateral manner, he considered our clarity superficial and tried to penetrate into the more obscure aspects of our field of consciousness. But our clear-obscure field of consciousness is constituted.

What is the original consciousness? Merleau-Ponty described it in a negative manner: it is not yet objective; it does not yet pose objects, just as objects; it is pre-reflective. In the present note he stresses that the original consciousness should not be called a "cogito"; it is not yet a real thought. He withdraws, therefore, the expression "silent cogito" which he used in *Phenomenology of Perception;* but he does not give a positive answer to the question what original consciousness really is. In the next chapter we will meet once again the same question.

Objectifying Consciousness is Not an Original Datum. Merleau-Ponty refuses to consider objectifying consciousness as an original datum. It has been constituted by speaking. It is Descartes' fundamental mistake that he has considered the cogito as the most original reality of man. This has also been the mistake of Husserl, who thought he could penetrate into man's ultimate reality by penetrating into the constituting consciousness. Both Descartes' cogito and Husserl's transcendental consciousness have been constituted by speaking.

In *Phenomenology of Perception* Merleau-Ponty was seduced into considering the cogito, the consciousness which from a certain distance confronts itself with reality, as the most original aspect of human reality. In his thinking there was, nevertheless, a tendency to see things differently; yet, when he faced the question whether or not man from the beginning is a consciousness, he assumed that man from the very beginning must have been a consciousness. Hence the "silent cogito." Even on the level where he does not yet speak, man already is consciousness.

Merleau-Ponty now breaks with this point of view. By speaking, man constitutes himself as a consciousness which, therefore, is not an original aspect of human life. It is a myth that the term "consciousness" refers to an aspect of human life which has always been there. By speaking man transforms reality into meaning, and by the same speaking he transforms himself into a consciousness to which an object can appear, or rather, to which reality can begin to appear as an object.[29]

It becomes clear how important Merleau-Ponty thought language to be for human life. By language man makes himself to be a consciousness, and reality to be meaning. The whole intellectual order is constituted by language. Language constitutes the whole realm of objectivity and of meaning.

Preverbal Meanings. There is, however, a preverbal level of life.[30] This is clear, for man develops himself into a being which speaks. Thus language itself must be understood from its preverbal level of existence. But on this preverbal level man is not yet consciousness and he is not yet confronted with meanings. It is quite understandable that in the second

---

[29] In the next chapter we will see that Merleau-Ponty makes a distinction between two forms of awareness; he indicates them with the words: *"il y a . . ."* and *"il m'apparaît que. . . . "* He finally accepts some kind of preverbal awareness.

[30] "Cependant il y a le monde du silence, le monde perçu." *V.I.,* p. 225.

part of his note Merleau-Ponty speaks about this preverbal level. There is, he says, the silent world, the perceived world. We find there meanings which do not yet have a linguistic character. He repeats: yes, meanings which do not yet have a linguistic character.[31]

Here Merleau-Ponty seems to contradict himself. He had said before that language constitutes meanings, and now he speaks of preverbal meanings. He explains, however, what he means. Preverbal meanings are not yet positive data. On this level our life is not yet a succession, a stream of acts which can be clearly distinguished from one another.[32] Clear and distinct meanings correspond with clear and distinct acts. On the preverbal level we do not yet find either clear and distinct meanings or isolated acts. We live in a field, in a visual, sonorous or tactile field. The more particular fields belong to a more general field. Every field has its own style, its own structure. This style, this structure, can be called a meaning. But it is a potential, latent meaning which has to be actualized by speaking.

Speaking produces meanings, but it does not create them from nothing. Originally meanings are the style, the structure, of the field in which we live. They are not yet separated from the field in which we exist. A certain separation takes place when we actualize the meanings by speaking. Color, e.g., is the style of our visual field. By speaking, we transform this style into a concept, into a meaning which has an ideal existence. Our actualized meanings are the expression of existential aspects of the field in which we live. We can speak of preverbal meanings insofar as our verbal meanings are the expression, the actualization, of preverbal aspects of our field of existence.

It is one of the tasks of the philosopher, Merleau-Ponty continues, to describe the existential characteristics of our field of existence which make possible the transcendental field. The transcendental field is not original, as Husserl sometimes seemed to think; it results from the verbal expression of our field of existence. The philosopher must show how, by expression, the transcendental field begins to exist.

No Purely Objective Meanings. Meanings, whether they are potential or actualized, are never purely objective data. They always

---

[31] "Le monde perçu, du moins, est un ordre où il y a des significations non languagières; oui, des significations non languagières, mais elles ne sont pas pour autant *positives.*" *Ibid.*

[32] "Il n'y a pas par exemple de flux absolu des *Erlebnisse* singuliers; il y a des champs, avec un *style* et un typique." *Ibid.*

imply a relationship between the active subject and its field. The human subject is active on two levels, first on the sensory level, secondly on the ideal level. We must distinguish, therefore, the sensory and the ideal subject. The sensory active subject is the body, the ideal active subject is the speaker. The potential meanings incorporate a relationship between the body and its field of existence; the actualized meanings incorporate a relationship between the speaking person and the ideal field.[33] The two levels of subject and field evidently are connected. The speaking subject is an actualization of the sensory subject, and the ideal field is an expression of the sensory field. Hence the sensory field, the world in which we live with our body, already has potentially a transcendental meaning. Man, who transcends himself, constitutes the transcendental field. The self-transcending movement of human life explains the evolution of the field in which we exist and work.

Conclusions. We have written several pages concerning a note of about thirty lines. But because the note is very condensed, this was unavoidable. We must now try to formulate some conclusions.

In this text Merleau-Ponty rejects his former idea of a "silent cogito," of thought which would be present on the preverbal level. Man becomes a thinker when he makes himself a speaker. Thinking and speaking are closely connected. On the preverbal level there is no real thought, no real cogito. Speaking actualizes all the aspects of ideal reality: meaning, objective consciousness, i.e., the awareness of objects, etc. It is wrong to place them already on the preverbal level. But the preverbal subject evidently is a potential speaker; if this were not the case, the preverbal subject could never become a speaker. The field of existence of the preverbal subject, therefore, is loaded with potential meanings; but on this level the meanings are still the style, the structure, of the field. The meanings are actualized when the potential speaker becomes an actual speaker.

Merleau-Ponty does not at all say that speaking is the only actualization of the preverbal subject. This subject is actualized also by art, by painting, by behavior, by work, etc. But the actualization which takes place when the preverbal subject begins to speak has a privileged position: by learning to speak, the subject becomes a thinker who places appearing reality at a distance. By speaking, the field of existence is

---

[33] "Décrire les existentiaux qui font l'armature du champ transcendantal—Et qui sont tjrs un rapport de l'agent (je peux) et du champ sensoriel ou idéal. L'agent sensoriel = le corps—l'agent idéal = la parole." *Ibid.*

transformed into objective reality, into a field of meanings.[34] The other forms of actualization do not coincide with the actualization by speaking, although they depend on it. If one did not develop himself into a speaking person, he could not become an artist, a painter, a worker. Being an artist, a painter, a worker implies more than being only a speaker, but speaking does condition the other actualizations of man. Merleau-Ponty always attached great importance to speaking and in his later period this importance becomes even more evident. Speaking not only reveals the aspects of human existence which cohere with thinking, but it even actualizes them. The central importance of speaking will become clearer in the following chapters.

3. Critical Note of February, 1959[35]

In this note Merleau-Ponty's self-criticism comes only after a rather long introduction. We have to study this introduction in order to understand the critical remarks.

"Embalmed Dialectics." Merleau-Ponty begins by speaking about dialectical philosophy which has become a thesis, a doctrine. We know this refers to Sartre because, in the text prepared for publication, we find a rather long exposition on this theme; and there the dialectical philosophy which has become a doctrine is explicitly attributed to Sartre. Although he does not mention Sartre's book, *Critique de la raison dialectique*,[36] in the text or in this note, there is no doubt that this is the book to which Merleau-Ponty is referring.[37] For, it contains the elaboration of Sartre's dialectical philosophy.

Kant wrote a criticism of theoretical and of practical reason; Sartre assumed the task of writing a criticism of dialectical reason. He makes a distinction between analytical and dialectical reason. Analytical reason places itself within a given field and tries to determine its structure. It does not consider this field as constituted in the course of history and,

---

[34] "Les idées sont la texture de l'expérience; son style, muet d'abord, proféré ensuite." *V.I.*, p. 159.

[35] *V.I.*, pp. 229-230.

[36] Jean-Paul Sartre, *Critique de la raison dialectique*, Gallimard, Paris, 1960.

[37] Merleau-Ponty refers to this book because there it becomes clear that Sartre considers dialectic thought to be the proper method of his philosophy. In his description of Sartre's philosophy, however, Merleau-Ponty has in view Sartre's *Being and Nothingness*.

therefore, does not penetrate into its ultimate intelligibility. It sees just one fixed picture without seeing this as a moment of a whole flowing movement. Dialectical reason views the whole, and it considers the field, which analytical reason isolated, as just one aspect of the whole historical reality.[38] Sartre's philosophy of dialectical reason then is at the same time a philosophy of history.[39] According to Sartre, dialectical philosophy is a doctrine which reveals the ultimate meaning of reality.

Merleau-Ponty objects that in this kind of philosophy everything is incorporated into the dialectical movement of history—except the dialectical thought itself.[40] Dialectical philosophy makes everything relative except itself. Dialectical philosophy is a non-dialectical view of a dialectical field. The dialectical philosopher sees the dialectical character of everything except of his view itself. Merleau-Ponty says that a hyper-dialectical philosophy[41] is necessary, viz., a philosophy which also recognizes the dialectical character of the philosophical view itself. Merleau-Ponty always radicalizes the situated character of every approach. Later on we will return to this point, for it is one of the most essential aspects of Merleau-Ponty's philosophy. Merleau-Ponty calls the dialectical philosophy which forgets its own dialectical character the "embalmed dialectics."

When Merleau-Ponty rejects "embalmed dialectical philosophy," he does not intend to say that everything is based on a ground about which we cannot say anything at all.[42] He rejects dialectical thought only when it is taken as the ultimate basis of all reality. The failure of the dialectical thesis, the fact that this thesis itself is incorporated into the dialectical movement of history, points to the *cradle of all theses,* viz., to the physico-historical world in which we live (the *Lebenswelt*).[43] We

---

[38] "Tout cela, pourvu qu'on prenne la précaution de définir les modes de rationalité qu'on utilise, reste parfaitement intelligible à la condition de dissoudre finalement la Raison analytique et la Raison économique dans la dialectique constituée." Sartre, *Critique de la raison dialectique,* p. 732.

[39] "Si la vérité doit être une dans sa croissante diversification d'intériorité, en répondant à l'ultime question posée par l'expérience régressive, nous découvrirons la signification profonde de l'Histoire et de la rationalité dialectique." Sartre, *op. cit.,* p. 755.

[40] "La dialectique devenue *thèse* (énoncé) n'est plus dialectique (dial. 'enbaumée')." *V.I.,* p. 229.

[41] See Chapter Two.

[42] "Ceci n'est pas au profit d'un *Grund* dont on ne pourrait rien *dire.*" *V.I.,* p. 229.

[43] "L'échec de la thèse, son renversement (dialectique) dévoile la *Source des thèses,* le *Lebenswelt* physico-historique, auquel il s'agit de retourner." *Ibid.*

will always have to return to this original world. We will always have to return to the field of perception; we will have to get a feeling for it (*Einfühlung*). We must always try to speak starting from this field, and we may never consider this task finished.

If we radicalize dialectical thought, Merleau-Ponty continues, we make human speaking impossible.[44] If at any moment I must be aware of the fact that my speaking is incorporated into the dialectical movement of history, I can no longer speak at all. Speaking views Being. It tries to say how things *are*. I take away the very ground of speaking if I am continually aware of the relativity of speech. I speak starting from the cradle of all speaking, and I make speaking impossible if I take away this cradle.

The Real Intersubjective Field. I cannot find in purely objective things (*Sachverhalt*) an ultimate ground for speaking. Realism tries to do so, but from the beginning Merleau-Ponty has broken with it. Realism places itself, without knowing that it does so, in the realm of the "spoken word." Such speech has given stability to the things about which we speak. We can have the illusion that this stability is based upon the real things themselves, while as a matter of fact it is based upon our speaking. Language, insofar as it has become an institution, gives us an illusion of stability and of established reality. We must consider the "speaking word," not the "spoken word."

The "speaking word" cannot be isolated from other persons. If we really speak, we speak to others. We are in contact with other persons without knowing how it takes place. We are ignorant of the psychic mechanism which makes this contact possible.[45] We experience the living words of the other person and he experiences ours without knowing how all this is possible. The "speaking word" constitutes for us a field of communication; in this field there is a place for meanings, for a common subject of meanings. As a particular subject, I participate in an intersubjective life. Without this intersubjective life real speaking is impossible. Intersubjective life is the real realm of speaking. It is included in the reality of speaking itself. It is not the "objective mind"

---

[44] "On sait simplement que la parole ne peut plus être énoncé, *Satz,* si elle doit rester dialectique." *Ibid.*

[45] "C'est bien la parole, non la langue, qui vise autrui comme comportement, non comme 'psychisme', qui répond à autrui avant qu' il a été compris comme 'psychisme'." *Ibid.*

of Hegel nor an objective reality. It is the intersubjective character of our being which becomes manifest in speaking.

The "Savage Spirit." We must rejoin, Merleau-Ponty continues, this intersubjective field which is there, both in the present and in the past. Then we will meet the real history of the world we live in. It is in this field that real culture exists. Dialectical philosophy has failed. This failure, however, can help us to discover the real intersubjective field, which, although it is extended in time, has a certain eternity in that it makes possible the dialogue of one who lives now with thinkers of the past. In this way we recapture the "savage spirit." We have already seen what Merleau-Ponty means by the expression "savage Being," i.e., Being insofar as it precedes the rational order and of which the rational order is one of the expressions. The "savage spirit" corresponds with "savage Being." It is the human mind in its most original life. We bring order into our life and into our world; both are necessarily connected, for we are intentional beings. By bringing order into our lives and into our world, we elaborate the contact, the communication we are living in; but we do not constitute it. The original contact with the world and with other persons belongs to the "savage spirit."[46]

It is rather difficult to say precisely what Merleau-Ponty means in this condensed text. We, adult persons, are living in a world of orderly communication. We have organized communication, but we could not do so unless communication was an original fact. We organize what is already there. Very young children communicate with one another; babies are aware of their mutual presence. Even in adult life there are real forms of communication which never have been organized. It happens that we feel that another, unknown person is looking at us, and we can answer his look by looking at him. There can be a struggle between the eyes. It sometimes happens that we feel a strong affinity with a writer who died a long time ago, and that we cannot explain this affinity. Our being is itself intentionality, communication. This original communication which precedes every explication and every organization belongs to the very essence of speaking. This original communication is situated in the realm of what Merleau-Ponty calls "savage Being" and "savage spirit."

---

[46] "L'échec de la dialectique comme thèse ou 'philosophie dialectique', c'est la découverte de cette intersubjectivité non perspective, mais verticale, qui est, étendue au passé, éternité existentielle, esprit sauvage." *Ibid.*

The Insufficiency of the "Silent Cogito." Merleau-Ponty now criticizes one of his former points of view. The "silent cogito," he says, does not resolve these problems.[47] When he introduced it, he posed a problem but did not resolve it. Merleau-Ponty indicates the reason why he did not, or rather could not, resolve the problem: he had neglected to connect the chapter about the cogito with the chapter about speaking.[48] This reminds us of the second note we discussed where, according to the later Merleau-Ponty, the real cogito comes into existence by speaking. In the chapter about the cogito in the *Phenomenology of Perception,* he concluded that the cogito had always been there. Even when man is silent, he is already a cogito; hence, the "silent cogito." In the chapter about speaking, however, there were certain elements which pointed at a different direction. Starting from the "spoken word," Merleau-Ponty penetrated into the "speaking word," and from there into our existence as an expressive power. The realization of this expressive power implies man's self-realization. If Merleau-Ponty had written the chapter about the cogito in the perspective of the chapter about speaking, he could have suspected that the cogito is not already there but that it is realized in speaking, that the "silent cogito" is not yet an actualized, but a potential, cogito. The "silent cogito" is a verbal but not a real solution, as we have seen in studying the preceding note.

The "silent cogito," continues Merleau-Ponty's note, should make us understand that language is not impossible, but it does not demonstrate the positive possibility of language.[49] As a matter of fact, the "silent cogito" indicates a cradle of speaking although it does not give us a real and a positive idea of this cradle. It indicates a reality without giving us a positive idea of it; it points to a reality which remains a darkness. It is the answer to an objection which takes away the strength of the objection but gives no real understanding. It makes us feel that language is not really impossible, because we see a fundament of it; nevertheless, it does not give us a real understanding of this fundament. The latest work of Merleau-Ponty, *The Visible and the Invisible,* could have offered us a clearer and more positive answer, but that answer remained unfinished.

---

[47] "Le Cogito tacite ne résout bien entendu pas ces problèmes." *Ibid.*

[48] "En le dévoilant comme j'ai fait ds Ph.P., je ne suis pas arrivé à une solution (mon chapitre sur le Cogito n'est pas rattaché au chapitre sur la parole) : j'ai au contraire posé un problème." *Ibid.*

[49] "Le Cogito tacite doit faire comprendre comment le langage n'est pas impossible, mais ne peut pas faire comprendre comment il est possible." *Ibid.*

In the lines that follow, Merleau-Ponty touches upon the inadequacy of his former answer. The question remains open, he says, as to how we make the passage from perceptive to verbal meaning, from behavior (and from the knowledge which is implied in behavior) to its thematic expression. This is the question which remained unanswered in his former works.[50] He himself admitted this in a note in *Sense and Non-Sense*.[51] He had analyzed the perceptive level of our existence but had not yet explained how we can pass from perceptive experience to verbal truth. He announced, therefore, a new book, *The Origin of Truth*. This book, published as *The Visible and the Invisible,* was to have given the answer. But, as a matter of fact, the answer has not been given, since Merleau-Ponty had no time to rework this theme in the unfinished manuscript.

Speaking and Silence. In this note he only makes precise the terms of the question. He speaks about the passage from behavior to its thematic expression. This thematic expression, however, must also be understood as behavior, but as behavior of a higher level. The relationship between the silent behavior and its transposition into words is a dialectical relationship. The silence of behavior is broken by language; in this manner language realizes what silent behavior intended to do but could not do. Speaking is the actualization of the latent intentionality of silent behavior. Behavior, as a matter of fact, does not remain enclosed within the realm of individual existence; it views the other person. The intersubjective character of behavior is highly actualized by speaking. Speaking actualizes and involves silent behavior. But silent behavior likewise involves our speaking.[52] In speaking itself there are essential elements which are not pronounced, which are silently presupposed. Speaking cannot exist without communication, but the aspect of communication itself is not expressed; even in the most perfect speaking there are elements of silence. By speaking we become aware of many things, but not of everything. Speaking and silence involve one another and, therefore, their relationship is dialectical.

This does not mean, however, that there is a philosophical observer situated above this dialectical relationship who transforms this into an

---

[50] "Reste le problème du passage du sens perceptif au sens langagier, du comportement à la thématisation." *V.I.,* p. 230.

[51] Merleau-Ponty, *Sense and Non-Sense,* p. 94, note 13.

[52] "Le language réalise en brisant le silence ce que le silence voulait et n'obtenait pas. Le silence continue d'envelopper le langage." *V.I.,* p. 230.

object. Otherwise we would arrive at an "unhappy consciousness" (Hegel) which has to admit its own failure. On the two levels, on the level of silence and on the level of speaking, a situated subject is at work; and this subject is the "savage spirit," viz., the spirit which never comes to complete awareness of itself. This "savage spirit" is the "practical spirit," the spirit which in practice does more than it knows, which is more than it knows about itself, which never comes to complete awareness of itself.[53]

On every level, including the level of speaking, we presuppose aspects of being which we take for granted. We place ourselves within a realm of constituted reality without knowing clearly how it has been constituted; we try to accomplish tasks without knowing how these tasks come into existence; we live within a practice without knowing where the absolute origin of this practice lies. We live, for example, in a speaking community of men. We take part in willing, speaking and thinking which exceed our particular being. The scientist elaborates a science which was there before he was born and which will continue to exist after he has died. We take over an intentional movement which exceeds us. Who is the final subject of this intentional movement? Who is the subject who intends, speaks and thinks in us? The note ends on this question without giving an answer.

Conclusions. This note makes it clear that, according to Merleau-Ponty, thinking is rooted in speaking and that speaking is rooted in a silent realm of our existence. This silence needs speaking because its inner intentionality can be realized only by speaking. Yet the silence remains always involved in speaking. It is impossible to understand human thought if we do not pay attention to language, and language is not understandable without the silent realm of our being.

Merleau-Ponty also emphasizes that speaking and thinking exceed the limits of our individual existence. Speaking at the same time presupposes and realizes a field of communication.

Finally, it is remarkable that in this short note Merleau-Ponty speaks twice about the "savage spirit" which is the final term of reductive thought. This "savage spirit" is a practical spirit, viz., a principle of self-realization. Intersubjectivity and communication are already there

---

[53] "Mais ces développements habituels sur le rapport dialectique pour n'être pas philosophie de *Weltanschauung,* conscience malheureuse, doivent aboutir à une théorie de l'esprit sauvage, qui est esprit de praxis." *Ibid.*

on the level of the "savage spirit." Man's self-realization presupposes, therefore, the intersubjective character of our existence and communication with other persons. Merleau-Ponty is far removed from the rationalistic trend of thought, according to which communication is constituted starting from the individual existence. There is communication on all levels of human existence, even on the most original one. We must also pay attention to the fact that Merleau-Ponty wants to correct himself in his doctrine about the cogito and that he thinks he is able to find the basis of this self-correction in his chapter about speaking. Hence there is continuity between his last work and the preceding ones.

4. Critical Note of July, 1959[54]

The Distinction Between Consciousness and Object. In this last critical note Merleau-Ponty formulates his most general and most radical self-criticism. The problems I have posed in *Phenomenology of Perception,* he says, cannot be solved, because I started in this book from the distinction between consciousness and object.[55] Before seeing how he works out this criticism, we must reflect on the preceding sentence. Two points come to light.

First, Merleau-Ponty in the last phase of his philosophical life refused to start from the distinction between consciousness and object. He did not deny, of course, that this distinction exists. We experience ourselves as subjects confronted with an object. Without this distinction, science could not exist. Merleau-Ponty did not deny the distinction itself, but its original character. The most original level of human life, therefore, must precede this distinction. This is most important for understanding Merleau-Ponty in the last phase of his thinking and we will return again to this point.

Secondly, the sentence tells us that, according to his own statement, Merleau-Ponty did not succeed in transcending this distinction in his phenomenology of perception. This sounds rather startling. It can hardly be denied that Merleau-Ponty tried to transcend the distinction between consciousness and object in his main work. He emphasized that the world exists already for our body before the things of the world are

---

[54] *V.I.,* pp. 253-254.
[55] "Les problèmes posées dans Ph.P. sont insolubles parce que j'y pars de la distinction 'conscience'—'object'." *V.I.,* p. 253.

constituted as objects. The original contact with the world takes place on the level of perception, and perception, he said several times, is pre-objective. He pointed out in *Phenomenology of Perception* that all kinds of misunderstandings are caused by the fact that objective thought —the reduction of the things we live with to objects and the reduction of human subjectivity to thought—does not leave room for the ambiguous adherence of the subject to pre-objective phenomena.[56] This is only one text, but it would be very easy to find many texts in his *Phenomenology of Perception* in which Merleau-Ponty affirms our pre-objective contact with reality. It seems that we must defend Merleau-Ponty against himself, and that we must qualify his self-criticism as unjust and exaggerated.

He probably accuses himself of inconsistency. Certainly he has written about the pre-objective level of human existence, and he has affirmed that this pre-objective level is the original one and that the objective level must be reduced to it. But he has been inconsistent because, in the exposition of particular points, he has forgotten his fundamental point of view; he has been seduced into placing himself again in the perspective of the cogito. We have already seen one example of this inconsistency. When Merleau-Ponty objected that man from the beginning must have been an awareness, for otherwise he is and will remain a thing, he answered that man originally is a "silent cogito."[57] The cogito, then, implies the distinction between consciousness and object, for there is no thought which is not a thought of something. Here Merleau-Ponty has implicitly withdrawn his fundamental point of view, that our life on its most original level is pre-objective.

The Visible and the Invisible. In the present note Merleau-Ponty gives another example. In *Phenomenology of Perception* he often posed the problem of bodily injury, which is a fact in the objective order, bringing with it a disturbance of our relationship with the world. This seems to imply that consciousness is only a function of the objective body. As a matter of fact, Merleau-Ponty raised this problem in many chapters of his main work.[58] He often spoke, e.g., about the famous Schneider

---

[56] *Phenomenology of Perception*, p. 336.

[57] *Phenomenology of Perception*, pp. 404-405.

[58] We wrote on this subject in *The Phenomenological Philosophy of Merleau-Ponty*, Chapter Two, "Merleau-Ponty's Approach to the 'Body-Subject,'" pp. 31-45.

case.[59]   Disturbances of human existence which are rooted in an injury of the body were often the starting-point of his existential analysis.   It is notable that he no longer uses this method in his last book.

In the note he rejects the problem itself.   Formerly he spoke of the objective conditions of existential disturbances.   Now he asks what such an "objective condition" really is.   He answers that this way of speaking is the expression of an event which belongs to a more fundamental order, viz., to the order of "savage Being" which precedes the distinction between subjective existence and the objective order.[60]   Speaking about the objective condition of existential disturbances does not penetrate into the ultimate realm of reality.   In speaking like this, we express ourselves in a superficial and confused manner.   And we ask, Which is the ultimate realm of reality?   There is a visible being, a body, which by its own development obtains an invisible meaning, an invisible aspect.[61]   We should not speak about two orders related to one another.   The invisible is just an aspect of the visible.   The two aspects belong together as do two sides of a piece of paper.   Unity precedes and prevails.

Here we touch the most essential aspect of the philosophy of *The Visible and the Invisible;* hence the title of this book.   We must not think that Merleau-Ponty reduces the subjective, existential realm to an objective one, nor does he reduce objective reality to the subjective order. He is convinced that both the subjective and the objective order are manifestations of a deeper realm of reality, which he calls "savage Being."[62]   The distinction between the two orders and the relationship between subject and object derive from a more primordial unity. Merleau-Ponty is convinced that formerly he did not and could not solve the above-mentioned problems because he had not yet penetrated into ultimate reality.   We cannot here describe this ultimate reality; this will be the difficult task of the following chapters.   It will be a difficult task, since Merleau-Ponty himself only started its philosophical approach. We limit ourselves here to the points of view which are exposed in the present note.

[59] *Op. cit.,* pp. 37-40.

[60] "Ce sont ces problèmes mêmes qu'il faut déclasser en demandant: *qu'est-ce que* le prétendu conditionnement *objectif?*   Réponse: c'est une manière d'exprimer et de noter un événement de l'ordre brut ou sauvage qui, ontologiquement, est premier." *V.I.,* p. 253.

[61] "Cet événement consiste en ce que tel *visible* convenablement agencé (un corps) se creuse d'un sens invisible." *Ibid.*

[62] This is the reason why we entitled this book: *From Phenomenology to Metaphysics.*   We will, of course, return to this point.

The matter out of which all structures have been composed, so continues Merleau-Ponty, is the "visible."[63] It is well-known that the concept "structure" is important in Merleau-Ponty's philosophy. Reality is accessible to us as a structure. The structure is not an effect of the causality of isolated elements. Everything which exists, exists within a structure, and the structure determines what things are. Accessible reality is identical with structured reality. Every structure, all accessible reality, is visible reality. Reality *is* visibility. The "visible," he continues, is not at all objective reality, not an object which exists in itself and which is independent of the subject. The "visible" is that which transcends the seeing subject. Its transcendence is identical with its being. This transcending reality is not opposed to the subject as an object; the visible cannot be conceived without the seeing subject. Here we are far removed from realism. One must not conceive the subject itself as nothingness, as Sartre does, nor as a thing.[64] The seeing subject itself is visible reality which becomes seeing and which, therefore, goes beyond itself. The subject is the actualized visibility, visibility becoming seeing. The seeing subject is the actualization of visible reality.

Conclusion. The preceding paragraphs must be rather obscure for those who have not yet read Merleau-Ponty's last book. In the interpretation of his self-critical notes I have had to make use of the points of view which come to light elsewhere in the book. While using them, I could not give a sufficient exposition of them. Several things which are now obscure will be explained later.

Our study of the last note has been very useful. We have seen that Merleau-Ponty's self-criticism has a very profound background. This was less clear in the preceding notes. The last note made us understand that Merleau-Ponty thinks he has penetrated into a deeper realm of reality which had remained concealed to him when he wrote *Phenomenology of Perception*.[65] He now thinks that his former approach remained superficial, and that, therefore, he was confronted with insoluble difficulties.

---

[63] L'étoffe commune dont sont faites toutes les structures, c'est le *visible,* qui, lui-même, n'est nullement de l'objectif, de l'en soi, mais du transcendant,—qui ne s'oppose pas au pour Soi, qui n'a de cohésion que pour un Soi," *V.I.,* pp. 253-254.

[64] *Ibid.*

[65] In this note Merleau-Ponty criticizes his former approach through psychic diseases. The analysis of such diseases fill many pages of *Phenomenology of Perception.*

5. *The Clutter of Concepts to Be Abandoned*

Five times in his latest book Merleau-Ponty enumerates concepts which should be removed from the dictionary of the philosopher. The concept of "perception" is among them. This certainly implies a self-criticism, because Merleau-Ponty entitled his main work *Phenomenology of Perception*. We will now study these five texts.

He says in the first text, that we must do away with notions such as "acts of consciousness," "states of consciousness," "matter," "form," and even "image" and "perception." We exclude, he continues, the term "perception," insofar as it implies a dissolution of real life into discontinuous acts, a reference to things, and an opposition between the visible and the invisible.[66]

In a note of December, 1959, he asks that the notions of concept, idea and representation be replaced by notions like dimension, articulation, level, hinge, axis and configuration.[67]

We must eliminate, he writes in a note of February, 1960, the whole positivistic clutter of "concepts," "judgments" and "relations," and turn to the unity of life which precedes this analysis.[68]

In May, 1960, he writes that we must demonstrate that the ontology of "experiences," "sensations," "judgments," "objects," "represented reality,"—briefly, the dissolution of psyche and nature into separated realities, the whole clutter of these pretended positive psychic "realities" —is as a matter of fact an abstract expression of a preceding unity.[69]

Finally, a note of December, 1960, states that the whole architecture

---

[66] "Il nous faut renoncer, en commençant, à des notions telles que 'actes de conscience', 'états de conscience', 'matière', 'forme', et même 'image' et 'perception'. Nous excluons le terme de perception dans toute la mésure où il sous-entend déjà un découpage du vécu en actes discontenus ou une référence à des 'choses' dont le statut n'est pas précisé, ou seulement une opposition du visible et de l'invisible." *V.I.*, p. 209.

[67] "Remplacer les notions de concept, idée, esprit, représentation par les notions de *dimensions,* articulation, niveau, charnières, pivots, configuration." *V.I.*, p. 277.

[68] "Tout le bric-à-brac positiviste des 'concepts', des 'jugements', des 'relations' est éliminé, et l'esprit sourd comme l'eau dans la fissure de l'Être." *V.I.*, p. 289.

[69] "Le sens d'être à dévoiler: il s'agit de montrer que l'ontique les 'Erlebnisse', les 'sensations', les 'jugements',—(les ob-jets, les 'représentés', bref toutes les idéalisations de la Psyché et de la Nature), tout le bric-à-brac de ces prétendues 'réalités' phychiques *positives,* (et lacunaires, 'insulaires', sans *Weltlichkeit* propre) est en réalité découpage abstrait dans l'étoffe ontologique, dans le 'corps de l'esprit'." *V.I.*, p. 307.

of psychological notions like "perception," "idea," "affection," "pleasure," "desire," "love," and "eros" becomes all at once clear, when we stop taking these notions as positive realities and see them as differentiations of one and the same massive attachment to Being.[70]

It is impossible to give a detailed explanation here of all these texts. We will only explain the general tendency which becomes manifest in them, and pay some special attention to perception.

Merleau-Ponty stresses the essential unity of the visible and the invisible. They belong together as the two sides of a sheet of paper. He protests against the separation of "psyche" and "nature"; he rejects that analysis of human psyche which starts from the hypothesis that the psyche is a positive reality able to be conceived in isolation from nature. Human life is the actualized visibility of nature, of Being itself, and if we analyze the human being, we must view it in its insoluble unity with nature. According to Merleau-Ponty, most of the notions enumerated in the five texts view the human psyche as an isolated reality.

Merleau-Ponty wants to abandon the notion of perception, insofar as perception is conceived as an isolated act which is confronted with nature as with an object. We feel that in this text he criticizes himself for having too frequently isolated perception in this way in his former works. In his last book he still uses the term "perception" often, but we also find the expressions "perceptive life," "perceptive faith." He does not consider perception as an isolated act, but as a stream of contact with the world.

6. Conclusion

In this chapter we have studied the explicit self-criticism of Merleau-Ponty. It has become clear that he thinks he has found a new philosophical approach. Human thought is not a reality which can be placed next to nature and next to Being. The distinction between object and subject is secondary and artificial. There is a primordial realm of reality, of "savage Being," which precedes all these distinctions. It is the task of the philosopher to reduce all these distinctions to the primordial unity.

---

[70] "Toute l'architecture des notions de la psycho-logie (perception, idée, —affection, plaisir, désir, amour, Eros) tout cela tout ce bric-à-brac s'éclaire soudain quand on cesse de penser tous ces termes comme des *positifs* (du 'spirituel' + ou − épais) pour les penser, non comme des négatifs ou négatités (car ceci ramène les mêmes difficultés), mais comme des *différenciations* d'une seule et *massive* adhésion à l'Être qui est la chair (éventuellement comme des 'dentelles')." *V.I.*, p. 324.

CHAPTER TWO

J'EN SUIS (I BELONG TO IT)

1. *Explanation of the Title*

It is somewhat strange to give a French title to the chapter of a book written in English. I think, however, that in this case there is a valid reason. The words *j'en suis* are not just a casual expression in Merleau-Ponty's last writings, but indicate his central point of view.[1] He came to realize that our human existence is not separated from nature or Being, that we are not opposed to it as subjects who know, but that we belong to it. He does not deny, of course, that we are subjects who know. Not a single aspect of man's spiritual being is denied by Merleau-Ponty. He often uses the term "spirit," perhaps more than in his former works. But along with the term "spirit" he now also uses the term "invisible." The human spirit is, according to him, an aspect of invisible reality. It is his main thesis that the invisible and, consequently, also the spirit is not opposed to the visible, but rather that the invisible is "the other side" of the visible. Hence his expression, *j'en suis:* "I belong to it"; I, human spirit, belong to Being.

Neither Materialism nor Spiritualism. At the very beginning we must clear away a misunderstanding, viz., that Merleau-Ponty's new philosophy is a kind of materialism. This misunderstanding could easily arise. If the invisible is merely the other side of visible being, if the human spirit is the other side of nature, the spirit seems to be only an aspect of nature, of matter. We should not forget, however, that if the spirit, the invisible, is the other side of visible nature, we can say just as well that visible nature is the other side of the invisible, of spirit.

The same reasons which could lead us to think that Merleau-Ponty's new philosophy is a kind of materialism could just as easily make us think that it is a spiritualism. For the visible and the invisible belong together as two sides of one and the same reality. The invisible cannot

---

[1] *V.I.,* p. 136; pp. 152-154; p. 155; pp. 156-157; p. 160; p. 164; p. 169; p. 175; pp. 177-178; p. 181; p. 237; pp. 247-250; p. 261; p. 302; p. 314.

be understood without the visible, but neither can the visible be understood without the invisible. Nevertheless, it would be wrong to speak either of materialism or of spiritualism, since it is the essential thesis of Merleau-Ponty that there is just one order of reality. Merleau-Ponty often says *"j'en suis,"* "I belong to nature, to Being." He could also have said: "Nature, Being, belongs to me."

Primordial Unity. This central awareness of Merleau-Ponty's new philosophy was introduced above where we spoke of his self-criticism. He now says that he takes up his former perspectives in a new and deeper manner. He accuses himself of having maintained the Cartesian cogito, the Cartesian distance from nature; he says he formerly did not see that the cogito must be understood in the light of the "speaking word," in the light of creative speaking. Finally he accuses himself of having considered the opposition between consciousness and object as an original one. He hesitates, therefore, to use the term "perception," since this term usually implies the distinction between consciousness and object. All these forms of self-criticism point in the same direction: Merleau-Ponty accuses himself of being blind to the primordial unity which is at the base of the distinction between consciousness and object, between spirit and matter, between the invisible and the visible. This primordial unity is expressed by the words *j'en suis.*

Merleau-Ponty would have written the entire book in the perspective of this primordial unity. It would have been a commentary on the words *j'en suis.* He intended to show how visible nature manifests itself as a body which feels itself and which actualizes the hidden sensitivity of nature, how visible nature becomes a seeing body, how in this body all the conditions are there for speaking and for other forms of expression, how the speaking body is a thinking body. He would have described all these developments as the manifestation of the intrinsic possibilities of visible nature. He would have shown that on all the levels of the human development it remains true that "I belong to it" (*j'en suis*). There can hardly be any doubt that this would have been the fundamental thesis of his book.

Unfortunately he did not finish it. But he started the execution of his program in the chapter *"L'Entrelacs—le Chiasme."*[2] The title of this chapter is composed of two metaphors. The *entrelacs* is a kind of medallion or network, composed of flowers, numbers or other decorative

---

[2] *V.I.,* pp. 172-204.

elements which are crossed and intermingled. The *chiasm* is a figure of crossed lines. It is clear why Merleau-Ponty uses these metaphors. He wants to indicate that the reality which he is going to describe is complicated, its elements commingled, and that the analytical attitude which isolates the elements endangers their essential unity. The elements have their identity only within the unity. Isolated from it, they lose their real being. With these metaphors Merleau-Ponty indicates the fundamental trend of his new thought.

We will follow the text of this chapter closely, for it contains the only systematic exposition of Merleau-Ponty's new approach.

2. Reflection Upon Seeing

Preliminary Remarks. Merleau-Ponty is opposed to analytic philosophy insofar as it starts from the results of preceding analysis. The philosopher must view the original totality. There has been, however, a long history of analytic philosophy. The philosopher who places himself within this trend of thought is inclined to accept the results of preceding analysis; and he will start from notions like idea, concept, judgment, consciousness, object, or act—briefly, from the "clutter of concepts" spoken of in the first chapter. Merleau-Ponty is afraid of such notions because they already contain a philosophical conception of the original totality of human life and of the world; thus they can prevent us from viewing the real original experience. If we make an uncritical use of these notions, we are prejudiced and remain ignorant about the ultimate basis of our philosophical thought.

One might object that it is also possible to make a critical use of such notions. This is true, but taking a critical attitude toward them means that we do not take them for granted, that we reconstitute them from their source. Whether a philosopher rejects these notions or makes a critical use of them, he always must return to their origin.

There are, continues Merleau-Ponty, other notions like seeing, speaking, and even thinking, which have a different character. They confront us with original experiences in which there is not yet a clear distinction between subject and object, between essence and existence.[3]

---

[3] "Il lui faut . . . s'installer . . . dans des expériences qui n'aient encore été 'travaillées', qui nous offrent tout à la fois, pêle-mêle, et le 'sujet' et l''objet', et l'existence et l'essence, et lui donnent donc les moyens de les redéfinir." *V.I.,* p. 172.

They indicate a vague experience in which everything still seems to be commingled. The experiences which are indicated by such words are at the same time both unavoidable and enigmatic. What exactly do I mean when, after having listened to a person and having observed his behavior, I say, "I see"? It can mean that I accept what he has said; it can also mean that I understand his intentions which he tries to hide from me; it can mean a radical agreement, but also a radical disagreement. Such notions are named in all languages, but they always have a large number of literal and figurative meanings.[4] They do not bring something to light in the way science wants to do so. Thinkers who want to speak in an exact manner are afraid of such notions because they can mean many things and do not have an exact meaning.

It is remarkable that while English or American analytic philosophers are afraid of such notions, Merleau-Ponty prefers them. He thinks that they indicate a mystery with which we are quite familiar but which cannot be explained in clear words. They remind us of the forgotten mystery in which we are living. Merleau-Ponty hopes that by reflecting upon these fundamental notions, he may find new instruments of reflection which will bring him into contact with the original, appearing reality. He starts with an analysis of seeing.

Analysis of Seeing. Visible reality seems to repose in itself. It seems to be there, independent of us.[5] It is as if our vision obtains its form from visible reality itself, as if we are joined to it as the sea is to the beach.[6] Still we must remain at a distance from visible reality, because otherwise both visible reality and vision would disappear.[7] Vision and visible reality come into existence when there is the right proportion between contact and distance. We cannot say that there are things which are just identical with themselves and which sometimes offer themselves to the seeing person. The seeing person is not an empty

---

[4] "Elles ont un nom dans toutes les langues, mais qui dans toutes aussi porte des significations en touffe, des buissons de sens propres et de sens figurés, de sorte que ce n'est pas un de ces noms, comme ceux de la science, qui font de la lumière, en attribuant à ce qui est nommé une signification circonscrite, mais plutôt l'indice répété, le rappel insistant, d'un mystère aussi familier qu'inexpliqué." *Ibid.*

[5] "Le visible autour de nous semble reposer en lui-même." *V.I.,* p. 173.

[6] *Ibid.*

[7] "Et pourtant, il n'est pas possible que nous nous fondions en lui, ni qu'il passe en nous, car alors la vision s'évanouirait au moment de se faire, par disparition ou du voyant ou du visible." *Ibid.*

reality opening itself to a visible reality that is inwardly consistent. We are most closely united with visible reality when we are at the right distance. We can only see the thing-at-a-distance, and not the naked thing as it reposes in itself. The visible thing exists as visible only when our look takes it up from the right distance, when our look takes it up into its own realm. Vision is appropriation. Our look takes up things and makes them visible.

If this is possible several questions arise. How is it possible that our look, although grasping the things, leaves them in their place? We appropriate them and yet we leave them where they are. It seems that our vision comes from the thing itself, and yet we have the feeling that its being-seen is a kind of down-grading of its being-in-itself, which seems to be more than being-seen. Color seems to be a "kind of mascot" because the colored visible reality, although it is actualized by our look, is more than its relationship to my vision. There is no color without vision, and yet colored, visible reality is there. How is it possible that my look, although it grasps the things, does not hide but reveals them?[8]

All these questions are different expressions of one fundamental question. How is it possible that the visible belongs to my vision and that still it exists in itself? My visible reality is a revelation of real things. Visible reality is mine, and still not mine. It is mine in such a manner that it exceeds me. The whole physiology of seeing presupposes this mystery without explaining it.

Instead of answering this question—is an answer really possible?— Merleau-Ponty continues his analysis, insisting upon the remarkable character of color. A color is sometimes conceived as a quality. This quality would be a kind of message without depth of Being, a message which resists further analysis; he who has received the message knows everything about it, whereas a blind person will never know it at all. He who knows it can express his knowledge by pronouncing, e.g., the word "red," but a further investigation would be meaningless.[9]

Merleau-Ponty rejects this conception. Color can exist for us in different manners. It exists first as a vague element on the horizon of our visual field. Frequently we do not know at once why our visual field is agreeable or disagreeable to us. The reason is that a gentle green or a hard red determines our visual field in such a manner that we do not

---

[8] *Ibid.*
[9] *V.I.*, p. 174.

pay attention to it. We then focus our attention on the predominant color, and by doing so we make it exist for us in a new manner. When we look at it for a long time, or when we look at other things, the color sinks back into the horizon of our visual field.[10]

We speak in an abstract manner as long as we speak about color in itself. Real color is always the color of a thing, and it participates in the structure of the thing itself, its form, its tactile qualities. It cannot be torn from these participations. Merleau-Ponty quotes Claudel who said that sometimes the sea is blue as blood is red.[11] The individual color, moreover, participates in the colors of its surroundings. It makes a difference whether it is dominant or whether it is dominated by other colors. The real color is a momentary nodal point within the simultaneous and successive totality of visible things. It is a kind of momentary contraction of the visible world, not an atom of visibility.[12]

The "Flesh of Things." The red color partakes of the structure of the visible things themselves. It makes a difference whether the red clothes we see are the clothes of custom officials, soldiers of the French Revolution, women, professors or judges. The red color can become a social symbol, as happened during the Russian Revolution.[13] If one takes into account these and many other participations, he will understand that color, visible reality in general, never is an isolated fragment of being offered to an isolated look.[14] The real color, the real visible reality, is a momentary contraction[15] of the visible world, situated between interior and exterior horizons which are always changing. It is something which touches us for a moment and which has an echo in several interior and exterior realms of our existence. It is a modulation of our world. Absolute, isolated being does not determine our vision, simply because absolute, isolated being does not exist. The difference of a color from the preceding, succeeding and surrounding colors is decisive. The colored visible reality is a momentary crystallization of colored and visible Being. People who think and speak about isolated colors forget

---

[10] "Le *quale* reprend son existence atmosphérique." *Ibid.*

[11] "Claudel dit à peu près qu'un certain bleu de la mer est si bleu qu'il n'y a que le sang qui soit plus rouge." *Ibid.*

[12] "C'est une concrétion de la visibilité, ce n'est pas un atome." *Ibid.*

[13] *V.I.*, pp. 174-175. See *Phenomenology of Perception*, pp. 208-212.

[14] "Si l'on faisait état de toutes ces participations, on s'apercevrait qu'une couleur nue, et en général un visible, n'est pas un morceau d'être absolument dur." *V.I.*, p. 175.

[15] "Cristallisation momentanée de l'être coloré." *Ibid.*

our real visual field. Between and below the alleged colors we find the tissue of Being which sustains and nourishes them. This tissue of Being is not, according to Merleau-Ponty, a thinglike reality but the "flesh of things."[16]

The expression "the flesh of things" is very often used by Merleau-Ponty. He holds that this way of speaking is not a vague analogy or metaphor,[17] and he wants us to understand this term almost literally. There is, according to him, a most remarkable affinity between our seeing body and visible reality. Our look envelops, feels and joins the things. The affinity between our look and the things makes one think of Leibniz' "preestablished harmony."[18] It is as if our look knows the things before knowing them; it adapts itself to them in order to see them, and it does so in a dominating way. The movements of our look do not cause chaos, but bring forward a visible world. We cannot say whether our look or the visible things dominate the visual field. Merleau-Ponty again finishes his analysis with a question: what is this remarkable visual prepossession of the visible world? How can we question the visible world in the way this world requires questioning? How is such an "inspired exegesis" possible?[19] These questions are undoubtedly most fundamental. They are presupposed, and even as a rule overlooked, by psychologists who organize experiments in their laboratories. They are the fundamental questions of the philosopher.[20]

3. Seeing and Touching[21]

Preliminary Remarks. In order to draw closer to an answer of the question how seeing as an "inspired exegesis" is possible, Merleau-Ponty now focuses his attention on touching. He makes this transition because in touching the interrogating body and the interrogated world are closer

---

[16] "Entre les couleurs et les visibles prétendus, on retrouverait le tissu qui les double, les soutient, les nourrit, et qui, lui, n'est pas chose, mais possibilité, latence et *chair* des choses." *Ibid.*

[17] *Ibid.*

[18] "Comme s'il était avec elles dans un rapport d'harmonie préétablie." *Ibid.*

[19] "Qu'est-ce que cette prépossession du visible, cet art de l'interroger selon ses voeux, cette exégèse inspirée?" *Ibid.*

[20] In an earlier book, we objected to Merleau-Ponty's neglect of these questions in his former works. See *The Phenomenological Philosophy of Merleau-Ponty,* pp. 242-243.

[21] *V.I.,* pp. 175-178.

to one another than in seeing. Their relationship is more accessible to our inquiry.

The term "interrogation" needs some comment. One of the essential topics of *The Visible and the Invisible* is the nature of "philosophical interrogation." Merleau-Ponty speaks about it in the introduction and often returns to this topic. It is striking that he calls the attitude of the seeing and touching body an "interrogation." This indicates that for Merleau-Ponty there is a continuity between the attitude of the seeing and touching body and the attitude of the philosopher. This topic will recur.

When passing from seeing to touching Merleau-Ponty makes another striking remark: our visual interrogation of the world is a very special manner of touching. In the preceding pages he used the expression *palper du regard,* viz., "to touch things with our look."[22] When speaking about seeing he made use of terms which belong to the realm of touching. This way of speaking presages his thesis of the reversibility of seeing and touching. Later on he will speak about a more general reversibility; in fact, the text which he had prepared for publication ends with the statement that "reversibility is the final truth about human life."[23] Merleau-Ponty looks for the unity which underlies distinctions. His thesis of reversibility manifests the fundamental tendency of his philosophical thought. It is true, indeed, that we touch things with our look. We rightly say, therefore, that some colors are soft and that others are hard. We not only see the light, but we also feel it. Light and color affect our eyes, and the whiteness of snow can really be painful.

Analysis of Touching. We must now follow Merleau-Ponty's analysis of touching. When touching or grasping a thing, I move my hand and my fingers. These movements are adapted to the things I am going to touch. There is a certain quickness in my movements and they have a certain direction. The quickness and the direction of my movements are adapted to the things I am going to feel. I move my fingers differently when I am going to feel the quality of cloth or the softness of putty.[24]

There is, and there must be, a relationship between the manner in which I explore with my fingers and that which my exploration is going

[22] *V.I.*, p. 173.
[23] *V.I.*, p. 204.
[24] *V.I.*, p. 176.

to teach me, between my movements and the things I am going to touch. There is an affinity between them. The movements of my hands are quite different from the movements of the pseudopods of the amoeba. Our movements are an initiation into the tactile world, an openness toward it.[25]

Our feeling hand cannot be openness toward the world if it is not sensitive to itself and, at the same time, sensible to another feeling person, sensible also to our other hand. Our hand must be both sensitive and sensible at the same time.[26] If it were not sensitive to itself, it could not adapt its movements to the things it is going to feel. It could not extend itself toward tactile reality if it were not a tactile reality itself. Our hand is touching, but at the same time it belongs to the realities which can be touched. It opens us toward the tactile reality to which it belongs itself. Its movements enter into the world which it is exploring. The touching and the touchable aspects of our hand imply one another and they belong together as the two sides of a coin.

In my touching experience I must distinguish three aspects which together constitute my experience:

1. I feel the qualitative aspects of reality, e.g., softness and hardness;

2. in these qualitative aspects I feel the things themselves;

3. at the same time I have a real feeling of my feeling.[27] I can even feel my feeling hand with the other hand. This is a clear indication that my feeling hand belongs to the realities which can be felt.

Application to Seeing. Merleau-Ponty analyzed touching in order to better understand our seeing. He now applies the results of his analysis to our seeing.[28] Just as I explore the tactile world with my hands by moving them, I explore the world with my eyes by moving them. There seems to be, however, an important difference. The movements of my exploring eyes and the messages I receive in this exploration seem to belong to a different order of reality. They do not seem to belong, therefore, to the same sense-organ.

---

[25] "L'initiation et l'ouverture à un monde tactile." *Ibid.*

[26] "Ceci ne peut arriver que si, en même temps que sentie du dedans, ma main est aussi accessible du dehors, tangible elle-même." *Ibid.*

[27] "Déjà dans le 'toucher', nous venons de trouver trois expériences distinctes qui se sous-tendent, trois dimensions qui se recoupent, mais sont distinctes: un toucher du lisse et du rugueux, un toucher des choses, -un sentiment passif du corps et de son espace-, et enfin un véritable toucher du toucher." *V.I.*, p. 176.

[28] *V.I.*, pp. 176-178.

This difference, however, is not absolute but relative. Within our touching experience itself there are important differences. I feel my clothes and I feel my touching hand with my other hand; I can control my feeling right hand with my left hand. In the same way I control my visual field with the movements of my eyes. Just as I control my feeling hands, I control my moving eyes. I control the tactile field with my sensitive hands, and I control the visual field with my moving and sensitive eyes. If my eyes would not be sensitive, I could not control my visual field. The sensitivity of my eyes is of essential importance for seeing. Without this sensitivity my seeing would not be adapted to the intensity of the light, and without this adaptation I could not see. My seeing, therefore, is not isolated from tactile reality. Visible and tactile reality belong together.

We must accept, then, that visual and tactile reality belong to the same fundamental realm of Being. Visible reality belongs to tactile reality, and tactile reality contains the promise of visibility. When I feel something in a dark room, I light a lamp in order to see what I have felt. Visible and tactile reality belong together, just as the touching body and tactile reality belong together. There is a real mutual implication between all these fields. It is one and the same body which touches and which sees; tactile and visible reality belong, therefore, to one another.[29] We do not pay sufficient attention, says Merleau-Ponty, to the remarkable fact that every movement of our eyes, every movement of our body, has its place in the visible world which I explore with these movements.[30] The exploring movements belong to the explored world. In the same way, our vision takes place in the tactile world. The visual and the tactile field are both complete because they are coextensive with our world. They are distinguished from one another, and still they cover one another.[31] Merleau-Ponty calls them "total parts."[32] They are partial, since they are distinguished, but both of them cover the whole. We have accentuated their distinction too much, and have not sufficiently seen their mutual implication.

The touching body belongs to the tactile world. So, also, the seeing

---

[29] "Tout visible est taillé dans le tangible, tout être tactile promis en quelque manière à la visibilité." *V.I.,* p. 177.

[30] *Ibid.*

[31] "Les deux cartes sont complètes, et pourtant elles ne se confondent pas." *Ibid.*

[32] "Les deux parties sont parties totales et pourtant ne sont pas superposables." *Ibid.*

body belongs to the visible world. I cannot see without being visible as a seeing person. We see one another looking. We are sometimes ashamed when other people see us looking. It is not just an accident that seeing is visible; seeing belongs to the visible world. *"Il en est,"* says Merleau-Ponty.[33]

It now becomes understandable why our seeing takes place at a distance from the visible things, and why, at the same time, it reaches the things themselves. Distance from the visible things is not an obstacle for seeing, but its condition.[34] It is because of the distance we have from the things that we, as seeing persons, are near to them. Distance and vicinity in this case are not mutually exclusive but rather imply one another. Merleau-Ponty rightly says that they coincide. The optimal distance is the optimal vicinity. The reason is that we do not see worldly things from a point outside the world; we see the world as beings in and of the world. The "density of flesh," which exists between the seeing person and the thing that is seen, constitutes both the visibility of the things and the corporality of the seeing person. This density is not an obstacle for seeing, but its condition. We are in communication with visible things in the world and by the world. The reason why I belong to visible reality is exactly the same reason why I must be at a distance from the thing to be seen. Visible reality is destined to be seen by a body, and not by a bodiless spirit. The same corporal density which characterizes the visible world also characterizes me, and it makes seeing possible. When seeing, I belong to the world and the world belongs to me. I am a part of the world, and the world is an extension of my flesh.

We have entitled this chapter *"J'en suis"*: "I belong to it." Merleau-Ponty's analysis has begun to make the meaning of this phrase evident. His description of seeing and of touching shows that these are not bodiless activities, that only beings which belong to the visible and tactile world can see and touch.[35]

4. Body and World

Our Body as a "Perceiving Perceptible." The analysis of seeing and touching implies important consequences regarding the human body; Merleau-Ponty now indicates them. The body is distinguished from

---

[33] *V.I.,* p. 178.

[34] *Ibid.*

[35] "L'épaisseur du corps, loin de rivaliser avec celle du monde, est au contraire le seul moyen que j'ai d'aller au coeur des choses, en me faisant monde et en les faisant chair." *Ibid.*

things by the fact that it is sensitive to itself.[36] We should not think of such absurdities as a color that sees itself or a surface touching itself.[37] But the body is a whole of colors and of surfaces in which there is a seeing and a touching of itself. Merleau-Ponty calls it a *sensible exemplaire*,[38] i.e., a perceptible reality of an exemplary character, because it is a perceptible reality which perceives itself. It can open itself, therefore, to everything which is similar to it. Being a part of the world, it can assume everything into its own realm. It appropriates everything and, at the same time, it constitutes the difference between itself and the surrounding things. Hence it constitutes the distinction between the interior and the exterior world. This distinction would make no sense if there were not a perceptible body which perceives itself.

By the same activity the perceiving body constitutes the world into a field which has its own identity; the world, as a matter of fact, becomes a tactile, a visual, an auditive field. This identity which characterizes the world as a field, is not artificially superimposed; it is the actualization of the things themselves, the fulfillment of a promise which is inherent in the things. The perceiving body is a worldly reality which at the same time transforms the things into a world. Within this field the things do not lose their own identity, because they appear to the body themselves.

Our body unites us directly with the world, because it is a perceptible reality which perceives.[39] As a perceptible reality it belongs to the things, and as perceiving reality it segregates itself from them. Since the perceiving body is itself a perceptible reality, it remains open to all perceptible reality. Precisely because our body, as a "perceiving perceptible," essentially has these two dimensions, it leads us to the things themselves. These things are not completely exposed to the perceiving body, since this body is not an absolute look which surveys the things. The perceiving body remains perceptible reality, situated among other perceptible realities. It coexists with all things which appear to it, therefore, from a distance. They preserve their own density of Being and never become completely exposed.

No Total Visibility. Merleau-Ponty does not intend to speak in an anthropomorphic manner. He does not say that we cover the real things with human projections, thus making it necessary to distinguish the

---

[36] *"Sensible pour soi." Ibid.*
[37] *Ibid.*
[38] *V.I.*, p. 179.
[39] *Ibid.*

reality-in-itself from the reality-for-us. The perceiving body itself *is* perceptible reality which becomes perceiving. It has the "flesh of the world" in itself. Its self-revelation, therefore, is a revelation of all Being. What is revealed when the body becomes perceiving, is not limited to the body itself. The body is merely a remarkable case of perceptible reality, and perceptible reality therefore exceeds the body. All worldly beings have their own density of being; they are not dissolved into their perceptibility. When we see a cube, we never exhaust its visibility. There is always something more to be seen in the things we see.

What we call visible reality is a quality pregnant with a real density of Being, the surface of a reality which is more than this surface, an appearance which is the appearance of real Being.[40] Reality itself becomes visible, but in such a manner that it is never totally revealed. Visible reality is accessible to an experience which belongs to it, to a perceiving body which exceeds its own material limits. Our body has access to visible reality, not as the bearer of a spirit, but as a "perceiving perceptible."[41]

Our body does not explain the visibility of things. It is not a heterogeneous principle conferring something totally new upon worldly things. The perceiving body is the actualization of a potentiality, of a promise, which is there in things themselves. The visibility of things is a mystery of Being in general, not an exclusive mystery of man.[42] In these words Merleau-Ponty grounds the point of view which the title of this chapter expresses: *j'en suis.* I see, not because I am a principle of being which is heterogeneous to the world, but because I belong to it. I am the actualization of the visibility of the world.

Rejection of the Cartesian Cogito. Now Merleau-Ponty poses an objection which refers to the philosophy of Sartre.[43] Merleau-Ponty has made a distinction between the body as perceptible and as perceiving reality. This distinction coincides, he says, with his former distinction between the objective and the phenomenal body. Sartre says that the body as perceiving, as a phenomenal body, is nothingness, confronted

---

[40] *V.I.*, p. 180.

[41] "C'est à ce titre, et non comme porteur d'un sujet connaissant, que notre corps commande pour nous le visible." *Ibid.*

[42] "C'est bien d'un paradoxe de l'Être, non d'un paradoxe de l'homme qu'il s'agit ici." *Ibid.*

[43] *Ibid.*

with the density of Being. Merleau-Ponty admits the weight of this objection. Our perceiving body is also a thinking body. It is a real question whether human thought can be explained as Merleau-Ponty tries to explain it. He sees man as the actualization of the visibility, of the perceptibility of things themselves. Can we also explain human thought in this manner? Are we not obliged to accept Sartre's thesis that human consciousness is in the end nothingness, radically distinguished from the density of Being?

Merleau-Ponty promises to confront himself with this question.[44] But he refuses to place his analysis in the light—rather, in the confusion —of an *a priori* point of view, namely, that human consciousness is nothingness, radically distinguished from the density of Being. This Cartesian point of view has confronted us with difficulties which cannot be solved, and Merleau-Ponty tries to overcome these difficulties. He speaks of a "classical impasse" which must be overcome. It is not right to begin with difficulties arising from a point of view which must be surpassed.[45]

This text proves that Merleau-Ponty rejects the traditional doctrine of the cogito, which considers it a reality of the spiritual order, radically distinguished from the being of the body. He always doubted it, as was pointed out in my first book about the philosophy of Merleau-Ponty.[46] He considered man as a body-subject and tried to reduce the total reality of man to this body-subject. But now he realizes that in his preceding works he could not overcome the classical impasse for two reasons. First, he did not penetrate sufficiently into the reality of the body-subject; according to his new views, his analysis remained superficial. Secondly, he was seduced into reintroducing the traditional concept of the cogito, e.g., when he spoke about the "silent cogito." Now he refuses to consider any objection which starts from the traditional concept of the cogito. He wants to give an interpretation of human thought, but not in the light of the traditional doctrine. He continues, therefore, his present analysis in the hope that this analysis will give him the fundaments for a

---

[44] "C'est une question, et nous ne l'éviterons pas, de savoir comment le sentant sensible peut être aussi pensée." *Ibid.*

[45] "Mais ici, cherchant à former nos premiers concepts de manière à éviter les impasses classiques, nous n'avons pas à faire acception des difficultés qu'ils peuvent offrir quand on les confronte avec un *cogito* qui, lui-même, est à revoir." *Ibid.*

[46] Kwant, *The Phenomenological Philosophy of Merleau-Ponty,* pp. 46-48.

new concept of the cogito.   In short, he refuses to be confronted with a concept of the cogito which badly needs revision.

We have, continues Merleau-Ponty, a body which is not a mere object, but which has the character of a subject since it suffers pain, since it has hands which touch the thing.[47]   It is true that in order to touch it is not sufficient that we have only hands; other aspects of our being play a role in touching.   But this does not justify the conclusion that our hands themselves do not touch, that they belong to the world of pure objects, that they are merely instruments.   Were we to think like this, we would again place ourselves within the separation of subject and object, and we would be unfaithful to the results of the preceding analysis.[48]

Perceiving and Perceptible as "Aspects" of Our Body.   The fact that our body is a perceptible reality which perceives implies that it is at the same time both an object and a subject.   These two orders are united, therefore, in the reality of the body.[49]   This cannot be just an accident.[50] It teaches us that the two orders are not really two; rather, they belong together.   It is not an accident that the perceiving body is perceptible; it could not be perceiving if it were not perceptible.   It belongs to the order of things in a new and stronger sense than other worldly beings. The fact that it perceives does not mean that it belongs less, but that it belongs more and in a new manner, to the world.   It is in the world as a center which concentrates things around itself.   It transforms them into a field, into a world.   It belongs to the family of things but it makes use of its own being in order to participate in the being of all.   The body and things compenetrate one another.   The body belongs to the order of things, and things are assumed into the realm of the body's being.   The body is a thing and the world is the "flesh" of the body.[51]

Merleau-Ponty has said that there are two aspects to our body, since it is perceptible and at the same time perceives.   Yet it is not quite right to speak of two aspects, for they essentially belong together and constitute

---

[47] *V.I.,* p. 180.

[48] "On le sait: des mains ne suffisent pas pour toucher, mais décider pour cette seule raison que nos mains ne touchent pas, et les renvoyer au monde des objets ou des instruments, ce serait, acceptant la bifurcation du sujet et l'objet, renoncer par avance à comprendre le sensible et nous priver de ses lumières."   *Ibid.*

[49] "Sa double appartenance à l'ordre de l'objet' et à l'ordre du 'sujet' nous dévoile entre les deux ordres des relations très inattendues."   *Ibid.*

[50] "Ce ne peut être par un hasard incompréhensible."   *Ibid.*

[51] "Le corps appartient à l'ordre des choses comme le monde est chair universelle."   *Ibid.*

together the identical being of the body. The body is not just visible and not just seeing. It is visibility itself, existing on different levels of actualization, because our body sometimes sees, and sometimes does not see; sometimes it is merely looking around and sometimes it becomes a determinate look.[52] The human body is not *in* the world in the sense that it is an isolated being which assumes the world into its own interior realm. It sees the world itself, the real world in which all men live together. It sees the world without leaving itself, since its organs, its eyes, its hands, are innerly directed toward the world.

If we are allowed to say that the world has a voice, we must say that our body is the ear which hears the voice of the world. When it sees and feels it is the magical actualization of the potentialities of the world.[53] Merleau-Ponty uses the word "magical" for we will never completely understand how seeing and touching are possible. If we look for metaphors, we should not say, according to Merleau-Ponty, that our body as perceptible and our body as perceiving are two aspects of one and the same reality; rather we must say that they are two sides of one and the same piece of paper, that they are two parts of one and the same circle.[54]

What has been said about the body as perceptible reality must be extended to all perceptible reality. The body is a part of perceptible reality and, at the same time, unites itself with it. We must reject the old prejudices, according to which the world enters into the body, according to which seeing is an activity which would take place within the body. There is no clear boundary between the perceiving body and the world, for the world is the continuation of our own visibility, of our own "flesh." The body is not "in" the world, neither is the world "in" the body.[55] These overly material expressions make us blind to the essential togetherness and mutual participation of body and world. I see

---

[52] "Il ne faut même pas dire, comme nous le faisions toute à l'heure, que le corps est fait de deux feuillets, dont l'un, celui du 'sensible', est solidaire du reste du monde; il n'y a pas en lui deux feuillets ou deux couches, il n'est fondamentalement ni chose vue suelement, ni voyant seulement, il est la Visibilité tantôt errante et tantôt rassemblée." *Ibid.*

[53] "Ses mains, ses yeux, ne sont rien d'autre que cette référence d'un visible, d'un tangible-étalon à tous ceux dont il porte la ressemblance, et dont il recueille le témoignage, par une magie qui est la vision, le toucher mêmes." *V.I.*, p. 181.

[54] "Si l'on veut des métaphores, il vaudrait mieux dire que le corps senti et le corps sentant sont comme l'envers et l'endroit, ou encore, comme deux segments d'un seul parcours circulaire." *V.I.*, p. 182.

[55] *Ibid.*

the surface of things, but this surface is the revelation of a depth of Being. This depth of Being which constitutes things, however, constitutes also my body and therefore supports my vision. As a visible reality my body is a part of the great spectacle of the world, but my look actualizes this spectacle and supports it. There really is *entrelacs* and *chiasme*.[56]

Summary. At the end of this analysis Merleau-Ponty reviews what he has explained.[57] There is, he says, seeing and touching when one of the visible and touchable beings opens itself to the visible and touchable reality to which it belongs, when all at once it finds itself surrounded by it. Then the visible, the touchable, is actualized; and the actualized visible and touchable does not belong exclusively to the body, nor to the world. It belongs to both together and unites them into one field, one world. The actualization of the visible and the touchable is not a physical fact; it belongs, although it exceeds man, to the human realm of existence. Man and world belong together in what could be called "the visible in itself," "the touchable in itself."[58] Man and world are assumed into one realm which begins to exist for man.

Merleau-Ponty uses this comparison: when two mirrors are opposed to one another, there come into existence two indefinite series of images which do not exclusively belong to the one mirror or to the other, since the images in the one are the reflection of the images in the other.[59] In this way man and world belong together within the visible and the touchable. The seeing man is taken up into the entire spectacle of visible reality. Since we see ourselves, there is a fundamental narcissism in our vision.[60] Several painters have said that things look at us.[61] This way of speaking is quite understandable, since we are the object of our own vision; we undergo what we do; we are assumed in the spectacle we constitute. By seeing we make ourselves visible. Our own visibility is the very condition of seeing.

This analysis of Merleau-Ponty concerns the most ordinary reality of

---

[56] "Où mettre dans le corps le voyant, puisque, de toute évidence, il n'y a dans le corps que des 'ténèbres bourrées d'organes' c'est-à-dire du visible encore?" *Ibid.*

[57] *V.I.*, p. 183.

[58] "Par leur commerce, se forme une Visibilité, un Tangible en soi, qui n'appartiennent en propre ni au corps comme fait ni au monde comme fait." *Ibid.*

[59] *Ibid.*

[60] "Il y a un narcissisme fondamental de toute vision." *V.I.*, p. 183. See also pp. 185, 303, 309.

[61] *V.I.*, p. 183.

our human life.   He does not make use of difficult psychological experiments, as he did in his former works.   Yet his analysis is extremely difficult, for he speaks about fundamental realities which as a rule are overlooked.

5. The "Flesh of the World"

The perceptibility which is actualized, but not created, by human perception and which characterizes all worldly reality, both the human body and other things, is often called by Merleau-Ponty the "flesh of the world."   He already used this term in some of the articles included in *Signs;* but in the present chapter he explains this rather myserious term. Merleau-Ponty often uses metaphors and new expressions, but this one is undoubtedly one of the strangest.

What the "Flesh" is Not.   Merleau-Ponty first indicates what the "flesh" is not.[62]   Certainly it not matter, viz., a number of particles which by their cohesion constitute a material being.   Neither is the "flesh" a kind of "psychical material" caused in us (only God knows how this could happen) by exterior things.   The manner in which Merleau-Ponty speaks of "psychic material" clearly shows his fundamental dislike of this term and of what it is supposed to indicate.   He stresses the unity of man and world and rejects the clear distinction between the material and the so-called psychic world.   In his criticism of physics and psychology, which we will study later, he says that there is a close connection between Cartesian dualism and the distinction between a physical and a psychic realm of being.   Since he rejects Cartesian dualism, he must also reject the distinction between physical and psychic reality.   The "flesh" is neither a fact nor a collection of facts.   Neither is it a representation of the human mind; the human mind could not be captured by its own representations like the perceiving person is captured by the "flesh of the world."   Thus, the "flesh" is neither matter, nor spirit, nor substance.[63]

The "Flesh" as "Element" of Being.   Merleau-Ponty turns to the Greek notion of "element" to make clear what he means by the term "flesh."[64]   The oldest Greek philosophers looked for the element which

---

[62] *V.I.,* p. 184.

[63] "La chair n'est pas matière, n'est pas esprit, n'est pas substance." *Ibid.*

[64] *Ibid.* It is remarkable that the term "element" also plays an important role in the book of Emmanuel Lévinas, *Totalité et Infini*, Martinus Nijhoff, La Haye, 1961. Lévinas, too, emphasizes the essential unity of man and world and calls the world the "element" of our existence.

would constitute and penetrate all things. Convinced of the fundamental unity of Being, they tried to explain this unity with the help of the element. The element is conceived by them as a *general thing*, viz., as a reality which is not a particular being next to other particular beings, but which is yet the essence of all. The element is neither a particular spatio-temporal being nor an abstract idea of our mind; yet it is similar to both because it has the generality of the idea and the reality of spatio-temporal beings. It is a kind of embodied principle which gives a style of Being to everything in which it is present. The element is not a particular appearing thing, but it appears in all appearing reality. It is the general style of Being participated in by all particular beings. It appears everywhere and in everything, and yet does not itself appear, since it is not a particular being. The element explains the interior unity of different beings. Experience teaches us that there is a plurality of beings. But the plurality is possible only within a fundamental unity. It would make no sense to speak of plurality if the many things did not belong together. We always presuppose this fundamental unity but usually do not make a problem of it. Metaphysicians traditionally say that all things belong together since they all participate in Being. Merleau-Ponty gives a more material name to the worldly unity of all beings, speaking, therefore, of the "element."

The "flesh" is an "element" of Being[65]—Merleau-Ponty himself capitalizes this word. The "flesh" is not a fact or a collection of facts. Yet it coheres with the "here" and "now." We sense here the reason why Merleau-Ponty avoids abstract metaphysical terms; his Being is corporal, worldly. The "element," the "flesh," is not a concrete thing appearing here and now, but it makes possible every appearance which is here and now. It inaugurates the fundamental realm of the "here" and of the "now." It is not a particular fact, but it makes the appearance of facts possible.[66] He calls the "flesh" a "facticity," i.e., that which makes possible all the facts. The "element" is not a particular meaning, but it makes meaning possible since it concentrates all partial facts around their source.

Conclusions from the Description. Although Merleau-Ponty's description remains rather vague, some conclusions can be drawn. The

---

[65] "La chair est en ce sens un 'élément' de l'Être." *V.I.*, p. 184.

[66] "Inauguration du *où* et du *quand*, possibilité et exigence du fait, en un mot facticité, ce qui fait que le fait est fait." *Ibid.*

"element," the "flesh," is certainly not a psychic reality immanent in our mind. But neither is it an objective reality quite independent of man. Merleau-Ponty excludes this by saying that the "flesh" concentrates around us all beings as meaningful.[67] The field of meaning cannot be independent of man. The "element" therefore is at the same time both a worldly and a human reality. It brings all reality, including man, into a field. It is the field-character of all Being. This field-character does not depend on man only, nor does it depend on the world only. It depends on both. The "element," the "flesh," makes it possible that all things belong together. This togetherness is not constituted by any particular human act, since it is presupposed by all of them.[68]

Merleau-Ponty never explained why he expressed this fundamental unity, this "element," by the word "flesh." The reason, however, is quite obvious: the flesh constitutes the unity and the cohesion of our body. The unity which embraces all the things of the world and also our body is conceived by Merleau-Ponty as a kind of prolongation of our body. Hence, he uses the word "flesh."

Merleau-Ponty's terminology and the way in which he explains himself make it clear that his thought represents a kind of metaphysics which tries to find its basis in matter, or rather, in the corporal order. His thought is metaphysical because he is looking for the principle of unity of Being. He thinks he can find this principle of unity in the corporal order. Nevertheless, it would be entirely wrong to say that his metaphysical thought is materialistic. This would be true only if Merleau-Ponty distinguished the corporal order from the spiritual and if he opposed them. We know that this is not the case for Merleau-Ponty. There is no reason, therefore, to accuse him of materialism.

6. *"Intercorporality"*

Merleau-Ponty has analyzed our seeing and touching and has demonstrated that these human activities belong to the world and imply a relationship to the world. Hence he has concluded that our body belongs to the world and concentrates the world around itself. This is possible because both are united within the same "flesh of the world," which is the realm of existence of both body and world. These

---

[67] "Et du même coup aussi, ce qui fait qu'ils ont du sens, que les faits parcellaires se disposent autour de 'quelque chose'." *Ibid.*

[68] "Lui et moi, ensembles, sommes pris dans un même 'élément'." *Ibid.*

fundamental points of view imply two consequences which are closely
connected, viz., the universality of our seeing and touching and also their
intersubjectivity, which Merleau-Ponty calls "intercorporality."

The Universality of Our Seeing and Touching. My seeing always
has a particular character. I cannot see all things together, nor can I
even see one thing totally. Still I presume that the things which I do
not see are also visible: when I look at a cube and see only several of its
sides, I presume that its other sides also are visible. There is a *visibilité
de principe,*[69] viz., a visibility which not only exists as a matter of fact
but which has the character of a principle. We all take the essential
visibility of worldly things for granted. When scientists descend into a
cave, and when in the future they land on the moon, they bring
themselves into a situation never before existing. Yet they still suppose
that their new surrounding will be visible, provided certain conditions
are fulfilled. How is it possible that we are certain about a visibility
which we have never verified? It is quite possible that I look hastily and
superficially and that, therefore, I look wrongly; the essential visibility of
things does not preclude my look being superficial and wrong. Still I
suppose that my vision can be corrected.[70] My inexact and incorrect
vision can always be replaced by one that is more exact and more correct.
It is as if there were a certain "horror of emptiness" in our seeing and in
our touching; we presume that the emptiness can always be filled, that
our potentiality can always be actualized.[71]

This is not difficult to understand if we accept Merleau-Ponty's
theory about the "flesh of the world." The fact that all worldly reality,
our body and things, is penetrated by the same "flesh of the world,"
explains how all things are visible and touchable in principle. My body
is a "perceiving perceptible," and it must be conceived as the actualization of a possibility which is inherent in the "flesh of the world."

It is possible to neglect these fundamental questions, as many scientists
do. But then we presuppose an essential visibility which is not
explained. We move in a fundamental darkness, as many theories of
human knowledge do, especially the theories of knowledge which are

---

[69] *Ibid.*

[70] *Ibid.*

[71] "Selon le principe de la visibilité, qui, comme par une sorte d'horreur du
vide, appelle déjà la vision et le visible vrais, non seulement comme substituts de
leur erreurs, mais encore comme leur explication." *Ibid.*

implicit in science.[72] A theory of vision must include an ontology of vision. Merleau-Ponty's philosophy of the "flesh of the world" tries to give us such an ontology of vision.

"Intercorporality." Another most important consequence follows from Merleau-Ponty's theory. The notion of the "flesh of the world," he says, is an ultimate notion,[73] not deduced from other notions, but rather supposed by them. As a matter of fact, the "flesh of the world," is not composed of other, heterogeneous substances but is the realm of existence of all substances. It is understandable in itself. In me there is a relationship of the "flesh of the world" to itself; in me the visible is related to itself; in me perceptible reality becomes a perception of itself— this is the reason why I am seeing. My seeing does not depend on my private, personal initiative, but it is indebted to the relationship of the visible to itself which constitutes me and which makes me seeing.[74] Vision is realized in me, independently of me, in the sense that it does not depend on my personal initiative.

If this is true, it becomes quite understandable that the relationship of the visible to itself which makes me see is also realized in other beings. My seeing is not my personal possession, but an ontological mystery realized in me independently of me and which I take up into my personal life. The mystery of seeing is mine, but not exclusively mine. It can be realized in every body in which its ontological conditions are fulfilled.

Because the same relationship of the visible to itself is realized in many bodies, an "intercorporality" arises. I can touch my touching hand. I am then contacting a corporal being which contacts things. In the same way I can touch the touching hand of another person. Then also I am contacting a corporal being which contacts things.[75]

Merleau-Ponty refuses to accept the theory which would make a worldless consciousness the universal principle of coherence. According to this theory, the world would be one field because it would be the totality of all the objects of consciousness; consciousness would constitute the unity of the world. It would also constitute the unity of the body; this would be a unity because it would be the totality of all the

---

[72] *V.I.*, p. 185.

[73] "La chair est une notion dernière." *Ibid.*

[74] "Me constitue en voyant." *Ibid.*

[75] "S'il s'est laissé capter par un de ses fragments, le principe de la captation est acquis, le champ ouvert pour d'autres Narcisses, pour une 'intercorporeité'." *Ibid.*

instruments which consciousness uses in order to contact the world. Our hands would touch the same world, since they would be the instruments of the same consciousness which contacts the world. The unity of consciousness would not depend on the unity of the body, but the unity of the body would depend on the unity of consciousness. Perceiving would be the activity of consciousness and the body would only be its instrument. As a consequence, the problem of intersubjectivity becomes insoluble. If consciousness is an absolute point which reduces every other reality to an object, how is it possible that there are many conscious beings? The problem of intersubjectivity can no longer be solved.[76]

Merleau-Ponty rejects this theory, for it neglects a number of simple facts. It brushes aside the fact that my seeing is really embodied in my eyes, my touching in my hands; it does not see that my body feels, enjoys and suffers, that my body has its own interior unity. My two hands touch the same things because they are the hands of the same body, and still each hand has its own tactile experience.[77] My two eyes work together to effect cyclopic vision because they belong to the same face, not because they are the instruments of the same consciousness.[78] The collaboration of the two eyes was already there before any human consciousness knew anything about it.

The theory which ascribes the unity of the body and of the world to consciousness makes things too easy and forgets their really complex nature. In the body there are many organs which feel, two eyes which see, two hands which handle the world. The body has a subjective character wherever it is a "perceiving perceptible," and it is a "perceiving perceptible" in many ways, in many organs. Moreover, it has its own interior unity which is not caused by an extrinsic principle.[79] The unity of my consciousness, on the contrary, is supported by the intrinsic unity

---

[76] *V.I.*, p. 186.

[77] "Mes deux mains touchent les mêmes choses parce qu'elles sont les mains d'un même corps." *V.I.*, p. 186.

[78] "Qui fait . . . de mes deux yeux les canaux d'une seule vision cyclopéenne." *Ibid.*

[79] "Relation difficile à penser, puisqu'un oeil, une main, sont capables de vision, de toucher, et que, ce qui est à comprendre, c'est que ces visions, ces touchers, cettes petites subjectivités, ces 'consciences de . . .' puissent s'assembler comme des fleurs dans un bouquet, quand chacune étant 'conscience de . . .', étant Pour Soi, réduit les autres en objets. On ne sortira d'embarras qu'en renonçant à la bifurcation de la 'conscience de . . .' et de l'objet." *Ibid.*

of the body itself. My body can be called a thing, but it is a thing which at the same time has the character of a subject. It has many experiences, but it unites them itself. The body itself gathers its manifold experiences into one life of experience. The dual vision of my two eyes is united by the body and it is the same body which gathers the tactile experiences of my two hands. Because of the body itself there is one experience of one world. The body itself translates our tactile experience into visual experience, etc. The appeal to a bodiless consciousness to explain the unity of our experience is an escape from reality which leaves the main problems unsolved, and which creates new problems, such as the problem of intersubjectivity and the plurality of conscious beings.[80]

We must understand the intersubjective character of human life, the connection between the experiences of many persons, in the same way we understand the unity of our own experience. In ourselves there is a connection between the manifold perceptive fields, between the visible and the touchable; the one is connected with the other without the intervention of an extrinsic principle. There is an intrinsic interchange between them which finally constitutes one general field of experience. The same interchange is possible between the experiences of many persons, since the same visible reality becomes seeing in many persons, since the same "flesh of the world" unites them as "perceiving perceptibles."[81] This does not mean that we all together are just one immense animal, but it does mean that the same "flesh of the world" makes us perceive, and that our lives are connected from within. The same "flesh of the world" which unites the manifold experiences of our body unites the experiences of many persons. Their seeing is the actualization of the same visibility. The same perceptible becomes perceiving in all of them. The "flesh of the world" enlightens not only what happens in me, but also what happens in others. We are all realizations of the same mysterious "perceiving perceptible."[82]

Thinkers sometimes maintain that another person's seeing or touching is completely inaccessible to me. I can never see what he sees, touch

---

[80] *V.I.*, pp. 186-187.

[81] "Pourquoi la synergie n'existerait-elle pas entre différents organismes, si elle est possible à l'intérieur de chacun?" *V.I.*, p. 187.

[82] "Cela est possible dès qu'on cesse de définir à titre primordial le sentir par l'appartenance à une même 'conscience', et qu'au contraire on le comprend comme retour sur soi du visible, adhérence charnelle du sentant au senti et du senti au sentant." *Ibid.*

what he touches. This would be true if seeing and touching were interior, worldless activities. But this is not true, for the same perceptible which makes him perceive also makes me perceive. It is not necessary that we exchange ideas in order to communicate with each other. The look of another person makes me look and his attention makes me attend. My body sometimes assumes the attitude of other persons without any intervention of my thought. What happens in me can pass over into the other. Our being is contagious. With the help of a few words we can enter into the field of existence of the other person.

There is no real problem of the other "ego" since it is not he or I who sees; an anonymous visibility lives and actualizes itself in us, and we share a general vision. The same "flesh of the world" constitutes all of us.[83]

Reversibility. Merleau-Ponty often uses the term "reversibility," and he attaches great importance to what he wants to express by this term. He ends this chapter, as we mentioned, with the sentence—the last sentence he wrote—that this reversibility is possibly the final truth.[84] He means by this term that the message we receive in one realm of our experience can be translated into another realm. This "translation" is sometimes the work of the intellect, e.g., when we are speaking. But very often the "translation" takes place on the pre-intellectual level. Our body translates tactile messages into visual language. The tactile message has a visual meaning also, and the visual meaning implies a tactile meaning. For our experience—and intellectual consciousness may not interfere on this point—there is an intrinsic communication between the visual and the tactile realm of our perception. Merleau-Ponty indicates this phenomenon by the term "reversibility."

If we look attentively, we become aware of the fact that this phenomenon of "reversibility" manifests itself everywhere. There is "reversibility" between the touchable and our touching, between the visible and our seeing, between seeing and touching, between all the ways in which we perceive.[85] This "reversibility" also manifests itself

---

[83] "Il n'y a pas ici de problème de l'*alter ego* parce que ce n'est pas *moi* qui vois, pas *lui* qui voit, parce qu'une visibilité anonyme nous habite tous deux, une vision en général." *Ibid.*

[84] *V.I.*, p. 204.

[85] *V.I.*, p. 188.

between the many "perceiving perceptibles";[86] we can exchange our experiences, and we do so, even more than we know, on the pre-intellectual level. "Reversibility" manifests itself between many perceiving bodies, between different persons. Our experience is not immanent but transitive. There is not only a transition between one realm of experience and another, but also between the experience of different persons.

When we see other seeing persons, we are not confronted with worldless looks, phantoms of what we take to be ourselves.[87] We see a look in which the world, our world, is involved. When we see other persons looking, we realize that our world, including ourselves, is visible to them. We realize that our eyes, which are not visible to us, are visible to them. We can experience this because we ourselves are seeing persons. If we would not have the experience of seeing, we could not see other persons as men who are seeing. We experience that in our seeing the depth of Being becomes manifest. This same depth of Being, then, reveals that seeing is not our own exclusive privilege. Solipsism is an impossible attitude.[88] The solipsistic thinker takes his own exclusive self as the starting-point of his philosophical thought. Having appropriated everything to himself, he asks whether his own experiences are shared by others. He cannot rightly come to a positive answer, since he has isolated his whole experience in himself.

When I realize, however, that I am a "perceiving perceptible," that I experience a mystery of Being which exceeds myself, I begin to understand that my experience does not necessarily belong exclusively to myself.[89] When I become aware of this, I understand that I am visible, precisely as seeing. My seeing returns upon me through the eyes of

---

[86] "Il y a un cercle du touché et du touchant, le touché saisit le touchant; il y a un cercle du visible et du voyant, le voyant n'est pas sans existence visible; il y a même inscription du touchant au visible, du voyant au tangible, et réciproquement, enfin il y a propagation de ces échanges à tous les corps de même type et de même style que je vois et que je touche,—et cela par la fondamentale fission ou ségrégation du sentant et du sensible qui, latéralement, fait communiquer les organes de mon corps et fonde la transitivité d'un corps à l'autre." *Ibid.*

[87] *Ibid.*

[88] "L'illusion solipsiste qui est de croire que tout dépassement est dépassement par soi." *V.I.,* p. 189.

[89] "Flotter dans l'Être avec une autre vie." *Ibid.*

other persons.[90]   In this way my attention is not limited to the things I see and to my seeing body, but I understand the human body in general; I see a reality which itself is seeing.   I am no longer exclusively confronted with an inhuman world, for there are other seeing persons; I am in the world with other seeing persons.[91]   What I am interiorly is also there, in the world; and what is there, outside me, the seeing of another body, is also in myself.   We communicate, since we are all "perceiving perceptibles," since the same "flesh of the world" makes us see, makes us perceive.

Merleau-Ponty accepts, of course, the intersubjective character of our human existence; but our intersubjectivity is first of all an intercorporality.   Our communication does not first proceed from an intellectual or from a voluntary act, but from the fact that we are all actualizations of the same visibility which is implied in the "flesh of the world."

7. The Speaking Body

The Transition to the Realm of Expression.   From "flesh of the world" Merleau-Ponty has come to "intercorporality."   In a rather poetic manner he writes that we "dwell in Being together with other living persons."[92]   Moving, touching, seeing are not limited to ourselves; we communicate in these activities and, thus, our own activities become transitive.   Man can become aware of the root of that which is simultaneously in him and transcends him.   In the patient and silent desire for awareness, the paradoxical activity of expression begins.[93]

We have seen that the "flesh of the world" exists as a seeing and touching body and that seeing and touching are reversible.   The reversibility, however, which characterizes the "flesh of the world," can also exist in other fields; and there it becomes even much more subtle. Between bodies relationships are constituted which not only enlarge, but which exceed, the realm of the visible.[94]

---

[90] "Pour la première fois, le voyant que je suis m'est vraiment visible; pour la première fois, je m'apparais retourné jusqu'au fond sous mes propres yeux." *Ibid.*

[91] "Pour la première fois, par l'autre corps, je vois que, dans son accouplement avec la chair du monde, le corps apporte plus qu'il ne reçoit, ajoutant au monde que je vois le trésor nécessaire de ce qu'il voit, lui." *Ibid.*

[92] *Ibid.*

[93] "Et dès lors, mouvement, toucher, vision, s'appliquant à l'autre et à eux-mêmes, remontent vers leur source, et dans le travail patient et silencieux du désir, commence le paradoxe de l'expression." *Ibid.*

[94] *Ibid.*

With these somewhat mysterious words Merleau-Ponty describes the transition toward the realm of expression. It is not his intention to give a historical description of the development of expression. His goal is to make the phenomenon of expression understandable, starting from the "flesh of the world." He does not really succeed, at least not in this chapter, in making this phenomenon comprehensible. But we must not forget that this chapter is only the beginning of the elaboration of his point of view. In his notes there are several remarks about the scheme of his book; there we read that he intends to return to the phenomenon of expression and language. Only at the end, in his final chapter, will he be able to formulate his final vision of language.[95] In the present chapter, we are disappointed in reading his remarks about expression and language; but here we have only a first statement of his new vision.

Some of my movements, he continues, are not directed toward any material being.[96] They do not even find their likeness and their example in other living bodies. Merleau-Ponty means the movements of the face and many gestures, especially the strange movements of the throat and of the mouth in the production of sound. I am a being which produces sounds, like the crystal, metals and many other beings. But I hear my sounds from within.[97] Merleau-Ponty quotes Malraux, who says that we hear ourselves with our throat.[98] On this point I am an incomparable being: my voice is connected with the mass of my body in a manner which I do not observe in other persons.[99] I experience my voice as most intimately connected with my corporal being; when I am speaking it is as if I am a voice. But when I am sufficiently close to another person who produces sounds, I can hear his breath, I can feel his impetuosity and his fatigue;[100] it is as if I were assisting at the birth of his voice, just as I am present at the birth of my own. There is, as we have seen, a reversibility

---

[95] In the last note, written in March, 1961, Merleau-Ponty says his book will be composed in the following manner: I. *le visible;* II. *la nature;* III. *le logos.* Thus he intended to write on language in the third and last part of his book. *V.I.,* p. 328.

[96] *V.I.,* pp. 189-190.

[97] "Je suis un être sonore, mais ma vibration à moi je l'entends du dedans." *V.I.,* p. 190.

[98] "Comme a dit Malraux, je m'entends avec ma gorge." *Ibid.*

[99] "Ma voix est liée à la masse de ma vie comme ne l'est la voix de personne." *V.I.,* p. 190.

[100] "Mais si je suis assez près de l'autre qui parle pour entendre son souffle, et sentir son effervescence et sa fatigue, j'assiste presque, en lui comme en moi, à l'effrayante naissance de la vocifération." *V.I.,* p. 190.

of seeing and touching; and this reversibility extends not only to our body, but also to other living persons. In the same way there is a reversibility in the production of sounds. My voice has an echo in the other person and his voice has an echo in me. This new reversibility, which comes into existence when the living body expresses itself in sounds, marks the point at which speaking and thinking begin to enter into the world of silence.[101]

Here we are at the border between the silent world and the world which expresses itself. When I am present to other seeing beings and they are present to me, I experience that my visible field is not exclusively my own, that the visibility of things exceeds me.[102] My visible field belongs to a visible reality which has a general character. Thus it becomes possible that the word "vision" contains a new and figurative meaning, viz., an intuition of the mind, an idea. During the entire history of philosophy the word "vision" has meant both the activity of our eyes and the intuition of our mind. The awareness of the general character of the visibility of things which I experience in my seeing approaches the intuition of the mind, the idea.

From Potential to Actual Thought. The presence of other seeing persons, however, could not provoke my thought or idea if it were not potentially there in my seeing.[103] My seeing cannot become an actual

---

[101] "Cette nouvelle réversibilité et l'émergence de la chair comme expression sont le point d'insertion du parler et du penser dans le monde du silence." *Ibid.*

[102] "A la frontière du monde muet ou solipsiste, là où en présence d'autres voyants, mon visible se confirme comme exemplaire d'une universelle visibilité, nous touchons à un sens second ou figuré de la vision, qui sera l'*intuitus mentis* ou idée, à une sublimation de la chair, qui sera esprit ou pensée." *V.I.,* pp. 190-191.

[103] "Mais la présence de fait des autres corps ne saurait produire la pensée ou l'idée si la semence n'en était dans le mien." *V.I.,* p. 191. The last two texts of Merleau-Ponty imply a most interesting and important question, namely, the question of the relationship between the "common" and the "universal." We become aware of the fact that one and the same visible reality is "common" to many bodies which see. The "common" character of visible reality does not coincide with the universality of the idea. Can we arrive, however, at the "universal" idea without the awareness of the "common" character of perceptible reality? Merleau-Ponty seems to think that the awareness of the "common" character of perceptible reality conditions, and perhaps even implies, the universality of the idea.

In a note of February, 1960, Merleau-Ponty writes: "Le concept, la signification sont le singulier *dimensionnalisé,* la structure *formulée,* et il n'y a

thought if it is not a potential thought. Thought begins to appear in the infrastructure of seeing; it is not introduced as a totally new and heterogeneous reality. Merleau-Ponty says he leaves open the question, at least in these pages, whether thought is already implicitly there in our vision; and he does not describe an empirical genesis of human thought.[104] Yet, does Merleau-Ponty really leave this question open? We must respect a writer when he gives us a reflective description of his own thought, but in this case it is undeniable that Merleau-Ponty's text itself points in a certain direction; it gives us the strong impression that for him thought is already implicitly present in vision.[105]

It is clear, Merleau-Ponty continues, that my touching experience is dispersed all over my body, since I have many organs which are in touch with the world. Therefore, I cannot ascribe my touching to a concentrated consciousness which would be distinguished from my touching body. But it is also clear that my touching is not a scattered plurality of separate experiences. There is an interior connection between my tactile experiences and between seeing and touching. There is a "central vision" which gathers my "scattered visions" and rules my perceptive life.[106] This center cannot be conceived as a worldless consciousness. For, the center would then be only an exterior reality, whereas all my preceptions are *intrinsically* connected. What is this intrinsic center which belongs to the very essence of all my perceptive experiences? Is it a potential thought? Is my actual thought a development of this potential thought? Merleau-Ponty does not yet

---

pas de vision de cette charnière invisible; le nominalisme a raison: les significations ne sont que des *écarts définis.*" *V.I.,* p. 291. In this text Merleau-Ponty says that the abstract meaning, the universal idea, is implied in the dimension, the structure of perceptible reality. But in order to become aware of the universal idea, it is necessary to formulate the dimension, the structure. This means that we "define" that which co-appears in appearing reality, that we focus our attention on the lateral aspects of perceptible reality.

[104] "Et c'est directement dans l'infrastructure de la vision qu'il faut la (la pensée) faire apparaître. La faire apparaître, disons-nous, et non la faire naître: car nous laissons en suspens pour le moment la question de savoir si elle n'y était pas déjà impliquée." *V.I.,* p. 191.

[105] Although Merleau-Ponty does not work out this point of view, he seems to think that the "universal" idea is the explicit awareness of the "common" character of the structure, the style of perceptible Being. See note 103. Visible reality is "common" to the seeing bodies, not only in fact, but in principle. Being actualizes its visibility in us. The awareness of this "common" character is the "universal" idea.

[106] This reminds us of the *sensus communis* of Aristotelian and medieval philosophy.

answer these questions, but he does say that our actual thought appears at the basis of the intrinsic coherence of our perceptive life, that the intrinsic unity of our perceptive life is the condition of thinking, that we men must see and touch in order to think, that our thought belongs to the "flesh of the world" which makes us see and touch.[107]

All these remarks point in a certain direction, viz., that our actual thought is the development of potential thought implicit in seeing, in touching, in the intrinsic coherence of our perceptive life. This interpretation agrees with the tendency of the preceding works of Merleau-Ponty and it is confirmed by a note which he wrote when reviewing the text we are now explaining.[108] In this note he asks whether he has not already introduced real thinking when describing the intrinsic coherence of our perceptive life. Certainly, he continues, our perceptive life does not belong to the order of "being-in-itself." When we describe seeing and touching, we are in contact with a realm of being in which there is already some kind of reflection, for the perceptible is perceiving and is, therefore, aware of itself. This means that we are already within the realm of thought. Here in the note Merleau-Ponty explicitly says that our perceptive life implies thought; he does not, therefore, really leave open the question he previously posed.

Is the "Silent Cogito" Reintroduced? We have seen in the first chapter that Merleau-Ponty accused himself of having introduced the cogito at the perceptive level. Is he again making the same mistake here? It is clear that Merleau-Ponty's philosophy remains ambiguous on this point.[109]

Merleau-Ponty tries to solve the difficulty by making a distinction between two kinds of thinking. The first one he describes with the words *"il y a . . ."* ("there is . . ."); the second one he indicates with the words *"il m'apparaît que"* ("it seems to me that . . .").[110] This distinction, however, is not at all clear. As a matter of fact, what is the thought indicated by the words "there is . . ."? The bare fact that being exists does not yet in itself constitute thought. The buildings on

---

[107] "Nous allons vers le centre, nous cherchons à comprendre comment il y a un centre, en quoi consiste l'unité, nous ne disons pas qu'elle soit somme ou résultat, et si nous faisons paraître la pensée sur une infrastructure de vision, c'est seulement en vertu de cette évidence incontestée qu'il faut voir ou sentir de quelque façon pour penser, que toute pensée de nous connue advient à une chair." *V.I.*, p. 191.

[108] *V.I.*, p. 190, note.

[109] We will speak of this question again in the last chapter.

[110] We are still commenting on the note of *V.I.*, p. 190.

the other side of the street are there, but their being there does not imply thought. There is no thought without some kind of awareness. If, then, there is an awareness, then there also seems to be the "it seems to me that . . . ," so that Merleau-Ponty's distinction no longer holds.

Still, we must make some distinction in our awareness; Merleau-Ponty has hold of something real and valuable here, although he does not succeed in expressing it. We have seen that in his note of January, 1959,[111] he rejected his own "silent cogito" because the cogito is constituted by language. But in the note reviewing the text, the note we are commenting upon now, which was written after 1959 toward the end of his life, Merleau-Ponty returns to the "silent cogito."[112] The verbal expression does not constitute my awareness but gives a new character to it. When expressing my awareness, I place myself at a distance from the reality of which I am aware. In speaking, my awareness becomes reflective and critical. But awareness precedes speaking. We often experience this transformation of simple awareness into reflective and critical awareness. Frequently it happens that we begin to know in an entirely new manner what we already knew. The child lives in space but has no reflective and critical awareness of space. It moves and adapts its own movements to the exigencies of the space in which it lives; it sometimes does this more easily than adult persons. It avoids dangers apparently without any critical awareness of these dangers.

We can *become* aware of realities of which we *were* already aware. The concept "awareness" is not univocal. Our reflective, critical and expressed awareness is preceded by a pre-reflective, pre-critical awareness which has not yet come to an expression of itself. This primordial awareness is not blind, but it does not yet clearly understand what it knows. Primordial awareness blends with the reality in which it lives. It is an awareness without its own inner life. It is an awareness which cannot be expressed in words, because as soon as we touch it with our words, it ceases to be what it is. The awareness that we give voice to is always awareness as changed by our speaking. We can say that this primordial awareness exists, but we cannot describe it. The described awareness is always awareness as changed by our speaking.

---

[111] *V.I.*, pp. 224-225.

[112] Merleau-Ponty conceives the *"il y a"* as a manner of thought (*penser*), although he distinguishes this implicit thought from thought in the strict sense (*pensée au sens restrictif*). Still the silent awareness is real thought.

Many of the problems which concern the "unconscious" are most likely problems of unexpressed awareness, which is not yet an awareness in the common sense of this word. Thinkers who speak about the unconscious seem to be considering a level of life which precedes every form of awareness. As a matter of fact, they are speaking about the awareness which precedes expression and which precedes, therefore, every form of critical reflection. Man is already openness in this awareness and here he is certainly not blind. But he knows without knowing that he knows. He is simply awareness without any reflection upon his thought. Perhaps it would be better not to speak here about a "silent cogito," since the term cogito reminds us of conscious thought, of thought which has reflective awareness of itself.

It now becomes understandable why Merleau-Ponty indicates this awareness with the words *"il y a . . ."* ("there is . . ."). There is openness toward Being without any reflective awareness, without any returning of this openness toward itself. Merleau-Ponty expresses this reflective return to itself with the words *"il m'apparaît que . . ."* ("it seems to me that . . ."). Although we criticized Merleau-Ponty for insufficiently expressing himself, it now appears that what he tried to say can hardly be said.

Perceptive Life as Beginning Thought. After this interruption we will continue our comment on Merleau-Ponty's note.[113] It is my thesis, he says, that this "there is . . . ," viz., this awareness without any reflection upon itself, this openness without critical distance, is strictly necessary, for we cannot conceive human life without it. His problem, however, is to demonstrate how our thought which views abstract meanings and which knows itself in knowing things is an accomplishment of this primordial awareness. In primordial awareness there must be a need for self-expression. By this self-expression we transform appearing reality into a realm of invisible ideas. This new realm, on the one hand, is the expression of a preceding realm and, on the other hand, implies the entrance into a new realm. Expression is at the same time fulfillment and renewal.[114] There is, consequently, a reversibility between the verbal expression and what is being expressed by it. It makes no sense to discuss the priority of one of these, since there is an interchange between our speaking and the reality about which we

---

[113] *V.I.*, p. 190.
[114] "Sublimation du *il y a.*" *V.I.*, p. 190, note.

speak.[115] This reality makes our speaking possible, and our speaking makes the reality exist in a new manner.

This reflective note of Merleau-Ponty's has been very illuminating. We have seen that, according to him, in man as a "perceiving perceptible" there is already latent thought. Our perceptive life is spread all over our body, and yet it belongs together and has its own interior unity; otherwise the "reversibility" which characterizes our perceptive life would be impossible. Our perceptive life, therefore, is already a kind of awareness, a beginning thought. I am confronted with other "perceiving perceptibles," and here is the beginning of the phenomenon of expression. Expression transforms our awareness into reflective consciousness. Merleau-Ponty stresses the continuity of our lives, refusing to accept the introduction of a radically new principle. He continues the line of his preceding works, notwithstanding his self-criticism.[116]

8. The Metaphysical Dimensions of the Visible

Merleau-Ponty repeatedly says that our ideas—ideas as the result of expression—belong to the invisible order. But our invisible ideas have something to do with the dimension of the visible. Before speaking about our ideas in this chapter, he first tries to penetrate into the dimension of the visible which our ideas reflect.[117]

Merleau-Ponty repeats that the "flesh of the world" is not identical with inorganic matter.[118] It brings about in me the return of the visible and the touchable upon themselves; it makes me a "perceiving perceptible." I am, therefore, a being which sees and touches itself. As visible and touchable, I belong to the world of which, as seeing and touching, I am the master. Thus perceptibles are concentrated around the perceiving body which exteriorizes itself toward things. With my eyes I transform the world into my scenery. There is an almost magical

---

[115] "De sorte qu'entre son et sens, parole et ce qu'elle veut dire, il y a encore rapport de réversibilité et nulle discussion de priorité, l'échange des paroles étant exactement différentiation dont la pensée est l'intégrale." *Ibid.*

[116] There is, however, a new point of view in *V.I.*, namely, that our lives are the self-manifestation of Being. We will stress this point of view in the following chapters.

[117] *V.I.*, pp. 191-195.

[118] "Encore une fois, la chair dont nous parlons n'est pas la matière. Elle est l'enroulement du visible sur le corps voyant. . . ." *V.I.*, p. 191.

relationship between my body and the world: I lend my body to the world, and the world gives itself to me.[119]

This remarkable relationship between the body and the world is not an accident. It appears that my body and the world belong essentially together, that my perception is an actualization of a potentiality which essentially belongs to things. My being is a kind of fulfillment of the world. There is something "systematic" in the world, and this constitutes my own being. As a "perceiving perceptible" I am not an accidental reality but the actualization of the potentiality of the world. The "flesh of the world" and my own flesh cannot be called contingent reality, chaotic being.[120] There is a fundamental structure of Being which matures in me.

Contingency is Not the Final Word of Philosophy. This is a most remarkable point within the whole of Merleau-Ponty's philosophy, implying a very important self-correction. In his former works Merleau-Ponty emphasized contingency as the final word of philosophy.[121] There is meaning, the result of the interchange between man and world; this interchange is the universal source of all meaning. Man, however, has no essence. He is a contingent being and his presence itself is contingent. All meaning exists, therefore, within the fundamental realm of contingency. If we would try to explain the presence of man, we would explain the reality which is at the origin of all explanation. Reason, therefore, is based on a fact—man's presence.[122]

---

[119] "Ce rapport magique, ce pacte entre elles et moi selon lequel je leur prête mon corps pour qu'elles y inscrivent et me donnent leur ressemblance, ce pli, cette cavité centrale du visible qui est ma vision. . . ." *V.I.,* p. 192.

[120] "La chair (celle du monde ou la mienne) n'est pas contingence, chaos, mais texture qui revient en soi et convient à soi-même." *Ibid.*

[121] "L'idée de l'Être nécessaire, aussi bien que celle de la 'matière éternelle' ou celle de l'"homme total', lui paraît prosaïque en regard de ce surgissement des phénomènes à tous les étages du monde et de cette naissance continuée qu'il est occupé de décrire." Merleau-Ponty, *Eloge de la Philosophie,* Gallimard, Paris, 1953, p. 62. See Kwant, *The Phenomenological Philosophy of Merleau-Ponty,* pp. 123-124.

Eloge de la Philosophie was translated into English by John Wild and James M. Edie, and the translation was published in 1963 by Northwestern University Press. We did not use this translation, however, because the text we quoted is translated there incorrectly. There is no question in this text of "religious phenomena" and of the "rebirth of the divine" (p. 45). Merleau-Ponty says that the continuous manifesting and rebirth of phenomena in general (and not of religious phenomena) is more interesting to the philosopher than any explanation of this basic fact.

[122] Kwant, *The Phenomenological Philosophy of Merleau-Ponty,* pp. 120-122.

Now Merleau-Ponty admits that contingency is not the final word of philosophy. Man's presence is not a contingent fact but the essential fulfillment of the world. In man the world comes to itself. Man is the actualization of the world. This most radical renewal of Merleau-Ponty's philosophy opens the way to metaphysics.

I do not know by experience the structure of my organism, but I know that it must be adapted to the world since the world becomes my scenery. The scenery of the world which belongs to me and to others, makes it clear that our bodies are adapted to the world. The universality of the scenery of the world, the fact that it is actualized in many organisms, points out that there are general conditions of visibility, that there are typical structures which are common to the world and to the different human organisms. At that point where the human organism meets the world, there is a realm of generality. And this generality is a light to our mind.[123] All these things are implied in the fact that our perception is not just an accident but the fulfillment of the world.

We come to the same conclusion when we study the physiological composition of our organism. Physiology has revealed important insights in regard to the material composition of our eyes. We must avoid, however, two extremes. On the one hand, the physiological composition of my eyes will never completely explain why I see; I cannot totally understand seeing through its physiological conditions. On the other hand, my vision is really the fulfillment of the physiological composition of my eyes.[124] It is as if my organism is just poised for the miracle of perception, for which it is not the complete explanation. It is as if my body from the beginning makes ready for the miracle of vision.

The "Flesh of the World" is a Fundamental Reality. The "flesh of the world" predestines me to see and to perceive. This "flesh of the world" is a most fundamental reality, which, Merleau-Ponty says, until now has not even been named in philosophy.[125] It is the fundamental reality in which both subject and object are constituted and which precedes, consequently, both of them. The "flesh of the world" is their "element."

---

[123] *V.I.,* pp. 192-193.

[124] "Comme si donc, à des moyens et des instruments matériels laissés çà et là sur le chantier, la vision venait soudain donner une convergence qu'ils attendaient." *V.I.,* p. 193.

[125] "Ce que nous appelons chair, cette masse intérieurement travaillée, n'a de nom dans aucune philosophie. Milieu formateur de l'objet et du sujet. . . ." *Ibid.*

The "flesh of the world" remains, however, a hidden reality. It becomes manifest in its results, but still hides itself. We can never transform it into a clear object.

We will understand this when we realize that reversibility, which has been strongly accentuated by Merleau-Ponty, is never perfect.[126] Reversibility is always imminent but is never perfectly actualized. I can touch my touching hand, but my touching of the things and my touching of my touching hand will never completely coincide. If my touching hand is really and completely touching, then I do not clearly experience it as being touched; if I really experience my touching hand as being touched, then it is no longer really touching. I can hear my voice when I am speaking, but I will never hear my voice like I hear the voice of other persons. Seeing and touching cover one another, but they never perfectly coincide. There is a real reversibility in my perceptive life, but this reversibility will never be perfect.

For Merleau-Ponty this is not a failure. The real reason why reversibility will never be perfect, notwithstanding innumerable transitions, is that the final unity of the body is hidden to me, that the final hinge of everything eludes observation. I seem to have a blind spot. It really is there; it is not just the absence of Being, an ontological vacuum; it is the "flesh of the world" which works in me and which constitutes me but which I cannot directly experience.[127] I find in myself realms of clarity, but also realms of obscurity; what is visible, accessible, in me has an inaccessible background. Is this background completely inaccessible to me? I cannot experience it directly, but somehow I can become aware of its role. And this in an intellectual awareness. Therefore, the primary visibility, the visibility which exists for my eyes, implies a secondary visibility which is not accessible to my eyes but only to my mind. This secondary visibility concerns the ultimate "hinges" of Being. The perceptible massiveness of my body points to a more subtle reality; the perceptible body implies an understandable body. There is, Husserl says, not only an exterior, but also an interior horizon. This interior horizon, which is not accessible to perception but only to thought, is a new type of Being.[128] This type of Being is reflected in our ideas.

---

[126] *V.I.*, p. 194.

[127] *V.I.*, pp. 194-195.

[128] "C'est un nouveau type d'être, un être de porosité, de prégnance ou de généralité, et celui devant qui s'ouvre l'horizon y est pris, englobé." *V.I.*, p. 195.

This exposition of Merleau-Ponty's has a metaphysical character. He accepts that the perceptible being is not understandable in itself, that it points to an "interior horizon," to a hidden Being which makes the perceptible being possible. Later on we will have to delve into the implications of this new point of view.

9. The "Flesh of the World" and Ideas

The Problem of Limits. In the preceding pages Merleau-Ponty has explained that our field of clarity is only a section of a larger field. We live in visible reality, but visible reality does not coincide with all reality. Here again man becomes aware of his limits. But Merleau-Ponty, too, is confronted with the eternal difficulty of the thinker who admits his limits. Is not the confession of the limited character of our realm of existence hypocritical? As a matter of fact, one who confesses his limits knows his limits as limits. This implies that he extends his look beyond the limits within which he confesses to be. This difficulty is well-known to everyone familiar with the history of philosophy. The problem of limits is also well-known to Merleau-Ponty, who wrote about it in his earlier works.[129]

Merleau-Ponty tries to overcome this difficulty by emphasizing that the invisible is not a realm of being which is separated from the visible. The invisible belongs to the visible as its "other side." The intelligibility of the visible depends on the invisible. In the pages which follow, he tries to explain this point of view. He is well aware of the difficulties implied in his philosophy. We are coming now, he says, to the most difficult point, viz., the connection between the "flesh" and the idea, between the visible and its interior "frame," which is manifested and, at the same time, hidden by the visible reality.[130] We are confronted here with a paradox: the invisible is at the same time manifested and hidden by the visible reality. The visible gives us an access to what it simultaneously hides.

There are two kinds of ideas: the abstract ideas of philosophy and science and the concrete ideas created, for instance, as artistic expression. The abstract ideas are to a large extent loosened from concrete, visible reality; whereas the concrete ideas remain connected with it. Merleau-Ponty begins by speaking about the more concrete ideas of art and then

---

[129] Merleau-Ponty, *Phenomenology of Perception*, Preface, p. IX.
[130] *V.I.*, p. 195.

reflects upon the more abstract ideas of philosophy and science. The reason for this procedure seems clear; it is easier to show the connection between visible reality and artistic ideas than the connection between the visible and the abstract ideas of philosophy and science.

Artistic Ideas. The French writer Proust, according to Merleau-Ponty, has penetrated deeper than anyone else into the relationship between the visible and the invisible, into the idea which is not the opposite of the visible but its double and its depth.[131] Proust speaks in one of his works about the musical idea, about the short melody which consists of only a few notes yet which presents to one of his characters, Swann—but also to everyone who can understand—the very essence of love.[132] Swann tries to analyze the simple melody, the sweet combination of a few sounds. There are five notes, only slightly different; the melody is concentrated on two of them. However, this analysis does not bring real clarity. As soon as we begin to analyze the melody, we lose sight of the melody itself. The melody is a whole and must be understood and heard as a whole. The intellectual analysis of a melody does not give us its very essence.

The melody does have an essence, a depth. It makes something present to us. That which is made present is indissolubly united with the material sounds.[133] Yet the essence of the melody is not fully identical with the material sounds. Hearing the melody we are in contact with its essence; but this essence is a depth which will never be completely present to us. Merleau-Ponty calls the essence of the melody "an idea." We find such ideas not only in music, but also in painting, literature, dancing, in all arts.

Artistic ideas are the revelation of the invisible, and on this point they are not inferior to the scientific ideas of Lavoisier and Ampère.[134] There is, however, an important difference between scientific and artistic ideas. While scientific ideas can to a certain extent be loosened from perceptive reality, artistic ideas remain united and have to remain united with perceptible reality. They cannot be raised to the separate order of

---

[131] "Personne n'a été plus loin que Proust dans la fixation des rapports du visible et de l'invisible, dans la description d'une idée qui n'est pas le contraire du sensible, qui en est la doublure et la profondeur." *Ibid.*

[132] *V.I.,* p. 196.

[133] "Simplement, cet invisible-là, ces idées-là, ne se laissent pas . . . détacher des apparences sensibles, et ériger en seconde positivité." *Ibid.*

[134] *Ibid.*

abstract ideas. Still, artistic ideas have their essence, their secret; but here perceptive matter *contains the secret;* there is a secret but this secret is contained in perceptive matter, although the secret itself is not a perceptible reality. The secret essence constitutes the order, the coherence, of the perceptive matter which in this way becomes the revelation of the secret essence. Imperceptible forces and laws are in this way revealed by perceptive matter. It seems to be the task of the artist to make us live in the secret essence.

The Essence of an Artistic Idea is Both Revealed and Hidden by Perceptible Matter. A direct apprehension of the secret essence is absolutely impossible; the secret essence is not a reality that is hidden to us merely as a matter of fact and that can be revealed by progress in human investigation. Its direct apprehension is absolutely impossible. Still we are in contact with it, though through a screen of perceptible matter. Our body is not an impediment to contact; on the contrary, it is the only means of contact.[135] If we would have no body, we could never understand the essence of music or of painting. Here we have ideas which are accessible only to a corporal experience. The perceptible matter is not the *occasion* which makes us think the secret essence but is its actual revelation. The secret essence is at the very heart of perceptible matter. It is absurd to attempt to understand the secret essence of artistic ideas by intellectual reflection.[136]

Artistic ideas are simultaneously revealed and hidden by perceptible matter. They are present without being perceptible in themselves. They assure us that the "great, inaccessible night of our soul" is not mere emptiness and nothingness;[137] the reality which is there, however, is accessible only through the visible reality to which the invisible remains attached. Just as the "hidden blackness" of milk is accessible to us only through its white color,[138] so too the artistic idea, its hidden reality, is

---

[135] "Ici, au contraire, il n'y a pas de vision sans écran: les idées dont nous parlons ne seraient pas mieux connues de nous si nous n'avions pas de corps et de sensibilité, c'est alors qu'elles nous seraient inaccessibles." *Ibid.*

[136] "L'explicitation ne nous donne pas l'idée même, elle n'en est qu'une version seconde, un dérivé plus maniable." *V.I.,* p. 197.

[137] "Ainsi il est essentiel à ce genre d'idées d'être 'voilées de ténèbres', de paraître 'sous un déguisement'. Elles nous donnent l'assurance que la 'grande nuit impénêtrée et décourageante de notre âme' n'est pas vide, n'est pas 'neant'." *Ibid.*

[138] *Ibid.* Here Merleau-Ponty quotes Valéry.

accessible only through perceptible matter. In this way we are confronted with the invisible aspect of visible reality. The invisible belongs to visible reality itself as its reality, as its depth. It is just the "other side" of the visible itself.[139] The invisible is the absence of what is present. We do not see the artistic ideas themselves, and yet we contact them through perceptible matter. They are present without being present. Merleau-Ponty adheres entirely to Proust's description.

The Fundamental Level of "the Idea." Until now Merleau-Ponty has analyzed the "invisible of the visible" especially in the realm of artistic creation. But the "invisible in the visible," the "ideal in the perceptible," does not begin to exist there alone. We entered into the invisible realm with our first look when for the first time we really touched reality, when for the first time we really enjoyed something. We could not actually see, touch or enjoy without being in contact with the "invisible in the visible."[140] It is the fundamental realm of our existence to which everything must be referred. Although it exists in a more evident manner in artistic creations, it is a general phenomenon.

Merleau-Ponty calls this fundamental level "the idea." It is not something which is invisible as a matter of fact, an object hidden behind another one; nor is it something absolutely invisible, having no relationship with the visible. It is the invisible aspect of this visible world. This invisible is inherent in the world, it supports the world, it makes possible the visibility of the world. Merleau-Ponty calls it *l'Être de cet étant,* the Being of this being.[141] When we live in the light of this idea, when the musician composes his melody, there is no emptiness in us. We live in a consistent reality which is just as explicit as the object of a positive thought.

What Merleau-Ponty calls "the idea," the "invisible of the visible," is much more consistent than the object of a positive thought. Such an object is nothing but an object, it has no depth. Hence it cannot fill us. As soon as we have seen it, our mind moves on elsewhere, for it does not

---

[139] "Leur texture charnelle nous présente l'absente de toute chair." *V.I.,* p. 198.

[140] *Ibid.*

[141] "L'idée est ce niveau, cette dimension, non pas donc un invisible de fait, comme un objet caché derrière un autre, et non pas un invisible absolu, qui n'aurait rien à faire avec le visible, mais l'invisible *de* ce monde, celui qui l'habite, le soutient et le rend visible, sa possibilité intérieure et propre, l'Être de cet étant." *Ibid.*

find rest in such a shallow being.[142] We possess the positive thought but it does not possess us. Musical ideas, on the contrary, and perceptive reality which is pregnant with the idea possess us. We cannot say that we possess them, but we must say that we are in their grip. The musician does not execute the sonata but feels that he is at the service of the sonata; it sings in him and through him.[143] All ideas, Merleau-Ponty says, belong together. Perception and art cohere, as do the different arts. As Proust remarks, there is necessity in this field. We must speak, sing, execute the music, create a character, as we actually do. The "invisible in the visible" rules us. There is a coherent essence in all these fundamental experiences, in the parts of the sonata, in the lines of a poem, in the beauty of a scene.[144] Their unity is similar to the unity of my body. There is an ideal cohesion without a concept. Is my body itself an idea or a thing? It is neither, for the body is the reality which makes both the things and the ideas exist.[145]

We must recognize, therefore, the existence of an ideality that is not separated from the "flesh of the world," an ideality that is its hinge, its axis, its depth, its most fundamental dimension.[146] Once we have recognized this most real ideality, it will be hard to withdraw from its attraction. We know now that corporal reality is animated by the idea. We know that the visible is penetrated by the invisible; that the visibility of things puts us into contact with a deeper realm which conditions the visibility itself; that the exterior world has an interior horizon. We reject, therefore, that dualism which separates the visible from the invisible, and we do so without reducing thought to quantity or quantity to thought. The visible and the invisible are the two sides of one and the same reality. How can we, knowing all this, fall back into dualistic conceptions?[147]

Abstract Ideas. The temptation to fall back into dualism is there, however, since we must still explain the presence of abstract intellectual

---

[142] "Une pensée positive est ce qu'elle est, mais précisement, n'est que cela, et dans cette mesure elle ne peut nous fixer." *Ibid.*

[143] *V.I.,* pp. 198-199.

[144] "Il y a une idéalité rigoureuse dans des expériences qui sont expériences de la chair." *V.I.,* p. 199.

[145] "Mon corps est-il chose, est-il idée? Il n'est ni l'un ni l'autre, étant le mesurant des choses." *Ibid.*

[146] "Nous aurons donc à reconnaître une idéalité qui n'est pas étrangère à la chair, qui lui donne ses axes, sa profondeur, ses dimensions." *Ibid.*

[147] "Or, une fois entré dans cet étrange domaine, on ne voit pas comment il pourrait être question d'en sortir." *Ibid.*

ideas, e.g., the ideas of philosophy and science. We have seen that there is a kind of generality in the perceptible world and that this generality explains the reversibility of our perceptions. But there is also the universality of abstract ideas. The realm of abstract ideas seems to be a second world, a new world. This new world has its own importance. We make use of our ideas in order to transform the world we inhabit.[148]

Merleau-Ponty sees a connection between the ideality of the real world which he has described and the universality of our abstract ideas. He thinks that our intellectual life makes use of roads which it did not construct, that it places itself within horizons that it did not open, that the abstract ideas of our intellect are supported by the ideas which are connected with the "flesh of the world." He says, however, that he will explain this in a later chapter—a chapter which has never been written —and that now he will make only a few remarks.[149]

The pure ideality of our abstract ideas is not without any flesh and is not placed outside all horizons.[150] When we construct abstract ideas, the visibility of this world does not go beyond all corporal reality, but it is embodied in a new manner. Its new body is less heavy and more transparent, but nevertheless it is a body. Abstract thought is embodied in language.[151] Just as musical sounds have their depth, so too words contain their meaning. This is evidently the case when our language is conquering, active and creative, when something is being said, in the authentic sense of this word.[152] Merleau-Ponty speaks here about the "speaking word." Just as musical notation is an expression of creative music, the "spoken word" is an expression of creative language. Language as a constituted system of relationships is a result of creative language. In creative language the relationship between sounds and meaning is the same as between the musical notes and the melody.[153]

---

[148] "Certes, c'est une question de savoir comment s'instaurent par là-dessus les 'idées de l'intelligence', comment de l'idéalité d'horizon on passe à l'idéalité 'pure', et par quel miracle notamment à la généralité naturelle de mon corps et du monde vient s'ajouter une généralité créée, une culture, une connaissance qui reprend et rectifie la première." *V.I.,* p. 200.

[149] *Ibid.*

[150] "Disons seulement que l'idéalité pure n'est pas elle-même sans chair ni délivrée des structures d'horizon." *Ibid.*

[151] "Comme si elle changeait de chair, abandonnant celle du corps pour celle du langage." *Ibid.*

[152] *V.I.,* pp. 200-201.

[153] "Le langage comme système de relations explicites entre signes et signifiés, sons et sens est un résultat et un produit du langage opérant où sens et son sont dans le même rapport que la 'petite phrase' et les cinq notes qu'on y trouve après coup?" *V.I.,* p. 201.

Our constituted language is not useless, of course. In our creative language we suppose all that has been created before our own creating. But the whole objective system of language is animated by creative speaking which nourishes its life.

Meaning and Speaking. The question of the source of creative speaking now arises. Constituted language is certainly not the adequate source of creative speaking, since creative speaking essentially exceeds constituted language. For instance, the mathematician, using existing symbols, makes them say what they have never said; the same happens in all creative speaking. The creative speaker is supported by a new kind of visibility, and just as the ideality of the visible reality is its other side, so the ideas are the other side of the body of language.[154] The creative thinker is moved by his ideas just as the musician is by his melody. The ideas exceed the creative words as the melody exceeds the material sounds. This does not mean that the melody or the idea exists elsewhere, in a "heaven" of melodies or ideas. They exist as the "other side" of sounds and words. They maintain the openness of sounds and words.

Our seeing is supported by the visibility of the "flesh of the world," but at the same time our seeing actualizes this visibility. In the same way our creative speaking is supported by the idea, and still our speaking makes the idea exist. In other words, the idea produces the arrangements of our words, but the arrangement of our words makes the idea exist. The organization of language is not an absolute datum which would explain the existence of meaning.[155] The meaning, the idea, supports the organization of language. I could not see if I were not visible to myself. In the same way my speaking has a relationship to itself. The speaking person organizes his words in the light of the meaning in order to actualize this meaning. Meaning precedes speaking and, at the same time, is its result. The meaning is the "other side" of

---

[154] "Le système de relations objectives, les idées acquises sont eux-mêmes pris comme dans une vie et une perception secondes qui font que le mathématicien va droit aux entités que personne n'a encore vues, que le langage et l'algorithme *opérants* usent d'une visibilité seconde et que les idées sont l'autre côté du langage et du calcul." *Ibid.*

[155] "Comme il y a une réversibilité du voyant et du visible, et comme au point où se croisent les deux métamorphoses, naît ce qu'on appelle perception, de même, il y a une réversibilité de la parole et de ce qu'elle signifie; la signification est ce qui vient sceller, clore, rassembler la multiplicité des moyens physiques, physiologiques, linguistiques de l'élocution, les contracter en un seul acte, comme la vision vient achever le corps esthésiologique." *V.I.,* p. 202.

speaking. As we have seen, the visible and seeing are reversible; now in the same way meaning and speaking are reversible. The meaning supports our speaking and likewise is its result. All the physiological instruments of seeing come to their fulfillment in the act of seeing. In the same way all the material means of speaking reach their destination in the existence of meaning. The meaning which has come into existence effectuates the sense of all the words. We rightly antedate the meaning which results from speaking,[156] since meaning guides our speaking. When meaning has been created it is as if it had always been there. This impression is correct, since intellectual meaning is the actualization of the ideal side of visible reality.

The generality which characterizes the ideal aspect of visible reality becomes intellectual universality. When we speak, we can be both spoken to and spoken about. When we speak we are plunged into a universal Word.[157] The silent world is translated into a world of language.

We are constantly confronted with the phenomenon of reversibility. When the world of silence is translated into the world of language, we become aware that our concepts originally existed in the "flesh of the world" and that the "flesh of the world" has been sublimated into the realm of abstract ideas. We become aware of the fact that all the conditions of speaking are fulfilled in our body.[158] We are "perceiving perceptibles" who belong to the world and who make the world exist for our perception; we produce sounds and at the same time hear our own sounds. We are sensitive to ourselves and to the world. These primordial facts contain all the essential conditions of speaking.

We must notice also the remarkable way in which we understand a sentence. We understand a sentence when we really understand the words in all their implications. The meaning is not "on" words as butter is "on" toast.[159] The meaning is the intrinsic reality of the words

---

[156] "La signification . . . s'antidate par un mouvement rétrograde qui n'est jamais complètement déçu." *Ibid.*

[157] "Nul locuteur ne parle qu'en se faisant par avance allocutaire, *ne serait-ce qui de soi-même,* qu'il ferme d'un seul geste le circuit de son rapport à soi et celui de son rapport aux autres, et, du même coup, s'institue aussi *délocutaire,* parole dont on parle: il s'offre et offre toute parole à une Parole universelle." *Ibid.*

[158] *V.I.,* p. 203.

[159] "Comprendre une phrase ce n'est rien d'autre que l'accueillir pleinement dans son être sonore, ou, comme on dit, si bien, *l'entendre;* le sens n'est pas sur elle comme le beurre sur la tartine." *Ibid.*

themselves and we cannot really understand the words if we do not grasp the meaning. The meaning is the whole which is expressed in many words. Without the meaning words would not belong together. Words are just nothing when they are separated from the idea, from their meaning. Language produces a new realm of invisibility, but this new realm of invisibility is the actualization of the "invisible of the visible." Language can penetrate, therefore, into our whole realm of existence. We speak about the world in which we live and we live in the world about which we speak. There is reversibility between the world of silence and the world of speech. Language is almighty since it is in the end, not the voice of particular persons, but the voice of Being itself. The reversibility of all the aspects of our life is the final truth of philosophical reflection.[160]

10. Summary

All the important new ideas of Merleau-Ponty are concentrated in the chapter *"L'Entrelacs—le Chiasme."* This chapter is the core of the whole book. In its light, all the preceding chapters must be read. As a matter of fact, the criticism of science and of other philosophical currents that it contains complements the positive development of Merleau-Ponty's thought. This is the reason for our extensive comment on this chapter.

Merleau-Ponty's ideas are contained in this chapter, however, only as in embryo. This chapter is loaded with promises which have not been fulfilled. It implicitly contains a new philosophy of nature, the development of which is promised in the notes but was never accomplished. Further, Merleau-Ponty made only a few remarks about the passage from the ideality and generality of the visible towards the universality of abstract concepts.

But notwithstanding its unfinished character, this chapter clearly indicates the fundamental movement of Merleau-Ponty's thought. His starting-point is the analysis of the visibility of the world and his central idea is reversibility. Vision implies that man belongs to the visible and that the visible is actualized in man. He discovers reversibility in his analysis of vision and of perceptive life in general, and he thinks that reversibility is a comprehensive truth which can be applied everywhere. Reversibility manifests itself in the relationship between man and world:

---

[160] "La réversibilité qui est vérité dernière." *V.I.,* p. 204.

man is a part of the world, but he is a part which possesses the whole; man is worldly and the world is human. There is an interpenetration of man and world. Merleau-Ponty's former concept of dialectical exchange has been more or less replaced by the concept of reversibility. This is quite understandable since the idea of dialectical exchange seems to imply a certain duality, which Merleau-Ponty now rejects. Also, reversibility reveals itself in all the aspects of human existence. There is reversibility between seeing and touching, between all the forms of perceptive life, and finally between perceptive life and speaking. Reversibility appears to be a universal and final truth.

Merleau-Ponty tries to give a metaphysical foundation to his concept of reversibility. Our human life is not just an accidental realization of Being, but the fulfillment of the fundamental potentiality of the world, of Being. He says that Being sees itself in man, that Being speaks in man,[161] that Being comes to awareness of itself in man. It is as if in Being there is a fundamental tendency which comes to fulfillment in man. Moreover, the fundamental structure of Being becomes evident in man. Does this imply that philosophical anthropology should be based on a preceding metaphysical doctrine, that we should attempt to understand man by starting from Being? I do not think so. Merleau-Ponty did not return to metaphysical realism, according to which man can be understood in the light of an understanding of Being which precedes an understanding of man. It is true that Being precedes man. But Being becomes understandable only in man. Man is the revelation of the structure of Being. If we would abstract from man, we could never understand the structure of Being.

It has been difficult to understand this chapter and to comment upon it. But we hope that by treating it first we have thrown open the fundamental light that illuminates the other parts of the book.

---

[161] "Et en un sens, comme dit Valéry, le langage est tout, puisqu'il n'est la voix de personne, qu'il est la voix même des choses, des ondes et des bois." *V.I.*, pp. 203-204.

CHAPTER THREE

MERLEAU-PONTY'S CRITICISM
OF OTHER TRENDS OF THOUGHT

Introduction: the Purpose of This Chapter

Whoever builds a new philosophy must come face to face with past philosophy. It is not necessary, of course, that he confront all the philosophers who have ever lived. So long and rich is the philosophical tradition that no single man can assume it in all its aspects. He will have to confront, therefore, particular currents of the rich philosophical tradition. Also, every philosopher views reality in a particular manner, and this implies that he participate in the philosophical tradition in his own particular manner. Merleau-Ponty has done so in his preceding works. As a French philosopher who was particularly interested in phenomenology, he confronted the French philosophical tradition and other phenomenological thinkers.

In regard to the French tradition, he confronted especially Descartes and the late nineteenth century French rationalism. The entanglement with Descartes was unavoidable, since Merleau-Ponty presented his own philosophy as a radical break with the dualism Descartes introduced into modern philosophy. Merleau-Ponty had to confront rationalism also for another reason. He rejected realistic philosophy and placed himself in a reflective attitude. The question arose, therefore, whether his reflective attitude was really different from the reflective attitude of rationalism.

Concerning phenomenological philosophy, Merleau-Ponty confronts especially Husserl and Sartre. It it is quite natural that he studied the works of the father of phenomenological thought. Moreover, the same trend of thought was also taken up by his friend Sartre, with whom he edited *Les Temps Modernes*. And since Sartre placed phenomenological analysis in the rationalistic style of thought, a confrontation with Sartre became unavoidable. Merleau-Ponty had certainly also read some of Heidegger's works. It is undeniable that he was influenced by

Heidegger, but it appears that he did not feel sufficiently competent to confront Heidegger's philosophy explicitly.

Merleau-Ponty was of the opinion that his philosophy had not only a theoretical, but also a practical interest. Inspired by his philosophy, he took part in discussions concerning social and political questions, and his thought undoubtedly belonged to the left wing. He therefore had to study Marxist philosophy. He was convinced that there was some relationship between the philosophical thought of Karl Marx, especially the younger Marx, and phenomenological thought; and it is quite understandable, therefore, that he critically analyzed Marxism.

Finally Merleau-Ponty was interested in science, especially psychology. He tried to penetrate into the hidden aspects of human life, into the obscure reality of the body-subject. Psychological experiments and psychological research of disturbances in human life helped him to know more about man's bodily life. His interest in scientific research, therefore, forced him to raise the question whether the attitude of the scientist and of the phenomenological philosopher are the same.

In his preceding works Merleau-Ponty had already confronted Descartes, French rationalism, Husserl, Sartre, Marx and the attitude of science, especially of psychologists. He spoke, of course, of other philosophers, but he did not confront them as explicitly and extensively.

But now Merleau-Ponty has deepened his philosophical perspective, and this implies important changes. A new confrontation with other currents has become necessary. The major part of his last book, *The Visible and the Invisible,* is this new confrontation. Consequently, he presents in a new manner his attitude toward science, toward reflective-rationalistic philosophy, toward Sartre and Husserl. His criticism of Descartes is contained in his study of reflective-rationalistic philosophy. There is no new criticism of Marx and Marxism, since Merleau-Ponty returns to the basic questions of philosophy, leaving aside the practical questions of the social-political field. In this chapter we will study, therefore, Merleau-Ponty's new attitude toward science, toward the reflective-rationalistic trend of thought, toward Sartre and Husserl.

In this book we have changed the order of procedure. Merleau-Ponty first describes his new attitude toward other trends of thought and then explains his own deeper way of thinking. We, on the contrary, have first presented the new basic ideas of Merleau-Ponty and only now describe his new criticism of other ways of thinking. This inversion is

justified, however, for Merleau-Ponty's new criticism of other philosophies is made possible only by the deepening of his own philosophy. The
intrinsic deepening of a philosophy determines its developing stance
toward other philosophies.

1. Merleau-Ponty's Attitude Toward Science

A. THE ONE-SIDED CHARACTER OF MERLEAU-PONTY'S APPROACH TO SCIENCE

It is well-known that both Heidegger and Merleau-Ponty usually
speak about science in rather negative terms. Hence, the objection
raised against phenomenology in general is that it takes too negative an
attitude toward science. Merleau-Ponty's negative attitude toward
science seems to have become even stronger in his last book.

Science and Its Self-Interpretation. We must make a distinction,
however, between science as such and the self-interpretation of science.
Man constructs his sciences, but he can do so without asking what
science is. A person can be an excellent mathematician without knowing
what mathematical science is. In almost every realm of human activity
this distinction can be applied. Innumerable people are engaged in
work, yet they would not be able to say what work is. There are many
artists who do not develop reflective concepts about the nature of art,
and even if they do, it is quite possible that they are excellent artists
although their reflective ideas about art may be very poor. One who is
engaged in some activity must have practical knowledge about this
activity. Man does not work blindly as do inorganic beings, but
practical knowledge which is not reflected upon is sufficient for human
activity.

It is quite obvious, however, that a person who is engaged in some
activity will raise reflective questions about his own activity. For man is
interested in his own being, and especially in the nature of the activity in
which he specializes. It is quite understandable, therefore, that many
scientists develop reflective ideas about the nature of their science and
about its place within the whole of human knowledge. It happens that
scientists not only construct their own scientific field, but that they also
develop an ontological interpretation of it. They sometimes identify
their own scientific field with the whole of understandable reality.
There have been physicists who advanced the thesis that every person

who pretends to have valuable knowledge in any field should make use of the exact method of physics, that all the so-called knowledge which does not make use of this method is not real knowledge but some kind of poetic fiction.

As soon as the scientist no longer moves within his scientific field but theorizes about it, as soon as he thinks about the place of his scientific field within the whole of human knowledge, he is no longer a scientist but a philosopher. To inquire about the nature and the place of science is a philosophical activity.

A Source of Misunderstandings. When Merleau-Ponty speaks negatively about science, he usually speaks, not about science, but about the (philosophical) self-interpretation of science. While he sometimes says so explicitly,[1] most frequently he does not. His negative judgment, consequently, does not concern science itself but the implicit or explicit self-interpretation of science by scientists.

Merleau-Ponty undoubtedly recognizes the value of science. In a note dated February, 1959, he wrote that the objectifications of science make sense and are true.[2] He also stated that only scientists can give demonstrations in the mathematical sense and that they, and they alone, can judge the value of such demonstrations.[3] It is the task of the scientists to construct the fields of science and to work according to methods which they make and which they control. The philosopher has no right whatsoever to interfere with the scientist in his own scientific work. Merleau-Ponty recognizes the truth and the value of science.

Some misunderstandings would have been avoided, however, if he had accentuated more this distinction between the pursuit of science and (philosophical) reflection upon it, and if he had written more explicitly about the positive value of science. Since he has not done so, at least not regularly, since he has mainly emphasized the false self-interpretations of scientists, he creates the impression of denying the positive value about which he seldom writes. In this, he has neglected a most important field of philosophical reflection.

---

[1] "Aucune ontologie n'est exactement *requise* par la pensée physique au travail." *V.I.,* p. 34.

[2] "La reconquête du *Lebenswelt,* c'est la reconquête d'une *dimension,* dans laquelle les objectivations de la science gardent elles-mêmes un sens et sont à comprendre comme *vraies." V.I.,* p. 236.

[3] "Si l'on prend 'démonstration' au sens mathématique, les savants, seuls en mesure d'en fournir une, sont seuls aussi en mesure de l'apprécier." *V.I.,* p. 34.

The Value of Science. It cannot be denied that human knowledge has to a high degree been actualized by modern sciences. By their very existence the sciences reveal to us what human knowledge is and what it can perform. It belongs to the nature of science, of course, that it is a *partial* actualization of human knowledge; the bare fact that there exist many sciences is a clear proof of the partial character of science. But notwithstanding its partial character, science is a real actualization of knowledge, a real manifestation of the potentialities of man.

Science has also contributed much to the self-understanding of the philosopher and to his modesty. When modern sciences did not yet exist, philosophers considered the whole of reality in all its aspects to be the field of philosophical research. In the past, philosophers have almost always exceeded their limits, trying to solve scientific questions in a philosophical manner. By their very presence the sciences have made the philosopher aware of the limits of philosophy. Philosophy has been purified by the very existence of science. Science, moreover, has revealed numerous facts which expose the premature character of several philosophical constructions.

Finally, the sciences have a practical value which can hardly be overestimated. Man is a being who situates himself. He is not condemned to accept the situation in which he finds himself; he can change and better it, since he lives in the light of reason. With the help of his critical reason he can make a distinction between the meaningful and the meaningless aspects of his own situation, removing the meaningless aspects and favoring the meaningful ones. To a large extent it is scientific reason that helps man to situate himself. The fact that in some countries poverty has been overcome and that we have, at least in principle, the possibility of overcoming it in the whole world, is due to modern methods of production; and these methods are due to modern science. The modern sciences have an immense practical meaning.

Merleau-Ponty's One-sided Approach. All these statements are obviously superficial. But we did not intend to present a theory about the positive value of science as a value in itself, as a value for philosophy, as a value for human practice; we only wanted to indicate a realm of reflection which has been neglected by Merleau-Ponty. One might object that not every philosopher can consider all possible themes of philosophical reflection, that every philosopher has the right to choose his own themes, and that we cannot criticize Merleau-Ponty for not writing about the subjects we just mentioned. This is true. Nevertheless, when a philosopher speaks about science frequently, and when he regularly accentuates only its negative aspects, then he treats his subject in a very unilateral way, certainly creating a wrong impression. This is the case with Merleau-Ponty. Before explaining his point of view, I have had to clarify the unilateral character of his approach. We must look not only at the statements of a writer concerning some reality, but also at his fundamental style. Merleau-Ponty himself is very sensitive to this style when he deals with other writers. The style of Merleau-Ponty's approach to science is extremely negative. This does not mean, of course, that Merleau-Ponty's negative statements about the self-interpretation of science are necessarily wrong. It does mean that the negative statements need completion by more positive ones; then the total impression would have been more objective.

B. THE OBJECTIVISM AND OPERATIONALISM OF NATURAL SCIENCES

Objectivism. Our knowledge, Merleau-Ponty says, is in a situation of crisis, for it is still dominated too much by the idealizations of Descartes.[4] This philosopher made the famous sharp distinction between quantity and thought and reduced the appearing world to a mere object of thought, an object opposed to pure, worldless thought. We understand matter as quantity and movement; Descartes concluded that matter *is* quantity and movement. The reflective philosopher experiences himself as a thinking being; Descartes concluded that man in his inmost reality *is* thought. He conceived the appearing world, therefore, as an entirely objective process.

This Cartesian way of thinking, according to Merleau-Ponty, still pervades the self-interpretations of scientists. Scientists understand their object as a datum independent of man. This conception also spoils the self-interpretation of psychology. As a matter of fact, the human body is conceived as a part of objective nature. Sensation is evidently an activity of our body. Sensation is conceived, therefore, as an objective process. This conception is extended to the whole psyche of man, which is often studied as an object by the objectifying methods of natural sciences. Nature is conceived as an objective process, while the human body is taken to be a part of nature. The crisis of human knowledge can only be

---

[4] "Ce n'est qu'en revenant à la foi perceptive pour rectifier l'analyse cartésienne qu'on fera cesser la situation de crise où se trouve notre savoir." *V.I.*, p. 46.

ended, says Merleau-Ponty, when we break with these idealizations.[5] In order to do so, we must return to our perceptive life, our original openness toward nature.

It is clear that the natural sciences have an objectifying character. They are inclined to think that truth can be found only in the objective order,[6] and they call "objective" whatever can be verified by their scientific operations. They attempt to free their science from all notions which express our contact with things.[7] From the beginning the natural sciences have had a preference for the most objective concepts, for concepts which abstract as much as possible from the presence of man. Philosophy aided the natural sciences by making a distinction between primary and secondary qualities. We can say that, by restricting themselves to the order of primary qualities, the natural sciences could use mathematical language. However, the predicates which express our contact with things could only be provisionally excluded since the measuring attitude of science is essentially human. It became clear that the position of the measuring man influences the result of his measurement. Thus the contact between man and world, after having been removed by abstraction, was necessarily reintroduced. But then the scientist tried to consider the relationship between man and world as a special case of objective relationships.[8] The contact between man and world became a special case of science's general object.[9]

The "Ontology of the 'Cosmotheoros'." There is one fundamental hypothesis supporting the natural sciences, viz., that the world, including the human body and even human perception, is an object[10] and that man, in his scientific attitude, is a worldless subject, a *"cosmotheoros."*[11]

All this is not the mere scientific attitude, but the result of the

---

[5] *Ibid.*

[6] "Le vrai, c'est l'objectif." *V.I.,* p. 31.

[7] "Ainsi la science a commencé par exclure tous les prédicats qui viennent aux choses de notre rencontre avec elles." *Ibid.*

[8] "Des vérités qui ne devraient pas laisser sans changements son idée de l'Être sont,—au prix de grandes difficultés d'expression et de pensée—, retraduites dans le langage de l'ontologie traditionelle, —comme si la science avait besoin de s'excepter des relativités qu'elle établit." *V.I.,* p. 33.

[9] "L'exclusion n'est d'ailleurs que provisoire: quand elle aura appris à l'investir, la science réintroduira peu à peu ce qu'elle a d'abord écarté comme subjectif; mais elle l'intégrera comme cas particulier des relations et des objets qui définissent pour elle le monde." *V.I.,* p. 31.

[10] "Nous serons devenus parties ou moments du Grand Objet." *Ibid.*

[11] *V.I.,* p. 32.

scientist's interpretation of his scientific attitude. It is a kind of scientific ontology. This scientific ontology is becoming increasingly untenable because of the evolution of science itself. It is becoming more and more evident that the elements cohering with the presence of man are not just a particular case of objective relationships, but an original datum which influences the so-called objective relationships themselves. Still the "ontology of the *'cosmotheoros'* " appears to be extremely obstinate; many scientists continue to consider the formulas which express the relationships between man and world as a mere case of universal, objective truth.

In order to penetrate into realms of reality inaccessible to common experience, science has been extremely inventive. But notwithstanding his progressiveness in scientific practice, the scientist remains conservative in his theory of knowledge.[12] In regard to discoveries concerning either astronomic space or microphysical realities, he continues to use the same objective language. When he speaks about particles which exist for only an extremely small fraction of a second, he considers them just as real as all the other objects of his scientific field.[13] It is as if his blindness to real Being is the price he pays for his success in the determination of beings.[14] He often refuses to accept the fact that his object is not just a reality, but something which is essentially connected with his own scientific attitude. The discussion as to whether there is only determinism and necessity in real and objective nature or also contingency and freedom, shows to what extent the "ontology of the *'cosmotheoros'* " is maintained.[15] The microphysical field remains a macroscopic field of extremely small dimensions.[16]

Operationalism. In another text Merleau-Ponty speaks of a second type of self-interpretation of the natural sciences. Some scientists have become aware of the fact that science is an operation. While the classical interpretation felt that science reflected reality—and this interpretation still exists, as we have seen—some modern scientists

---

[12] "Autant la science a montré d'invention dans le maniement de l'algorithme, autant en ce qui concerne la théorie de la connaissance elle s'est montrée conservatrice." *V.I.,* p. 33.

[13] *V.I.,* pp. 33-34.

[14] "Comme si la cécité pour l'Être était le prix dont elle doit payer son succès dans la détermination des êtres." *V.I.,* p. 33.

[15] *Ibid.*

[16] *V.I.,* p. 34.

exaggerate the operational character of science.[17]   Science, they say, merely constructs models; the question whether these models do or do not reflect reality in itself, is entirely unimportant.   The model is neither true nor false; it is only right or wrong.   It is right whenever, and as long as, the model is successful in controlling nature.   In this scheme science would be nothing but a refined operation of nature.

In this way science hopes it can avoid all kinds of false dilemmas. The world is nothing more than an anonymous field of our operations.[18] There is a danger that the sciences of man will adopt this self-interpretation of the natural sciences; as a matter of fact, some psychologists have already accepted it.   Man himself then becomes a being which is manipulated by science.   "In the United States a decadent psychoanalysis and culturalism have done so."[19]   Man then becomes the victim of his own theories.

C. THE ONTOLOGICAL INTERPRETATION OF SCIENCE

Merleau-Ponty confronts the scientists with a choice.[20]   In the first place, it is possible that science be considered a special kind of operation, a manipulation, that it makes use of formulas and algorisms in order to bring about something in nature.   The scientists, and they alone, are the judges of their methods.   But they then have neither the obligation nor the right to formulate a concept of Being; within this framework they cannot determine whether and to what extent their field of action is a field of Being.   As a second choice, it is possible that scientists pretend to describe *Being,* that they consider their science a science of Being.   In this case they are wrong if they straightaway describe their object either as a real Being or as a pure field of operations.   For they must first analyze their own methods; they do not have the right to accept blindly the concepts of classical philosophy, the concepts of Descartes.

In order to make his objection precise, Merleau-Ponty refers to

---

[17] "Il y a aujourd'hui—non dans la science, mais dans une philosophie des sciences assez repandue—ceci de tout nouveau que la pratique constructive se prend et se donne pour autonome." *"L'Oeil et l'Esprit,"* p. 193.

[18] "Dire que le monde est par définition nominale *l'objet X* de nos opérations, c'est porter à l'absolu la situation de connaissance du savant, comme si tout ce qui fut ou est n'avait jamais été que pour entrer au laboratoire. La pensée 'opératoire' devient une sorte d'artificialisme absolu." *"L'Oeil et l'Esprit,"* p. 194.

[19] "Comme l'ont fait aux Etats-Unis une psychoanalyse et un culturalisme décadents." *Ibid.*

[20] *V.I.,* p. 35.

Einstein's refusal to recognize the ontological value of our experience of the simultaneous perceptions of different persons.[21] We experience, as a matter of fact, that we are looking together at the same time and at the same object. This simultaneity is not real, according to Einstein. There is only an impression of simultaneity, and this impression belongs to the psychological order; it does not give us the right to say that there is real simultaneity. The physicist alone determines real simultaneity, and according to him there is a real simultaneity only when it can be established and measured with the help of scientific methods. Einstein attaches an ontological value to the object of natural science. This science is a contact with reality. In the name of natural science Einstein determines whether our daily experiences have an ontological value.

Merleau-Ponty is right when he says that very often scientists try to give an ontological interpretation to their scientific field. Einstein does so in saying that the physicist establishes real simultaneity, that every simultaneity which has not been established with the help of physical methods is uncertain, or even unreal. Despite Einstein's statements, judges will continue to realize that two cars arrived at the corner simultaneously, viz., at the same time, and that, since one of the drivers should have waited, he is, thus, responsible for the collision. The judge will accept the testimony of the policeman and of other people who attest to seeing the simultaneity. The physicist may make use of exact methods to establish simultaneity, but he has no right to deny that we see simultaneity in daily experience.

Merleau-Ponty is also right in stressing the question of the ontological value of the field of natural sciences. Many scientists are aware of this question. They know, on the one hand, that they are working in an abstract field, that this field has been constituted by scientific abstractions, that this field cannot be simply identified with the real world. On the other hand, they maintain that their science reveals reality. Their science is not just a song or a poem which expresses the world in an arbitrary manner. They know that their science has an operational character, but still they maintain that their operations reveal something about the real Being of things. Technology is partially based on the natural sciences. But technology could not be successful in our real world if the natural sciences had nothing to do with reality itself. Today's scientists are aware of all these questions and usually feel rather

---

[21] *V.I.*, pp. 35-36.

confused about them. They know that these questions vitally concern their science, but they cannot answer them.

D. THE FAILURE OF PHILOSOPHY IN THE ONTOLOGICAL INTERPRETATION OF SCIENCE

It seems, however, that Merleau-Ponty is wrong when he says that the scientists are responsible for this situation and that science itself is in a situation of crisis because these fundamental questions have not been answered.[22] It is not the task of the scientist, but of the philosopher, to answer these questions. If an adequate answer does not yet exist, philosophy has failed, not natural science. By their very existence, the natural sciences offer the philosopher a most important field for reflection; but the philosopher has failed to reflect upon it. Tradition- ally philosophy has been rooted in the humanities, and when the natural sciences arose the philosophers were not very interested in them. For a rather long time there was little philosophical reflection upon the natural sciences. There is indeed a crisis today in the interpretation of the ontological value of natural sciences; but this crisis is due to the negligence of the philosophers, not to the negligence of the scientists themselves.

It is quite understandable that, since philosophy did not ontologically interpret the field of science, the scientists themselves interpreted it. It is also quite understandable that their interpretation was one-sided, based as it was upon the light of their own science. The dialogue between philosophy and science is very important. When the philosopher, however, tries to give an ontological interpretation of science, he must understand its particular character; he must know a great deal about the methods of science. How can he see the ontological importance of scientific statements if he does not thoroughly understand them? Accusations by an outsider have little value. A real and valuable criticism is possible only when a thinker really enters into the field of scientific thinking itself.

Merleau-Ponty has never done so. He has never really been engaged in the natural sciences. He speaks about them as an outsider. His statements, therefore, do not have great importance for the philosophy of natural science. He does confront us with a real problem. The question of the ontological importance of scientific statements must be

---

[22] "La situation de crise où se trouve notre savoir." *V.I.,* p. 46.

answered. Merleau-Ponty is right in holding that the answers given by the scientists themselves are often unilateral and even wrong. But he himself does not move us closer to a real answer. He could not do so, since he has never seriously involved himself in the field of natural sciences.

I doubt whether Merleau-Ponty is right in saying that the natural sciences themselves are in a crisis because of the lack of this ontological interpretation. This fact implies a crisis, indeed, but not a crisis of the natural sciences themselves; the crisis is, rather, in an important section of philosophy. The natural sciences have found their way and their method—this cannot be said about the sciences of man—and they are making great progress. There is definitely a crisis concerning, not the natural sciences themselves, but their ontological interpretation and man's use of them. The crisis is in the philosophical and the practical fields.

E. SOME OF MERLEAU-PONTY'S VIEWPOINTS ABOUT NATURAL SCIENCE

Perceptive Ambiguity and Scientific Certainty. Merleau-Ponty formulates some positive points helpful in constructing a philosophy of science. He says that the "Being" which is the object of science is not and cannot be conceived as an independent, original and autonomous "Being."[23] It has been constituted by the scientific attitude, whose point of departure is Being as it reveals itself in our perception. Merleau-Ponty planned to write a chapter about the relationship between Being as it is revealed by perception and Being as it is conceived by natural science.[24] The re-examination of Being as the object of natural science can be of some help in understanding Being as revealed in our perception, although the latter is quite understandable in itself.

Merleau-Ponty hopes that his analysis of perceptive Being will clarify the Being which is the object of science. Perceptive Being is loaded with ambiguities. It reveals itself to *me,* and still it is evidently the same Being which is the object of perception for other persons. I cannot

---

[23] "Le montrer en faisant voir que l'être de la science ne peut ni être ni être pensé comme *selbstandig.*" *V.I.,* p. 230.

[24] "C'est le chemin inverse que nous avons à suivre, c'est à partir de la perception et de ses variants, décrites telles qu'elles se présentent, que nous essayerons de comprendre comment a pu se construire l'univers du savoir." *V.I.,* p. 208.

loosen it from my own presence; yet it reveals itself as independent of me. It gives me a pre-reflective certainty; however, when I come to reflect, my certainty seems to be dissolved into a collection of doubts. The ambiguities of perception are not really transcended by the scientific attitude, Merleau-Ponty says.[25] The so-called certainty of science is supported by the pre-reflective certainty of perception. Generally, scientists are certain that the object of their science has something to do with real Being; this certainty arises not from scientific methods, but from the intrinsic certainty of perception. The ambiguity of our perception reveals itself in the many difficulties which become quite evident when we try to establish the ontological value of scientific knowledge. The field of scientific knowledge is loaded with all the confusions that cling to the poorly developed ontology of the visible world. Merleau-Ponty hopes that his ontology of the visible world will also clarify the field of science.

Both philosophers and scientists have attempted to make a clear distinction between facts and essences or ideas. They think that we arrive at essences or ideas either by induction (empirical philosophy) or by eidetic reduction (Husserl). It is urgent, Merleau-Ponty believes, to reject both myths,[26] as well as the clear distinction between facts and essences.[27] Between the facts themselves there is an intrinsic coherence which creates realms of facts belonging together. The essence is to be found, not above or beneath the facts, but at that point of cohesion at which different facts constitute one realm. The essence or idea is nothing other than the intrinsic coherence of the facts.[28] Science has learned to arrive at a "common opinion" about this intrinsic coherence.[29] This *opinio communis* is rooted in perceptive experience. Science does not leave the realm of perception; it does not introduce us into another realm where the ambiguity of perception is replaced by the certainty of science. Science is the expression of certain elements within the ambiguous field of perception.[30]

---

[25] "Le Kosmotheoros . . . bien loin de dissiper les obscurités de notre foi naïve dans le monde, en est au contraire l'expression la plus dogmatique, la présuppose, ne se soutient que par elle." *V.I.*, p. 32.

[26] "Il serait temps de rejeter les mythes de l'inductivité et de la Wesenschau." *V.I.*, p. 155.

[27] "La question reste indécise dans le savoir scientifique parce qu'en lui vérités de fait et vérités de raison empiètent les unes sur les autres." *V.I.*, p. 146.

[28] *V.I.*, pp. 149-155.

[29] "Cette *opinio communis* qu'on appelle la science." *V.I.*, p. 156.

[30] *V.I.*, pp. 156-157.

Scientific Deduction and Facts. There is, Merleau-Ponty writes in a note of January 4, 1960,[31] a most remarkable parallel between scientific deduction and experimental facts. Starting from a certain number of facts, the scientist formulates an hypothesis and deduces a large number of conclusions from his hypothesis. Verification shows that, in turn, such scientific deductions are often valuable in the world of facts. This remarkable parallel does not justify the conclusion that our ideas are a mere reflection of reality; it does not justify a realistic philosophy. It is based on the fact that deductive science is an explicitation of the structure or the axis of experienced reality. Neither reality itself nor the intrinsic light of our ideas alone explains this parallel between scientific deduction and facts. The structure of our experience in which subject and object are united, or rather, in which they coincide, explains it to us. It is the task of the philosopher to show how this is possible.[32]

Experienced Reality. In a note of January 20, 1960,[33] Merleau-Ponty points out the phenomenon of the "scale." It often happens that in different realms of reality, e.g., in the macro- and microworld, the same proportions are found. Both the astronomic world and the realm of the smallest elements of matter appear to be fields of force, and in these different fields the same proportions are valid, at least to a certain extent. This phenomenon sometimes prompts the idea that the same objective reality repeats itself on the most different scales, that the same objective model appears on different levels.

Merleau-Ponty of course rejects this conclusion, for he rejects realism in general.[34] Some thinkers reject the objective model but still conceive the phenomenon of "scale" as the reflection of an objective reality. Merleau-Ponty thinks that philosophy has yet to explain this phenomenon, although science establishes its existence. There is here neither a reflection of objective reality nor the projection of a human idea. The phenomenon belongs to *experienced reality,* to the world of which

---

[31] *V.I.,* p. 279.

[32] "Le parallélisme déduction scientifique—faits experimentaux n'est ni à contester ni à comprendre comme preuve d'un *réalisme* de la science. Il est fondé sur ceci que la science déductive explicite les structures, les *pivots,* certains traits de membrure du monde. Cette *vérité* de la science, loin de rendre inutile une philosophie, n'est fondée et garantie que par un rapport de transcendance à l'Être, une inhérence du sujet et de l'objet de science à un Être préobjectif." *V.I.,* p. 279.

[33] *V.I.,* 279-281.

[34] "On fait un pas de plus en supprimant *l'En soi modèle.*" *V.I.,* p. 280.

experiencing man is a part, but a part which makes the whole exist.   The phenomenon should be explained, not in an appeal to some mysterious factor of the objective or subjective order, but by starting from experienced reality itself.   There is nothing besides the experienced reality to which our experience itself belongs.   Experienced reality is the field of Being, and I belong to it.   Being is essentially dimensional.   The scale-phenomenon belongs to the dimensionality of experienced Being itself.[35]   It manifests itself already on the level of perception.   On this point the scientific concept itself is based on perceptive evidence, which evidence is purified and exactly verified by science.

Concluding Remarks.   These few remarks of Merleau-Ponty about the philosophy of science are found in different parts of his works, sometimes in his notes.   He did not have the opportunity to develop his ideas, and therefore they remain vague.   He intended, as has been said, to write a chapter on the relationship of Being in general and Being as the object of science.   Would he have been able to formulate a new philosophy of science, one of considerable value?   Personally, I doubt whether this hope would have been fulfilled.   Merleau-Ponty certainly knew something about the natural sciences, but he did not know enough about them to write a significant philosophy of science.   He clearly felt the need for it, but he was probably not the philosopher to accomplish this.

There are several phenomenologists who are interested in philosophy of science.   And phenomenology could undoubtedly contribute to the development of a philosophy of science because of its insight into the interaction between man and world.   But this contribution can be given only by a phenomenologist who at the same time is a competent scientist.

F. MERLEAU-PONTY'S CRITICISM OF PSYCHOLOGY

Psychism.   Psychology, in its beginning, was introspective.   However, it very soon moved away from introspection because, insofar as introspection really is present in consciousness, it gives access only to the psychic life of the thinking individual and not to the psyche of other persons. The fact, however, that the method of introspection has been officially

---

[35] "Ce qui remplace la pensée causale, c'est l'idée de la transcendance, c'est-à-dire d'un monde vu dans l'inhérence à ce monde, grâce à elle, d'une Intra ontologie, d'un Être englobant-englobé, d'un Être vertical, dimensionnel, dimensionnalité." *V.I.*, pp. 280-281.

abandoned, does not guarantee[36] that psychologists have eliminated all traces of the introspective method. It would be interesting, says Merleau-Ponty, to analyze the concept of "psychism" which still prevails in psychology.[37] The human psyche is often understood as an invisible reality, a deeper stratum of reality hidden somewhere behind the living body.[38] The whole question would be to find the view-point which guarantees access to this hidden reality. How is the hidden reality of psychic life accessible to scientific knowledge? As a "thinglike" reality it is hardly accessible to itself; it must be understood starting from its exterior manifestations, from which it is presumed we can learn something about psychic life itself. Psychologists work with a large number of concepts without being aware of their real origin and without understanding to what extent their concepts are confused and confusing.[39]

Bifurcation of Subject and Object. Psychological concepts, like the concepts of the natural sciences, are rooted in perception; but the perceptive roots of psychological concepts have not been sufficiently clarified. The concepts of both natural science and psychology have lost their contact with perceptive evidence and are rooted in the false *a priori* bifurcation of subject and object, of subjective and objective order; and both are conceived in a "thinglike" manner. Both natural science and psychology conceive their object in terms of this bifurcation. Strangely enough, the two orders of reality are opposed to one another and yet are conceived in the same "thinglike" manner.[40] Hence arises the temptation to approach psychic reality with the methods of natural science and,

---

[36] "La critique de l'introspection détourne trop souvent de cette manière irremplaçable d'accéder à autrui, tel qu'il est impliqué en nous. Et par contre, le recours au 'dehors', par lui-même, ne garantit nullement contre les illusions de l'introspection." *V.I.*, p. 36.

[37] "Il serait instructif d'expliciter ce que les psychologues entendent par le 'psychisme'." *Ibid.*

[38] "C'est comme une couche géologique profonde, une *'chose'* invisible." *V.I.*, p. 37.

[39] "Une explicitation complète de l'attitude psychologique et des concepts dont le psychologue se sert comme s'ils allaient de soi, montrerait en elle une masse de conséquences sans premisses, un travail constitutif fort ancien qui n'est pas tiré au clair et dont les resultats sont acceptés tels quels sans qu'on soupçonne même à quel point ils sont confus." *Ibid.*

[40] "Le clivage du 'subjectif' et de l' 'objectif', par lequel la physique commençante définit son domaine, et la psychologie, corrélativement, le sien, n'empêche pas, exige au contraire, qu'ils soient conçus selon la même structure fondamentale." *Ibid.*

hence, follows the similarity of the fundamental attitudes of the physicist and the psychologist: they place themselves outside their objects, creating the illusion of surveying it without being related to it.

This, however, is an impossible attitude, since the physicist himself belongs to nature and the psychologist himself also has a psychic life and is, therefore, the object of his own science. The so-called "subjective" and "objective" orders have too hastily been abstracted from an original and integral experience to which they must again be reduced.[41]

Gestalt Psychology. Merleau-Ponty illustrates his point of view in a short description of the psychology of form (Gestalt psychology).[42] This type of psychology was initiated about a half century ago, and it seemed to give the psychologists a really scientific approach. The physicists studied structures, of which they discovered the laws. By changing an element of the structure, they could determine its influence on the whole. The psychologists hoped they could do the same. As a matter of fact, behavior also has its own structure, and this can be made the object of psychological research. Within the structure of behavior there are functional relationships which seem to be universal. The psychologist must start, of course, with a description of behavior, but this description can set up the concepts of functional relationships which are able to be scientifically determined. When, e.g., certain conditions are fulfilled, man perceives in a certain manner; and this perception changes with the variation of its objective conditions. When this approach had been established, the psychologists expected to see real progress in their field, and at the same time a confirmation of its scientific character.

They have been disappointed. After fifty years of employing psychology of form many psychologists feel they have arrived at a deadlock.[43] It appears that the strict relationship between the conditions and what is conditioned by them functions only in the artificial situations of the laboratory.[44] We do not find there a real beginning from which the whole psychic life can be understood. Laboratory experiments do not

---

[41] "Cette physique du physicien, cette psychologie du psychologue, annoncent que désormais, pour la science même, l'être-objet ne peut plus être l'être-même: 'objectif' et 'subjectif' sont reconnus comme deux ordres construits hâtivement à l'intérieur d'une expérience totale dont il faudrait, en toute clarté, restituer le contexte." *V.I.,* p. 38.

[42] *V.I.,* pp. 38-42.

[43] "Mais l'enthousiasme n'y est plus, on n'a nulle part le sentiment d'approcher d'une science de l'homme." *V.I.,* p. 39.

[44] *Ibid.*

explain the real psychic life of man. In the experiences of real life there is no strict relationship between the so-called conditions and what is conditioned by them. Although it may be easy to explain the apparent movement of a spot of light by the conditions which have been created in the laboratory, it appears to be impossible to explain the real perceptive field in the same manner.

The impossibility is not due to our ignorance of the conditions of real perception; it is due to the fact that in real perception the conditions cannot be isolated.[45] They function in an essential interchange with one another. When in real perception I see a road which starts here and which extends to the horizon of my field, I see one and the same road, here and at a distance, although it does not appear to me in the same manner. Still I *see* one and the same road. I do not express myself fully when I say that I *know* it is the same road; I know it because I see it so. Here, at the place where I am, the road covers nearly my whole visual field; there, at a distance, near to the horizon, it is only a narrow strip, almost a line. Yet I see one and the same road. The size of the road there, in the distance, is not a question for me. It is the same road, here and there. My eyes do not measure the breadth of the line I see at a distance; and I do not coordinate the breadth of the line with the distance. I simply see one and the same road.[46] There are conditions which influence my vision, but that which is conditioned by them is like a conclusion which exceeds its premises.

All the conditions which can be studied in the laboratory do not explain the simple fact that I see the same road; and this fact co-determines the way in which I see the road there, at a distance. I organize my visual field, and I make use of what the psychologists call the objective conditions of vision. It is not completely right to say that I do so; it is rather my seeing body which does so. Well then, in my concrete vision the so-called conditions do not explain completely that which is conditioned by them. Only in the laboratory is there a strict relationship between the conditions and what is conditioned by them. The reason for this is that in the laboratory the natural horizon of my visual field is taken away. The scientists who organize experiments

---

[45] ". . . autant une détermination totale du champ perceptif concret de tel individu à tel moment apparaît non pas provisoirement inaccessible mais définitivement dépourvue de sens *parce qu'il offre des structures qui n'ont pas même de nom dans l'univers OBJECTIF des 'conditions' séparées et séparables.*" *V.I.*, pp. 39-40.

[46] *V.I.*, p. 40.

create an artificial situation; they determine both the figure and the horizon. In this impoverished field the so-called conditions seem to function perfectly sometimes. But my real vision in my natural field is not merely a more complicated application of what takes place in the laboratory. In my natural field all the conditions of vision co-determine one another, and, therefore, cannot be isolated. There the structure of the situation is more than its components. There the influence of the isolated conditions never completely explain that which they condition. There what is conditioned makes us understand its conditions.[47] The confluence of the two images of my two eyes into one visual field cannot be deduced from the two images. The two images reach their fulfillment in the one visual field. The single field is the fulfillment of the two images, and the fulfillment makes what goes before it understandable.

The psychology of form initially grew out of the hypothesis that the schematism, condition-conditioned, could explain the structures of our psychic life. If we could understand all the conditions, we could also understand the structure. This hypothesis has not been verified because the conditions influence, not only the whole, but also one another and, furthermore, the whole influences the conditions themselves.

We must not conclude, continues Merleau-Ponty, that the reality of our psychic life exceeds the realm of science. We would then easily slip into the hypothesis that there is a realm of reality inaccessible to science. We would distinguish a realm accessible to science from one which is not, a realm of science from a realm of mystery. This would lead to a false spiritualism, to a kind of mysticism.[48] We must conclude, on the contrary, that psychology simply did not conceive its object in the right manner.

A Fundamental Misconception. There is, according to Merleau-Ponty, a relationship between the difficulties of the natural sciences and the partial failure of psychology. Both started from a false bifurcation of reality. Nature, the object of natural science, was reduced to a mere

---

[47] ". . . et que donc le 'conditionné' conditionne ici la condition." *V.I.,* p. 41.

[48] "Le 'psychisme' n'est pas objet; mais,—notons-le bien—, il ne s'agit pas ici de montrer, selon la tradition 'spiritualiste' que certaines réalités 'échappent' à la détermination scientifique: ce genre de démonstration n'aboutit qu'à circonscrire un domaine de l'anti-science qui, d'ordinaire reste conçu dans les termes de l'ontologie qui précisément est en question, comme une autre 'ordre de réalités'." *Ibid.*

object independent of the subject; and the subject's life, the psychic life, was conceived as a reality of a different order. The result of this bifurcation was a world without psyche and a psyche without world. Both were considered as objective fields. The most fundamental truth is here forgotten, the truth expressed in Merleau-Ponty's words: *j'en suis.* I am the world which has come to awareness of itself. I cannot separate the world from my awareness, neither can I divorce my awareness from the world. I am present in the world of physical research, and the world is present in my awareness.

The crisis of psychology, for Merleau-Ponty, is not due to a lack of development, but to the fact that psychology is on the wrong path.[49] It thinks of a separate realm of reality which it calls "psychic life." It considers this realm a new kind of object and looks for the scientific methods to approach this object correctly. Just as the natural sciences must recognize the essential presence of man in their field of research, so the psychologists must recognize the worldly character of the psyche. The psyche *is* world which comes to awareness of itself. The psyche is the "other side," the "interiority," of the world itself. Merleau-Ponty does not explain how psychology should be constructed according to his own principles. Perhaps he would have done so in the chapters which have remained unwritten.

G. THE DEADLOCK OF SOCIAL PSYCHOLOGY

The Stimulus-Response Scheme. Merleau-Ponty views social psychology as in a situation of conflict.[50] Insofar as it is a real access to social life, it exceeds the methods to which it wishes to remain faithful. The social psychologist, like every psychologist, wants to make use of the stimulus-response scheme, which is nothing but the cause-effect scheme applied to the psychic order. But if he really restricted himself to this scheme, he could not practice social psychology.[51] Were man a collection of responses, of effects, then he could not influence other men in his own manner. The person's own character could not be introduced into social

---

[49] "Nous nous sommes adressés à la psychologie de la perception en général pour mieux montrer que les crises de la psychologie tiennent à des raisons de principe, et non à quelque retard des recherches en tel domaine particulier. Mais une fois qu'on l'a vue dans sa généralité, on retrouve la même difficulté de principe dans les recherches spécialisées." *V.I.,* p. 42.

[50] *V.I.,* pp. 46-50.

[51] "Du seul fait qu'on pratique la psychologie sociale, on est hors de l'ontologie objectiviste." *V.I.,* p. 43.

psychology.   Moreover, it would be impossible to speak of the real influence of social and historical surroundings.

But social psychology does speak of the influence of persons and of the existence and influence of social surroundings.   As a matter of fact, they are considered a Gestalt which is more than all the particular stimuli. The social psychologist recognizes the existence and influence of social totalities which cannot be considered as the sum of effects of many causes.   Social psychology knows that these totalities have an existence which differs from the physical existence of things, that they are temporal and spatial in their own manner, that they have their own code, and that very often they are symbols rather than causes.   In practice social psychology exceeds the objectivistic trend of thought which, frequently, it still professes in theory.   If social psychology would really remain faithful to the objectivistic manner of thinking, it would be forced to betray its own object.

The actual development of social knowledge directly opposes the scientific principles which are often still professed.   According to these principles, magic and myth were to have been surpassed by the scientific attitude.   They could not have their own truth, since everything which really happens must have its own objective causes; thus what is conceived as magical and mythical should be ascribed to subjective illusions.   This is a current scientific postulate.[52]   Yet if social psychology wants to approach our society as it really is, it cannot start from this postulate, which itself is a social phenomenon of our Western world.   The ethnologist is well aware that in primitive societies time is not experienced in the same manner as in our Western society, that mythical events there are not conceived as belonging to the past, but as an eternal present which is still working.   The social psychologist does not have the right to deny that the mythical conception of time is still active.   How can he deny that magical and mythical elements really play a role in social and individual life?

The Insufficiency of the Scientific Method.   Since real social life is the object of the social psychologist, he has no right to subject it *a priori* to all the claims and all the postulates of Western scientific thought, which itself is only one of the components of Western social life.   There is no guarantee that this component element gives access to the whole.   The social psychologist must, of course, work according to the current

---

[52] *Ibid.*

scientific methods. He must accept them as they are, viz., as methods by which Western science exists and which must be used as much as possible. These methods embody man's endeavor to transform pre-rational reality into rational statements. But the social psychologist must be ready to admit that his object exceeds these methods; he must be ready to correct his methods when his object demands it.[53] As a matter of fact he does so, but generally without being aware of it.

The social psychologist is confronted with questions which he cannot solve as long as he restricts himself to the traditional scientific methods. What is the other person? What is the character and place of a social and historical event? What is a group, a society? These questions cannot be solved as long as the scientist thinks according to the stimulus-response scheme. This scheme is surpassed by the social psychologist, and he is right in doing so. But how does he then proceed, and what justifies the procedure?

Scientism. Previously Merleau-Ponty stressed that physicists often try to include within an objective ontology a science which goes beyond this way of thinking.[54] The same happens in psychology. It even seems that the psychologist clings more strongly to the mechanical way of thinking than does the physicist.[55] The physicist sometimes admits relationships in nature which exceed the mechanical scheme; the psychologist, however, hesitates to admit that relationships between the body and the world exceed the causal relationships. The reason is that as soon as we admit that perception cannot be explained in a causal manner by the action of things on the body, all the traditional explanations of human science are undermined. Then truth can no longer be a reflection of reality, and scientific knowledge is no longer a reflection of nature. The causal relationship between stimulus and perception is the final stronghold of scientistic philosophy, which for a long period has dominated scientific life.[56] Thus the renewal of scientific life filters with more difficulty into psychology[57] and biology[58] than into physics. But the question whether our perception can be explained in a mechanical

---

[53] *V.I.*, p. 44.

[54] Merleau-Ponty quotes Arthur Eddington as an example of this attitude. *V.I.*, p. 45, note 1.

[55] *V.I.*, p. 45.

[56] *V.I.*, pp. 45-46.

[57] "La physiologie participe moins activement que la physique au renouveau méthodologique d'aujourd'hui." *V.I.*, p. 46.

[58] "Les biologistes restent plus matérialistes que les physiciens." *Ibid.*

manner, by the causal action of things on the body, appears to be unavoidable.   When this question is faced and the negative answer given, the last stronghold of scientism will have surrendered and a new philosophy of science will be possible.

Our perception gives access to the world, and it offers us a world which has a structure, which is a whole of coherent facts.   We believe firmly, therefore, in a structured and coherent world.   We have believed in it so firmly that we have absorbed our perception into the world, transforming our access to the world into a simple fact of the world. We have forgotten the final source of our knowledge and of the knowable world itself.   We will have to re-examine our access to the world and, hence, also our knowable world itself.   This is the task of philosophy, which not only asks questions, but reflects upon the questioning being itself.[59]

H. CONCLUSION

In this criticism of science Merleau-Ponty indicates many tasks to be accomplished.   Science is inclined to reduce its subject matter to a mere object.   Perception, our primordial access to the world, is also conceived as an objective fact, as the effect of the action of stimuli.[60]   Since the object cannot exist without a subject, science implicitly sets up a subject who is distinguished from all the objects.   The subject of science is a worldless "surveyor" who makes both the physical and the psychic world his object.   On this point Merleau-Ponty applies his fundamental thesis: *j'en suis*.   The subject of scientific knowledge must be seen as the perceiving subject, and the perceiving subject must be seen as belonging to the world.   When the absolute subject has thus disappeared, the absolute object can no longer be maintained.   The scientist, the perceiving subject, belongs to the world.   But this world is no longer the mechanical field, the realm of causal relationships.   The radicalization of Merleau-Ponty's *j'en suis* finally requires a new concept of the world, of nature itself.   And he intended to write a chapter about this new concept of world and nature.   This new concept would have been the foundation of a new philosophy of science.

---

[59] "La philosophie est l'ensemble des questions où celui qui questionne est lui-même en cause par la question." *V.I.*, p. 47.

[60] "Il faut réexaminer la définition du corps comme objet pur pour comprendre comment il peut être notre lien vivant avec la nature." *Ibid*.

2. *Merleau-Ponty's Criticism of Reflection*

A. THE PURPOSE OF REFLECTIVE PHILOSOPHY

Following his criticism of science, Merleau-Ponty examines what he calls, in short, "reflection."[61] With this word he indicates a style of philosophizing which he gives several names throughout his different works. He speaks of "reflective analysis," of "reflective philosophy," of "rationalism," and "idealism." He uses these terms again in the chapter we are dealing with now, but most frequently he simply speaks about "reflection." Merleau-Ponty criticizes reflection. This does not mean, however, that Merleau-Ponty rejects reflection. Criticism is not identical with rejection. Criticism means making a distinction between what is valuable, good or acceptable and what is valueless, bad or unacceptable; criticism implies that one accept the former and reject the latter. Merleau-Ponty could not simply reject reflection, since philosophy itself cannot exist without it.

In this chapter Merleau-Ponty rejects a type of philosophy which has no confidence in our immediate knowledge and which professes that truth can be found only in the reflective order. This trend of thought has been rather common in modern Western philosophy. We find it in the works of Descartes and all his followers and in Kant and Hegel. In France there was a strong revival of rationalism at the end of the past century. Although Merleau-Ponty sometimes speaks of Kant, he generally has French rationalism in mind.

Distrust of Immediate Knowledge. Reflective philosophy distrusts our immediate knowledge. This distrust has been clearly expressed in the methodical doubt of Descartes. Our so-called immediate knowledge sometimes appears to be wrong; how do we know, then, that it is not always wrong? We sometimes confuse real perception with imagination and dreams; how can we be sure that we are not always imagining or dreaming?

This distrust of immediate knowledge is quite understandable for Merleau-Ponty. Our immediate or perceptive knowledge is the presence to the world of the being which belongs to it, which *"en est."* It is a presence without distance, and it cannot be called, therefore, real

---

[61] *V.I.,* pp. 48-74.

thought.   Merleau-Ponty calls it "perceptive *faith*" (*foi perceptive*).[62]

By "faith" Merleau-Ponty does not mean that we base ourselves on the authority of other persons or on God.   He simply wants to say that there is a presence, a contact without distance, awareness without thought.   We have already seen that Merleau-Ponty accepts the difficult idea of presence, an awareness without any reflective consciousness.   We know without knowing what we know.   We believe in the world, in the real world; we are aware of the presence of other persons; we experience them as an awareness of the same world we believe in.   Our immediate knowledge, our perceptive faith, is a knowledge without real criticism. It sometimes happens that we confuse real perception and imagination. Our "perceptive faith" is loaded with ambiguities.   When we reflect upon it, many questions arise.   The world to which I am present evidently is *my* world; how can it be, at the same time, the world of other persons?   How can my world be a common world?   How can my world be an objective world?   How can this ambiguous world help me to make a clear distinction between real perception and imagination?

Reflective philosophy starts from the hypothesis that our so-called immediate contact with the world is unreliable.   We are not even sure that there is real contact with the world.   For the so-called contact may be a dream, an imagination.   If there is any hope of having real and true knowledge, we must look for it in the reflective order.

Whether I perceive, imagine or dream, one thing is certain: something is present to my mind.   I may not be able to distinguish perception, imagination and dream, but I am absolutely certain that something is present to me.   The character of this presence is not important at the moment, since I am absolutely sure of the fact that I think and that my thought has an object.[63]   I can reflect on my object of thought.   I can try to make out what is clear to me, and what is not at all clear.   To Descartes it is clear that I think, and that my thought is confronted with quantitative objects between which there exist quantitative relationships. This certainty does not depend on whether or not the quantitative objects and relationships really exist.   I think them; they are present to me; they are clear to me as a "what," even if the question of the "that" is not yet resolved.

---

[62] "Elle est une foi, c'est-à-dire une adhésion qui se sait au-delà des preuves, non nécessaire, tissée d'incrédulité, à chaque instant menacée par la non-foi." *V.I.*, p. 48.

[63] "Par la conversion réflexive, percevoir et imaginer ne sont plus que deux manières de *penser*." *V.I.*, p. 49.

Perception and Thought. I do not find clarity in my immediate contact with the world, but I do find clarity in my object of thought. I must focus my attention, therefore, on the object of thought. In this way I transcend the obscure field of the so-called immediate contact with the world; I find clarity in the realm of reflection.

In this way reflective philosophy thinks it retains everything which is really valuable in our perception. Our reflective thought brings to light its most essential elements, or rather, it discovers this light. According to rationalism, perception *is* a hidden thought, a thought which is still unaware of itself. Both perception and illusion are forms of thought, but in them thought is still hidden in the darkness of materiality and corporality; we could say that there thought is alienated from itself. In the reflective attitude the hidden thought comes to itself. Thought is the manifestation of what they really are; and the distinction between perception and imagination consists in the level of thought: in perception our hidden thought constitutes an object, which must of course still be discovered by reflection; our imagination and our dreams are nascent and unfinished thoughts.

Human thought and its object are indeed important, and reflection discovers these essential elements. The naive and impossible illusion of a bodily activity able to give us real knowledge of real things is exposed by reflection. How could it be possible for the body to be a being which knows realities distinguished from itself? If this were true, the same things would be simultaneously outside and inside the body; they would be outside the body since it is distinguished from them; they would be inside the body since the body would know them. An "external object" is a contradiction, for being an object implies interiority. The external thing exists in itself, and the object exists for the mind. The primitive notion of perception which conceives it as a bodily activity transforming real things into objects is not only an ambiguous idea, but is even weighted down by contradictions.[64]

Where is the Object of Thought? The essence of perception is thought and what perception gives us is the object of thought.[65] Where

---

[64] "Je ne crois plus voir de mes yeux des choses extérieures à moi qui les vois: elles ne sont extérieures qu'à mon corps, non à ma pensée, qui le survole aussi bien qu'elles." *V.I.,* p. 51.

[65] "L'existence brute et préalable du monde que je croyais trouver déjà là, en ouvrant les yeux, n'est que le symbole d'un être qui est pour soi sitôt qu'il est, parce que tout son être est d'apparaître, donc de s'apparaître, —et qui s'appelle **esprit**." *V.I.,* p. 51.

is the object of thought? The question itself is meaningless. The object of thought is nowhere. It is not in space, since it is incorporeal. We are here in the realm of ideality, which transcends both space and time. There is real light in the field of perception, but this light is the light of the ideas which are not *in* a field. The field of perception is a materialization of the ideal light, and the latter is discovered in reflection.

In this way the illusory distinction between my world and the world of other persons is transcended.[66] As long as reflection has not yet reduced perception to its truth, we are inclined to oppose our world to the world of other persons. The ideal world, however, which is the truth of the perceptive field, is essentially common. The word "common" is not quite correct. We must say that the ideal world is strictly unique. The triangle which was thought of by the Greeks is not different from the triangle we think about. Real thought about the triangle is always confronted with one and the same ideal phenomenon. The ideal phenomenon, which is the object of thought and the truth of perception, is neither outside me nor inside me. It is nowhere, since it has no place.

I must say, of course, that things of the world are outside my body. But I can say so only because I understand what space is. Spatiality means a network of relationships, and relationships are an ideal reality, objects of thoughts. As long as I am living on the level of perception and have not yet penetrated into its ideal truth, I blindly believe that space exists for my body, that my body gives me access to space. Reflection makes me understand that both my body and all corporal things are assumed within the network of ideal relationships. Bodies are situated in space in different ways; but, on the level of thought, space is unique for all thinking persons.

As soon as there is real thought, as soon as reflection has discovered the real truth of perception, the distinction between myself and others becomes unimportant, or rather, it completely disappears. We think, and both thought and its object transcend plurality.

The Role of Reflection. Is there no darkness, no confusion? Yes, there is. There is darkness and confusion as long as the truth of perception has not yet been discovered by reflection. We do not always live on the level of thought. Thought is not always revealed by reflection, and even when the thinking person reflects, he does not do so

---

66 *V.I.*, pp. 53-54.

in all the aspects of his life.   There seems to be an almost natural movement toward the darkness of perception which forgets its own truth.   Descartes discovered the truth of perceptive life by what he called "metaphysical reflection," but he also confessed that this activity is exceptional, that man has to return to the darkness of common life.   Man is an embodied being, and this implies that he cannot always or in every aspect of his life ascend to the light which is the truth of his own being. We have to live in the darkness of perception which has forgotten itself.

How is this possible?   According to reflective philosophy the ideal world of thought is not here, in the world, as a material object.   The object of thought cannot be separated from thought itself.   Thought constitutes its own ideas, it is the source of its own light.   Thought is not centripetal and it does not collect the light it finds in the world; it is centrifugal, for it constitutes the light.   The centrifugal movement of thought explains why thought so easily forgets itself.   Its attention is focused on the light it constitutes.   Since we are embodied beings, the light of thought finally descends into perception and sensations.   In them thought almost completely forgets itself.   It falls into the illusion that the object of thought is here, outside me, in the real world.   The centrifugal movement of thought makes it understandable that thought forgets itself, that it becomes alienated from itself.

Reflection implies that our thought which has forgotten itself returns to itself.   By reflection we trace back the way we have come. Constituting thought becomes aware of itself.   It transcends the illusions it has occasioned by its centrifugal movement and returns to its own essence.   It understands what it has always been.   Hence, it is understandable that the reflective attitude is a difficult one.   It is not obvious for man to place himself in the reflective attitude, since he must break with the centrifugal movement of his thought which is ingrained in him.   Metaphysical reflection is, therefore, an activity we exercise only a short time, and then we return to the common attitude of human life.   The reflective movement of our mind would not be necessary if a constitutive movement had not preceded it.   By reflection we gain back the clarity we had lost.   Reflection is the struggle against our own imagination.   The reflecting philosopher returns to the light which he originally was.   In philosophy man returns to his own original being. Philosophy is a kind of redemption.

Merleau-Ponty's description of reflective philosophy in *The Visible and the Invisible* is both condensed and clear.   But it is not the first time he has given this description; it is present already in the concluding chapter of *The Structure of Behavior* and in *Phenomenology of Perception*. However, we felt it necessary to summarize this description of reflective philosophy before passing on to Merleau-Ponty's criticism of it.

Why does Merleau-Ponty again describe and criticize reflective philosophy? The reason becomes clearer when we read his criticism. The philosopher always has to place himself within the reflective attitude. Philosophy *is* reflection. In order to explain what philosophy ultimately is, Merleau-Ponty has to examine the function of reflection in philosophy.

B. MERLEAU-PONTY'S CRITICISM OF REFLECTIVE PHILOSOPHY

Immanence of Knowledge. Reflective philosophy is right, according to Merleau-Ponty, insofar as it denies that human knowledge is a relationship between separated realities.[67] Realism conceives human knowledge as such a relationship: the knowing person is here and the things which are known are there, outside him, in the world. Consequently, knowledge must be conceived either as an action of wordly things on the knowing subject, or as an exteriorization of the knowing person into the world. Both ideas are unacceptable; they are a materialization of knowledge. In the first hypothesis the physical action of wordly things must explain knowledge; this implies that knowledge is ultimately reduced to a physical process. In the second hypothesis knowledge is conceived as a physical exteriorization of the knowing subject; this, too, is materialistic. Hence the reflective philosopher concludes that we must conceive human knowledge as an immanent activity. The real knowing subject is not the body separated from other worldly things; the real object is not the thing which exists outside the body.

The knowing subject is mind, spirit, and the object of knowledge is the ideal reality, which is neither inside the body nor outside it. The ideal reality is neither here nor there; it is not located at all; strictly

---

[67] "Ce qui fera toujours de la philosophie réflexive, non seulement une tentation, mais un chemin qu'il faut suivre, c'est qu'elle est vraie dans ce qu'elle nie: la relation extérieure d'un monde en soi et de moi-même, conçue comme un processus du type de ceux qui se déroulent à l'intérieur du monde, qu'on imagine une intrusion du monde en moi ou, au contraire, quelque voyage de mon regard parmi les choses." *V.I.*, p. 53.

speaking, it is nowhere. All spatial relationships are transcended in knowledge. Even the word "immanent" is confusing, since it makes us think of a local relationship. The object of knowledge appears to the mind. We cannot separate its Being and its appearing. Its Being *is* its appearing to the mind. I have the illusion that something which is separated from me, which exists there, in the world, appears to me. Reflection reveals the truth of this illusion. This illusion is an exteriorization of the appearance of Being to my mind; this is an ideal fact which belongs to another realm. Thought is the truth of vision, of hearing, of perception. Perception *is* thought which has forgotten its own spiritual character.

Merleau-Ponty rejects, as does reflective philosophy, any physical interpretation of knowledge. He does not agree that knowledge can be explained by the impressions that things of the world cause upon us, nor by any movement on our part into physical things. He already rejected these ideas in the final chapter of *The Structure of Behavior* and never returned to them. He has always been opposed to what he calls "realism." With this term he indicates any materialistic interpretation of knowledge.

Rejection of Reflective Philosophy. What has always remained the real problem for Merleau-Ponty has been avoiding the perspectives of "reflective analysis," of rationalism and idealism. If knowledge is not conceived in a materialistic way, must we not then accept a spiritual interpretation? Should we not then conceive knowledge to be an ideal event? Knowledge seems then to be the presence of ideal reality to spiritual thought. Merleau-Ponty has often said that rationalism, idealism, is a more profound philosophy than realism. Reflective philosophy, he says in his last book, is not only a temptation but a road we must follow, insofar as it denies realism, that is, any materialistic interpretation of human knowledge. Why, then, is reflective analysis not the final truth which we must accept?[68] This is not just an academic question for Merleau-Ponty. In opposing his own philosophy to materialism and realism, he did not experience many difficulties; yet he did have difficulties in distinguishing his philosophical perspectives from reflective analysis.

There are two main reasons why Merleau-Ponty rejects reflective philosophy. First, according to him the reflective attitude of mind,

---

[68] *V.I.*, pp. 53-54.

although it pretends to coincide finally with the constitutive attitude, can never succeed in doing so. The second reason is that reflective philosophy always presupposes a basic certainty which it does not explain.

The First Reason. According to reflective philosophy we do not *find* the ideal light of truth, but we constitute it. If we could *find* the ideal light in a real world, we would have to accept realism. Man is the source, the origin, of the ideal light; but he has forgotten this. We have forgotten the constituting character of our mind and we have exteriorized the ideal light into the material world of sensation and perception. Reflection tries to recover what we have lost. It travels the same path as the constitutive movement of our mind, but in the opposite direction. Constitution starts from the reality of the mind, the spirit itself, and ends in perception and sensation. Reflection starts from sensation and perception and hopes to return to the final source of ideal light.

This return to the source can never coincide, according to Merleau-Ponty, with the constituting movement of our mind. To illustrate what he means, he uses a metaphor. We can walk from Place de l'Étoile to Notre-Dame and then return from Notre-Dame to Place de l'Étoile. In both cases we go the same way, and yet it is not the same way.[69] We have quite a different experience in both cases. This metaphor can be applied to the relationship which exists between the so-called constitutive and the reflective movements of our mind. Reflective philosophy explains everything except reflection itself.[70] Reflection is necessary since we have lost the awareness of what we really are. The original light has been dissolved into darkness. Reflection is the rebirth of the light, and it tries to return to the original birth which we have forgotten. Thus reflection is *for us* the origin of the ideal light. True, reflection is not the final origin, since by reflection we return to the final origin; but *for us* who have forgotten the final origin, reflection really is the origin of light.

The subject of reflection is not the constituting subject who is the origin of light, but the empirical, perceiving subject who has been lost in the darkness of the material world. The act of reflection is an empirical act which has its own place in the history of the subject's life. I move, reflective philosophy says, from the darkness to the light. But I cannot

---

[69] *V.I.,* p. 55.

[70] "La réflexion récupère tout sauf elle-même comme effort de récupération, elle éclaire tout sauf son propre rôle." *Ibid.*

do so if I do not find a real light in the darkness itself. Having lost the original light, I must find some light in the darkness in which I live.[71] This light is my starting point, and I have no other light when I begin to think, when I begin to reflect.

Reflective philosophy holds that the way of reflection is not the original way, that it is only a way back. It is important, not in itself, but only insofar as we recover the original way, the way of constitution. Reflective philosophy, in this way, devaluates the real movement of my thought by appealing to a preceding, hidden way of thought, of light. It depreciates the real light which is available to me; it ignores the real, empirical subject who struggles for light, appealing to a hidden subject who, for some obscure reason, has made the struggle necessary. Reflection, on the one hand, is the source, the origin of light, at least *for us* in our empirical situation. But on the other hand, reflection becomes completely unimportant when I have returned to the original source of light. The way back, in which philosophy would be engaged, is due to an accident. Reflective analysis explains everything except the central act of philosophy, viz., reflection.

The Second Reason. There is a second reason why Merleau-Ponty cannot accept the type of philosophy which he calls "reflective" analysis: this philosophy appeals to a clear, ideal world in order to explain the perceptive field, but in doing so, it presupposes the inner light of the perceptive field itself. Reflective philosophy is looking for a source of light; it could not do so if, before finding its source, it were not already confronted with real light. The latter cannot be found elsewhere than in the perceptive field. Reflective philosophy tries to reduce the existing world to an ideal world which is the object of thought; in doing so it presupposes the presence of the world itself. Reflective analysis depends on the inner light of the perceptive world.

Kant often prefaced his important statements by saying: "If a world is possible . . .";[72] he thus professed that he knew what a world was before he found its ideal source. The presence and the structure of this world was not revealed to him, therefore, by the ideal thought, but by perception. Thought is not the final source of the world, but its

---

[71] "En tant qu'effort pour fonder le monde existant sur une, *penseé* du monde, la réflexion s'inspire à chaque instant de la présence préalable du monde." *Ibid.*

[72] *V.I.*, p. 95.

secondary expression. If I shall ever know how the world is possible, this understanding will find its foundation in the simple fact that I perceive the world. Even when the reflective philosopher has the illusion that he is returning into himself and finding there the source of all light, he is still continually appealing to the perceptive field. If we can withdraw into ourselves in order to make clear what we know, we can only do so because we are already perceiving the world. We can reflect because we already know. Our capacity to reflect is conditioned by pre-reflective knowledge. The constitution of an ideal world presupposes the presence of a real world.[73]

An Objection. The objection can be raised that every great reflective philosopher has been aware of all this. Spinoza continually refers to "true ideas" which precede reflection and Kant consciously makes use of the light of the world which is already there before we begin to reflect.[74] They understood that there is a circular movement between the immediate field of perceptive knowledge and the field of ideal thought. We must begin with an analysis of the perceptive field, for thought only brings clarity into its own confused beginning. Analysis of the perceptive field is like a stairway which one can remove after having mounted it.[75]

If this is true, then reflective philosophy has denied its own essence, says Merleau-Ponty. If this is true, there is no longer a hidden source of light which must be recovered. There is then a mutual relationship between the immediate field of perception and reflection, since reflection both presupposes the inner light of the perceptive field and, at the same time, enlightens it. Consequently, the final term of reflective analysis is already present in its beginning, and the beginning remains present in the final term.[76] However, this is precisely Merleau-Ponty's thesis. He does not intend to deny all reflection in order to remain within the realm of immediate knowledge, for the meaning of immediate knowledge is

---

[73] "Toute l'analyse réflexive est non pas fausse, mais naïve encore, tant qu'elle se dissimule son propre ressort, et que, pour constituer le monde, il faut avoir notion du monde en tant que préconstitué." *V.I.*, p. 56.

[74] *Ibid.*

[75] *Ibid.*

[76] "Mais s'il en est ainsi, il n'y a plus de philosophie réflexive, car il n'y a plus d'originaire et de dérivé, il y a une pensée en cercle ou la condition et le conditionné, la réflexion et le réfléchi, sont dans une relation réciproque, sinon symétrique, et ou la fin est dans le commencement tout autant que le commencement dans la fin. Nous ne disons pas autre chose." *V.I.*, pp. 56-57.

revealed only in reflection.[77]   The original datum of philosophy is
neither a world which is complete darkness nor a field of thought which
is nothing but light.   We are reflecting beings who search the semi-dark
world in order to enlighten it.   But if reflection enlightens the world, it
finally restores to the world the light which belongs to it.   This,
however, is not what reflective philosophers really mean.

There is real thought, and there is a relationship between thought and
its ideal object.   This ideal relationship expresses to some extent my real
relationship to the world; but it is certainly not its adequate expression.
For, I am related to the world before I begin to think, and this relationship has more aspects than my ideal thought expresses.   I am an openness
to the world before I begin to think.   I deny this original openness as
soon as I pretend to know all about it by abstract thought.   By abstract
thought I know something about it, but at the same time it always exceeds
abstract thought.   As soon as I want to understand what seeing is, I can
no longer surrender myself to my vision.   My endeavor to understand my
vision implies that I "translate" my vision into a realm of ideal meaning.
But then I must say that my vision itself is the original "text."   This
metaphor, however, can be only partially applied, since in this case the
ideal version, on the one hand, makes no sense without the original text
and, on the other, makes the original text accessible.[78]

It is entirely false to think that we are never certain until we have
reflected.[79]   There would be no certainty in reflection if there were no
certainty in immediate knowledge.   Reflection is not the source, but the
awareness, of certainty.   In reflection already existing certainty comes to
its fulfillment.   But reflection is always rooted in pre-reflective knowledge.   Reflection certainly is a renewal, but a renewal and a prolongation of what already existed.

Reflection makes use of words.   Our ideal thought cannot exist
without the abstract meanings of language.   These abstract meanings,
however, are not self-sufficient.   Reflection is rooted in a pre-reflective
field.   The abstract meanings of language are the expression of a preverbal world.   When they are drawn away from the pre-verbal world,
they lose their real meaning.   As soon as we enclose our abstract

---

[77] "Les remarques que nous faisions sur la réflexion n'étaient nullement
destinées à la disqualifier au profit de l'irréfléchi ou de l'immédiat (que nous ne
connaissons qu'à travers elle)." *V.I.*, p. 57.

[78] *V.I.*, p. 58.

[79] *V.I.*, p. 59.

meanings in themselves, their real meaning is lost. By speaking we try
to bring things to light, but the light of our words is connected with an
original darkness.[80] When this connection with original darkness is
dissolved, the light of speaking itself disappears, or rather, we move in a
world of imaginary light. Language transforms darkness into light, and
still it must remain connected with original darkness. This essential
paradox of language is usually forgotten by philosophers who concentrate
on the meaning of words. Reflection is rooted in immediate experience.
In the same way, the world of speech must remain connected with the
silent world. If we fail to do so we fall into a "dogmatism of
reflection";[81] and then philosophy is completed at the moment of its
beginning, since we are enclosed in a field of poor and imaginary light.
Then philosophy has lost contact with the real experience which is the
root of its renewal.

Rootless reflective philosophy is unfaithful to: a) the world about
which it speaks, viz., the perceptive world; b) the reflecting philosopher,
himself, since the origin of reflection is neglected; c) other persons who
look at the same world, for they all are brought together within the
absolute unity of the thinker.[82] Briefly, reality is dissolved into ideality,
losing its original density.

Why does the reflective philosopher do this? He begins with the
pretentsion that original experience is confused and uncertain, loaded
with doubts. He is afraid that the appearing reality may be unreal, and
so he tries to resolve his doubts. Like Descartes he is looking for a point
which resists all possible doubt, which he can make the starting-point for
all philosophy. He loses sight of what our original experience offers us,
and he looks only for what resists doubt. In this way he reduces positive
reality to the "negation of the negation"; he makes the innocent prove
that it is not guilty;[83] he reduces our original contact with the world to
the discursive activities of our mind; and he transforms our struggle
against possible illusions into the starting-point of all philosophy. He

---

[80] "Elle employe les mots *pour dire* ce lien prélogique, et non pas
conformément à leur signification préétablie." *V.I.*, p. 61.

[81] *V.I.*, p. 62.

[82] *Ibid.*

[83] "C'est identifier d'emblée le positif avec une négation de la négation, c'est
imposer à l'innocent la preuve de sa non-culpabilité, et d'avance réduire notre
contact avec l'Être aux opérations discursives par lesquelles nous nous defendons
contre l'illusion, le vrai au vraisemblable, le réel au probable." *Ibid.*

forgets that in immediate experience we usually distinguish real perception and illusions rather well.   The endeavor of discursive thought to
distinguish real experience and imagination presupposes, rather than
constitutes, this distinction.

Passivity of Human Thought.   Merleau-Ponty's confrontation with
reflective philosophy brings another difficulty to light.   Human thought
is discursive, active.   It cannot, therefore, subject itself to something
which it does not understand.   If it does so, it can no longer be called
real thought.   Merleau-Ponty criticizes himself for seeming to make
human thought passive.   As a matter of fact, thought seems to *find* its
original light.   It is subjected to something which it does not really
penetrate.   But as soon as some kind of passivity is introduced into
human action, this passivity will penetrate the whole of it.   In other
words, if human thought depends upon an order of pre-constituted, given
reality, it will be the continuation of an original darkness; and thus it
will never be real light, real thought.[84]

Merleau-Ponty admits the essential point of the objection,[85] viz., that
the introduction of real passivity into human thought makes real thought
impossible.   But he says that he himself does not really do so.   The
objection is directed against realism.   Realism, as a matter of fact, does
affirm that human thought is confronted with an order of reality which
is distinguished from thought itself.   Human thought is then really
passive.   Merleau-Ponty, however, wants to avoid choosing between
passivity and activity of thought.   As long as this choice is imposed, we
will have to accept either a philosophy which reaches truth, but loses its
contact with the world—reflective philosophy, rationalism, idealism—or
a philosophy which maintains its contact with the world, but which does
not arrive at real truth.   Merleau-Ponty refuses the choice between
activity and passivity of thought and is looking for a different starting-
point.[86]   We must now explain how he escapes from the dilemma.

---

[84] *V.I.*, p. 66.

[85] "Et il est certain en effet que toute tentative pour raccorder une passivité à
une activité aboutit ou à étendre la passivité à l'ensemble, ce qui revient à nous
détacher de l'Être . . . ou à restaurer dans l'ensemble l'activité." *V.I.*, pp. 66-
67.

[86] "Il s'agit de reconsidérer les notions solidaires de l'actif et du passif, de telle
manière qu'elles ne nous placent plus devant l'antinomie d'une philosophie qui
rend compte de l'être et de la vérité, mais ne tient pas compte du monde, et d'une
philosophie qui tient compte du monde, mais nous déracine de l'être et de la
vérité." *V.I.*, p. 67.

C. QUESTIONS RAISED BY REFLECTIVE PHILOSOPHY AND MERLEAU-PONTY'S ANSWER

We have arrived again at the question posed at the beginning of this paragraph. With reflective philosophy Merleau-Ponty rejects the primitive idea that a real world imposes itself upon our passive mind, or that our thought, in some wonderful manner, leaves its own interiority and extends itself into an exterior world. But at the same time Merleau-Ponty rejects the reflective alternative of the pure ideality of truth. How, then, does he conceive human knowledge? How does he avoid the classical alternative of passivity or activity? This is the most essential question remaining after Merleau-Ponty's confrontation with reflective philosophy.

"I Belong to It." Merleau-Ponty does not answer this question in this chapter. He only begins an answer in the chapter *"L'Entrelacs—le Chiasme,"* which we have already summarized. We know, therefore, in what direction we must seek. We have often quoted Merleau-Ponty's sentence: *"J'en suis,"* "I belong to it." The fundamental thesis of Merleau-Ponty is that the world, Being, comes to awareness of itself in man. Man is not opposed to the world, to Being. He essentially belongs to it. Man's awareness is not some strange, heterogeneous fact which has nothing to do with the world, with Being. Man's awareness is a fulfillment of the world, of Being itself.

The world is the realm of visible reality. For Merleau-Ponty the visibility of wordly things is their skin, their surface. But this surface of visibility cannot exist without the depth of Being. This depth of Being belongs to the visible things as their "other side," as their "invisible aspect." In human vision the visibility of worldly things is actualized; in man the visibility of things reaches its own fulfillment. Man is the "perceiving perceptible." He is the perceptible which in the full sense reaches its own truth. Man, therefore, can see, hear and feel himself. If he could not do so, he would not see, hear or feel at all. Man is the actualization of perceptible reality, perceiving both himself and the exterior world. But it is not right to make a distinction between man and the exterior world, since man essentially belongs to the world. *"Il en est,"* "he belongs to it."

We must even say that the distinction between man himself and exterior things comes into existence by man's awareness, by the actualization of the perceptibility of the world. Thereby man emerges from the world and obtains his individuality. Because man is actualized visibility, he finds himself surrounded by things which are exterior to him. It makes no sense to ask how it is possible that man sees exterior things, because the things become exterior by man's seeing. Our seeing constitutes the exteriority of things and does not presuppose it. If we ask how the vision of *exterior* things is possible, we forget that the exteriority is constituted by seeing. In this way, we take into consideration one of the results of seeing and, forgetting that it is a result, make the result exist prior to its origin; then—from this illusory point of view—we raise the difficulty.

Merleau-Ponty's Escape from the Dilemma. Now it becomes clear how Merleau-Ponty avoids the choice between the passivity or activity of our mind, between realism or idealism. According to realism the things of the surrounding world exist prior to our vision; the visible things are there before we see. When we see these things our vision must be passive, since the pre-existing visible things make us see. Realism extends this hypothesis to all forms of knowledge. Idealism, and reflective philosophy in general, cannot accept this hypothesis of the passivity of knowledge. Knowledge cannot *accept blindly* anything at all. It is absurd to speak of a light which would precede knowledge. Knowledge evaluates everything according to its own criteria, and it is, therefore, incompatible with a light exterior to it. When perceiving we have, indeed, the impression that our perception is confronted with a light exterior to it. This is, however, a superficial illusion because, on a deeper level, we have constituted the light we perceive. Consequently our knowledge is active.

According to Merleau-Ponty, it makes no sense to speak of activity or passivity in relation to knowledge. For both terms suppose some separation between the knowing body and the reality which is known. They suppose, moreover, that this separation precedes knowledge. Merleau-Ponty denies this hypothesis. According to him the distinction or separation is not supposed, but constituted, by knowledge. There is some separation between the body which sees and the things which are seen precisely because the body sees. In the fundamental realm of visibility which, of course, is presupposed by actual vision, there is not yet a distinction between the body and the surrounding world; on this level it does not make sense to speak of a "surrounding world." All visible reality reaches its fulfillment in the body which sees. The body which sees is the self-actualization, not only of its own visibility, but of the visibility of the world to which it belongs as a part. It ceases to be a mere part and emerges from the whole, just because it is seeing.

We must not say, therefore, that by seeing we appropriate exterior things, or that we emigrate to them in some mysterious manner. This way of speaking likewise forgets that our vision constitutes the distinction between interior and exterior reality. Vision is interiorization, and it therefore constitutes both the interior and the exterior reality—not as reality, but only as interior and exterior.

This is the reason why Merleau-Ponty uses expressions such as: the world sees in us, the world perceives in us, Being thinks in us, Being speaks in us, Being becomes conscious in us. These expressions are not metaphors. In such sentences Merleau-Ponty expresses his deepest view of human knowledge, and even of human reality itself. They must be understood in the light of *j'en suis*. Man does not belong to Being because he can make Being the object of his knowledge. Rather, he knows Being because he belongs to it. In man Being reaches consciousness of itself. There is a process of objectification, but the objectification is supported by a more fundamental identity. This identity is the deepest truth of all knowledge. Knowledge could not constitute the identity, because the identity makes knowledge possible.

Now we understand how Merleau-Ponty can be a metaphysician who does not fall back into realism. Being is more important to him than man, since man *is* the self-consciousness of Being itself. Our individuation is due to the self-awareness of Being, or rather, it *is* the self-awareness of Being. Nevertheless, it would be absurd, at least according to Merleau-Ponty, to say that Being imposes itself upon human knowledge, that exterior Being influences human knowledge. Man *is* the self-awareness of Being. Being is interior to man, not because man is identical with the whole of Being, but because the whole of Being reaches self-awareness in man, without any relationships between exterior terms. Interiority and exteriority are constituted because Being reaches self-awareness in man.

Reflective philosophy poses a serious question; and the answer, as we have given it in the preceding pages, had not as such been formulated by Merleau-Ponty. But the answer is implicitly there in a number of passages of his text and in several notes.

3. Merleau-Ponty's Criticism of Sartre's Dialectic Philosophy

A. INTRODUCTION

Understandably enough, during his whole philosophical life Merleau-Ponty had to confront the philosophy of Sartre. The two men were educated in the same French philosophical tradition with which they both partially broke at the same time. They experienced the same war, and during this war both studied the same philosophers, viz., Husserl and Marx. Likewise, the rather negative experience of the war inspired within them the same social-political ideas, and they worked together in publishing *Les Temps Modernes*. Their names were often mentioned together, and for some time Merleau-Ponty was considered a member of the "Sartrian school." This is not surprising. Both called themselves existentialists, and both adhered to phenomenology; furthermore, both sympathized with the leftist political movement, although they kept themselves at some distance from the communist party. Sartre, however, enjoyed much wider publicity, for he expressed his philosophical ideas also in novels. Existentialism became fashionable in Paris and revealed itself, not only as a trend of philosophical thought, but also as a style of living. Sartre was considered the representative of the new style of thought and life. It is quite obvious that for some time Merleau-Ponty remained in the shadow of Sartre. Their relationship was stressed, but their opposition was not generally known.

The opposition between them already existed during the war, when both were preparing their main works, *Being and Nothingness* and *Phenomenology of Perception*. Merleau-Ponty ended his book with a rather radical criticism of Sartre's notion of freedom, which undoubtedly is one of the key points of Sartrian philosophy. The separation between the two thinkers had been radical and deep from the beginning, although they tried to conceal their differences for some time. Merleau-Ponty in his chapter on freedom mentioned Sartre's name only a few times in notes, and later he published an appreciative article on Sartre's philosophy.[87] Sartre did not answer Merleau-Ponty's criticism, at least not publicly. After some years, however, their opposition became sharper. Merleau-Ponty stopped writing in *Les Temps Modernes*, and in the last

---

[87] "The Battle over Existentialism," *Sense and Non-Sense,* pp. 71-82.

and longest chapter of *The Adventures of Dialectics* he criticized Sartre's philosophy on almost every basic point. We should not say that the opposition between Sartre and Merleau-Ponty is recent; it always existed; only it has become ever more manifest and public. Many of their basic concepts were common, since they shared the same tradition. But each interpreted the common concepts in a quite different manner. Both spoke of Being, Being-in-itself and Being-for-itself, existence, subject, freedom, intentionality, time and the dimensions of time; but all these common words assumed different meanings in the two philosophies.

In the last chapter of *The Adventures of Dialectics,* Merleau-Ponty accused Sartre of destroying the dialectical character of thought when he placed this dialectical movement in the light of absolute concepts.[88] There Merleau-Ponty anticipated the chapter in *The Visible and the Invisible* entitled "Interrogation and Dialectics" which we will now treat.

The Adventures of Dialectics was published in 1955, and we may assume that Merleau-Ponty composed "Interrogation and Dialectice" in 1959 or 1960. In the meantime Sartre had published *Critique of Dialectical Reason,* which is a long exposition of dialectical thought as well as a philosophy of history. Merleau-Ponty was obviously aware of this book. In a note of June, 1960, he wrote that Sartre's philosophy of history is based on the practice of the individual;[89] this evidently refers to Sartre's *Critique of Dialectical Reason.* It is one of Sartre's main theses there that the practice of the individual is the *raison constituante,* i.e., the principle of the intelligibility, of history. This book implies some important changes in Sartre's philosophy. It is remarkable, therefore, that in the chapter in *The Visible and the Invisible,* Merleau-Ponty does not confront himself with the *Critique of Dialectical Reason.* Yet this was the book in which Sartre extensively and systematically speaks of dialectical reason. Merleau-Ponty criticizes Sartre as if he were the philosopher who wrote only *Being and Nothingness,* as if he did not write a separate work on dialectical reason. Merleau-Ponty bases his criticism on Sartre's concepts, "Being-in-itself" and "Being-for-itself,"

---

[88] Remy C. Kwant, *The Phenomenological Philosophy of Merleau-Ponty,* pp. 211-218.

[89] "Opposer à une philosophie de l'histoire comme celle de Sartre (qui est finalement une philosophie de la 'praxis individuelle'—et dans laquelle l'histoire est la rencontre de cette praxis avec l'inertie de la 'matière ouvrée', de la temporalité authentique avec ce qui la *fige*. . . ." *V.I.,* p. 312.

while Sartre hardly uses these concepts in his book on dialectical reason.

Merleau-Ponty has not said why he did so, and we can, therefore, only suggest reasons for this strange behavior. Did Merleau-Ponty have no time to read *Critique of Dialectical Reason* thoroughly? Or was he convinced that this book did not have the same value as *Being and Nothingness?* Did he think that the latter was still the most important contribution Sartre made to modern philosophy? We do not know the answer, but it remains strange that Merleau-Ponty in his criticism of Sartre's dialectical thought does not even mention Sartre's systematic treatment.

B. SARTRE'S BASIC NOTIONS

Sartre's philosophy is not a type of the reflective philosophy Merleau-Ponty has described. Sartre does not consider the realm of our existence the materialization of an ideal light. The mind does not alienate itself in its contact with material being. In order to seek truth we must, of course, reflect; but reflection does not imply that we withdraw from the material world. For, by such a reflection, we reveal the truth of our existence itself: our "existence" is not an alienation of our real being; our existence would not be real if it were not "existence," contact with the world. Our being is "ec-static." Sartre appreciates the play of words, and he understands the term "ec-static" in its literal sense: our being is a standing outside itself. We should not think that we are first something in ourselves, and that we then enter into contact with things. No, our being itself is "ec-static." Our being is "out-standing," it *is* contact with things.[90]

Our being does not affect or change things. Things do not become different because I enter into contact with them. Things are what they are, and their Being is not increased or diminished because I contact them. Being transcends me and it reposes in itself. It has its own density which is neither increased nor diminished by my presence. Being is indifferent to my presence. Being reposes in the density of its own identity. It is pure Being-in-itself.[91]

---

[90] "On dira donc qu'avant la réflexion, et pour la rendre possible, il faut une fréquentation naïve du monde, et que le *Soi* auquel on revient est précédé par un Soi aliéné ou en ek-stase dans l'Être." *V.I.,* pp. 76-77.

[91] "Si elle vient d'être perçu par quelqu'un, et en particulier par moi, cela n'est pas constitutif de son sens de chose, qui est au contraire d'être là dans l'indifférence, dans la nuit de l'identité, comme en-soi pur. Telle serait la description de l'Être à laquelle nous serions conduits si nous voulions vraiment retrouver la zone préréflexive de l'ouverture à l'Être." *V.I.,* p. 77.

According to Sartre, I could not contact Being-in-itself if I belonged to Being. I can contact Being-in-itself because I am nothingness. Real contact is not possible if something is interposed between myself and things; thus, were there any real Being in myself, I could no longer contact things. I am nothingness, and I do not find any real Being in myself. I do not find images, representations or ideas in myself.[92] I must not say that I *am* a subject, a mind, an ego. All these notions imply the affirmation of real Being in myself. As soon as I affirm the presence of these realities in myself, I deny what I am, viz., presence, contact, existence. I must not even say that I am aware of myself. I am awareness, but awareness of things. When Sartre says that I am awareness of things, he brackets the word "of." I am *conscience (de) choses,* awareness (of) things. The word "of" must be bracketed; otherwise there would be a separation between myself and the things, which would imply that I am something in myself. Even words like awareness, consciousness, presence and contact are dangerous, because they can make me think that I really am something.[93] I am nothingness. Our language makes it unavoidable that I say that I *am* nothingness. But the word "am" must be understood, not as the affirmation, but as the denial of Being. There is no positive reality in me. My reality is my nothingness. Our language fails to express this, because our language is always the affirmation of positive realities. When I express my nothingness in words, I always express my nothingness in terms of Being. I must, therefore, continually correct my way of speaking when I try to express my nothingness. There are no words which express exactly what I am.

C. SARTRE'S SOLUTION TO THE PROBLEM OF PERCEPTION

In the Introduction to this book we mentioned that, according to Merleau-Ponty, there are three fundamental certainties in "perceptive faith," viz., that we perceive the real world, that this real world is perceived also by other persons and that the real world is essentially a whole, a totality in which all things belong together. These certainties, however, are ambiguous. We become aware of this when we begin to reflect. Many difficulties then seem to undermine the fundamental certainties of perception. Each philosophy tries to give an answer to

---

[92] *Ibid.*

[93] "La seule manière d'assurer mon accès aux choses mêmes serait de purifier tout à fait ma notion de la subjectivité; il n'y a pas même de 'subjectivité' ou d' 'Ego', la conscience est sans 'habitant'." *Ibid.*

these difficulties. How does Sartre explain the three fundamental certainties of perception? Merleau-Ponty tries to answer this question in his chapter "Interrogation and Dialectics."

i. We Perceive the Real World

Sartre maintains the certainty of our "perceptive faith," maintains that we perceive the real world. But how does he explain this, starting from his basic notions?[94]

According to Sartre I have access to the real world precisely because I am nothingness. This explains why I am radically opposed to the fullness of Being and, at the same time, am open to it. If I would belong to Being, I could not be an openness to all Being. There is no interaction between me and Being; the interaction is possible only between beings themselves. There is no Being in me. In a certain sense I could say that I belong to Being, not because there is some Being in me, but because as nothingness I am openness to Being. My nothingness would make no sense, it could not exist, without the fullness of Being. Nothingness and Being belong together, not as two aspects of Being, but as complementary terms. Nothingness and Being are two sides of one and the same reality; nothingness calls for Being, and Being calls for nothingness. Being is the fulfillment, the actualization, of nothingness. Being is revealed, precisely as Being, by nothingness.

I have—or rather am—an intuition of Being. I cannot say that I have an intuition of myself; this would imply that I would be a Being myself, since we can have a positive intuition only of a positive Being. In explaining Sartre's ideas, Merleau-Ponty introduces, therefore, the concept of *"négintuition."*[95] This word does not exist in English, but neither does it exist in French. Thus, we may just as well presume to use it in English. The awareness of the fullness of Being implies a collateral awareness of my own nothingness. This awareness cannot be called a real intuition, since it is not an insight into Being. It is the collateral awareness, the co-experience of my own nothingness. The intuition of Being implies the "negintuition" of my own nothingness; this "negintuition" of my own nothingness is an essential aspect of my

---

[94] *V.I.,* pp. 78-84.

[95] "L'intuition de l'être est solidaire d'une sorte de négintuition du néant (au sens où l'on parle de négentropie), de l'impossibilité où nous sommes de nous réduire à quoi que ce soit, état de conscience, pensée, *ego* ou même 'sujet'." *V.I.,* p. 78.

intuition of Being. What Sartre calls "Being-for-itself" is not the object of a positive intuition, since it is not a positive reality; it is the object of a "negintuition"—even the term "object" should not be used here, but we simply have to use some word to express what cannot be expressed.

As nothingness I am not confronted with the whole of Being; I am always confronted with a particular Being. We could say that I am a "particularized nothingness."[96] This "particularity" at first sight seems to have a positive character, but this is not true. Some particular thing can only be present to me because other things are absent for the moment. Consequently the presence of a particular thing is always threatened with a possible absence. As a matter of fact, at any moment another thing can become present to me from the horizon of absent things. The thing which was formerly present will then be absent again. Every presence is a possible absence, because absence is a possible presence. Therefore, presence is the negation, the "suspension" of absence. Presence is the negation of negation. Even if absence, negation, is denied for a moment, it will return again. The reality of my nothingness is affirmed by the presence of things. My nothingness is affirmed by the negation of negation. The foundation of nothingness is the negation of negation.[97]

In this perspective we are no longer obliged to chose between monism and dualism. According to monism consciousness is only a part of Being; according to dualism consciousness and Being are radically opposed. Sartre thinks that he has transcended this choice. On the one hand, consciousness and Being are radically opposed, since the first is nothingness and the latter is the fullness of Being; on the other, there is no dualism, because consciousness is nothing but the affirmation of Being, the negation of its negation.

Because consciousness is nothingness, it does not add anything to Being. It is nothing but the affirmation of Being; it belongs to Being as its own affirmation. Because nothingness affirms Being, Being appears as it is. We could say that by consciousness Being is *affirmed,* that it *appears as it is.*[98] But this is not a real addition, because it does not change Being.

---

[96] "Je suis un rien déterminé." *V.I.,* p. 79.

[97] "Ainsi le fondement de la négation est négation de la négation." *V.I.,* p. 80.

[98] ". . . à quoi je n'ajoute rien que l'infime doublet 'tel qu'il est'." *V.I.,* p. 84.

All the classical problems of the philosophy of knowledge disappear in this way of thinking.[99]   Where knowledge and worldly things were opposed as two positive realities, the question of their meeting had been posed.   According to realism worldly things influence our knowledge, and according to idealism active consciousness communicates its own light to the worldly things.   Terms like "union," "influence" and "communication" were generally used.   These terms and the problems they intend to solve have disappeared in Sartre's perspective.   According to him Being and nothingness are, on the one hand, absolutely distinguished and any reduction of the one to the other has become strictly impossible; on the other hand, Being and nothingness belong together, since nothingness is nothing but the affirmation of Being.   Because I am nothingness, I am immediately present to things as they are.   There is no distance between me and things.   There is no causal relationship between nothingness and Being or between Being and nothingness; neither of them is active or passive; yet there is still knowledge, immediate presence.   There is infinite distance, and still immediate presence, and the two terms express the same reality.

I do not know myself immediately because I am nothingness.   It is not that anything separates me from myself, but there is nothing to see in me. I know myself, therefore, in things, in the world.   My intuition of Being is the "negintuition" of my own nothingness.   I need no longer choose between the immanence and the transcendence of thought, between my presence to myself and my presence to things.   They coincide perfectly, because to be nothing is the same as to be in the world.[100]

Being nothingness, I make the world appear.   My nothingness constitutes the truth of the world without adding anything to it.   In this way Sartre explains how I know the real world.   My nothingness belongs to the world as its affirmation.

ii. My World is Accessible to Other Persons

Merleau-Ponty continues his exposition of Sartre's philosophy.   The world I perceive is, according to Sartre, not strictly mine.[101]   What could it mean that the world is mine?   As we have seen, I am

---

[99] *V.I.,* pp. 81-82.

[100] "C'est la même chose de n'être rien et d'habiter le monde." *V.I.,* p. 83.

[101] *V.I.,* pp. 84-91.

nothingness. Even if the world were mine, this would not add anything to the world itself. Being nothingness, I reveal the world as it is in itself.[102] There is only one thing which is mine, viz., my nothingness.

I only experience, or rather co-experience, my own nothingness which is the object of my "negintuition." If there are other persons, I cannot experience them in the way I experience myself. I am present only to my own nothingness. If I see another person looking, I do not experience his look as "another nothingness." The things I see do not need his affirmation in order to be what they are. The other man's perception does not compete with mine,[103] for I live my perception from within, and from within I experience that by my presence the negation of things is denied. Consequently I cannot experience the other person's perception. I seem to be reduced to a solipsistic world. Although I have no reason to call the world mine because I make it appear as it is, still I have no access to another access of the world, and I seem to be enclosed, therefore, within my own access.

Still the other man's look is there. I can somehow understand his presence, according to Sartre, if I really understand my situation. I am nothingness and as such am accessible only to myself; and, if there were another nothingness, it would not be directly accessible to me. Still I am not an absolute nothingness but a situated nothingness. As we have seen, I cannot be present to the whole world at the same time. Why is this? There is a part of the world which belongs to me in a special manner, viz., my body.[104] My body belongs to the world, as do all the corporal and psychic processes which take place in the body. As nothingness, I am not a part of the world, as is my body. Still my body belongs to me in a special manner. It conditions my access to the world. My nothingness is embodied. This is the reason why I am not present all at once to the whole world. My presence to the world is mediated by the body, and therefore it is a particular presence.

If I am a particular presence, there is no longer any reason why I

---

[102] "Ce *que* je vois n'est pas mien au sens d'un monde privé." *V.I.*, p. 84.

[103] "La perception du monde par les autres ne peut entrer en compétition avec celle que j'en ai moi-même: mon cas n'est pas assimilable à celui des autres, je vis ma perception du dedans, et, de l'intérieur, elle a un pouvoir incomparable d'ontogénèse." *V.I.*, p. 85.

[104] "Pour venir au monde, je prends particulièrement appui sur une partie de l'être." *V.I.*, p. 87.

should deny the presence of another nothingness.[105] Just as I am situated in a part of the world, the other nothingness could be situated in another part of the same world. This is not, of course, a positive argument for the existence of other persons; it only shows that the presence of other persons is not unimaginable, and even that it is obvious. I make use of a part of the world, viz., my body, in order to be present to the world as nothingness. But in this way I am exposed to the world itself. I assume my body in an active manner, but my body can undergo the influence of other worldly beings. Through my body I am exposed to the world.

By means of the body I experience the presence of other persons. I experience in the visible part of myself that I am seen;[106] but what I use in order to see is reduced by others to a visible object. Because I have a body I am exposed; I experience this exposure in the look of other persons. I know that other persons are there because I experience their looking at me. The other's presence does not teach me something which I did not already know. I know that I am nothingness, that my access to Being is conditioned by a part of the world which I call my body, that in my body I am exposed to the world. The other's look affirms what I already knew, viz., that I am nothingness belonging to Being; I am a parasite of Being; I live in the world as embodied nothingness.[107] Other persons could only be excluded if the whole world were my body. The particular character of my presence opens the possibility of the presence of other persons.

It is quite obvious, therefore, that I live with other persons in the same world, that my world is accessible to others. Sartre does not demonstrate the presence of other persons. He only analyzes our own being in order to show that there is room for other persons. In this way Sartre confirms the second certainty of our "perceptive faith" that we live with other persons in one and the same world.

---

[105] "Des lors, tout est prêt, non pour une expérience d'autrui, dont nous avons vu qu'elle n'est pas positivement possible, non pour une démonstration d'autrui qui irait contre son but en le rendant nécessaire à partir de moi, mais pour une expérience de ma passivité à l'intérieur de l'être." *V.I.,* p. 88.

[106] "Il n'y a pas d'expérience positive d'autrui, mais il y a une expérience de mon être total comme compromis dans la partie visible de moi-même." *V.I.,* p. 88.

[107] "L'expérience du regard d'autrui sur moi ne fait que prolonger mon intime conviction de n'être rien, de ne vivre qu'en parasite du monde, d'habiter un corps et une situation." *V.I.,* p. 89.

iii. My World is a Whole

In our perception there is a fundamental awareness that all perceived things, the perceiving "ego" and its perceived field, and even all human persons, belong together. Our term "world" indicates this rather vague, but comprehensive, unity. Reflective philosophy tries to explain this universal coherence but, in so doing, reduces the appearing world to a rational construction. There are, according to Descartes, many conscious beings; but all of them arrive at the same truth if they observe the laws of thinking which are innate in them and which have been caused by the Maker of the universe. We arrive at truth, according to Kant, if we observe the laws of thinking which are implied in the universal, transcendental mind which is present in all empirical persons.

The unity and universality of truth, the unity of the world, presents no problem for Sartre.[108] Conscious beings, just as consciousness, are nothingness. There is only one positive reality, viz., the reality of Being. This is, of course, one and the same reality. A synchronization of conscious beings is not necessary. They are nothingness, and one and the same Being is their common fulfillment. The absolute character of my nothingness, of my negativity, calls for the absolute positivity of Being. The philosophy of absolute negativity of consciousness is at the same time the philosophy of the absolute positivity of Being.[109]

Being and nothingness essentially belong together, although they are not, of course, two positive parts of a new totality. Nothingness is the affirmation of Being. Being is recognized, precisely as Being, by nothingness. Being and nothingness cannot be divorced from one another. There is no longer any reason to maintain the classical question: Why does Being exist?[110] Why is there something, instead of nothing? Nothingness could not take the place of Being, since nothingness itself calls for Being. Being and nothingness no longer exclude one another, but rather belong together. The metaphysical questions have been resolved.

In this way Sartre answers the problems posed by our perception of the world. We perceive the real world, the same world, the world

---

[108] *V.I.,* pp. 91-93.
[109] "Le négativisme, s'il est rigoureux, absolu, est une sorte de positivisme." *V.I.,* p. 92.
[110] *Ibid.*

which is a whole since it is Being. In his criticism of reflective philosophy Merleau-Ponty has demonstrated that reflection supposes a pre-reflective contact with Being, that this contact with Being must enable us to reflect. Now it seems that Sartre gives us what we were looking for. He seems to have answered all our questions. There is an immediate contact with the real world. I should not say that I *have* contact with the real world, but rather that I *am* contact with it. There is literally nothing in me to prevent me from contacting the world, since I am nothingness. Hence, there can be no distance between myself and the world. I am consciousness (of) Being. I am absolutely distinguished from the world and I can never be embodied into it, since I am nothingness. I am, therefore, a view of Being. But this view does not add anything to Being; it only makes Being appear as Being. My intentionality is not a reality.

There are no longer two movements, namely, my adherence to Being and my reflective distancing from Being. The intuition of Being and the "negintuition" of nothingness essentially belong together.[111] In other words, there is no longer any distinction between my immediate belonging to Being and my reflective self-awareness. As a matter of fact, I am nothingness, belonging to Being. There is nothing to be seen in myself.[112] All the positive aspects of my own being, my body, my experiences, belong to the world. Only one thing really characterizes me: I am nothingness which calls for Being. Sartre's philosophy is the most radical affirmation of Being, since it is the most radical affirmation of the nothingness of consciousness.

D. MERLEAU-PONTY'S CRITICISM OF SARTRE

Merleau-Ponty must have been deeply impressed by Sartre's philosophy of Being and nothingness, for his criticism extends through forty-seven pages,[113] more than one-fifth of the text he prepared for publication. It is impossible here to give a complete commentary on this part of Merleau-Ponty's book. We will try to summarize only the main points of his criticism.

---

[111] *V.I.*, p. 94.

[112] "C'est l'inexistence absolue du Néant qui fait qu'il a besoin de l'Être, et que donc il n'est pas visible, sinon sous l'apparence de 'lacs de non-être', de non-êtres relatifs et localisés, de reliefs ou de lacunes dans le monde." *Ibid.*

[113] *V.I.*, pp. 93-141.

i. The Two Opposed Movements of Sartre's Philosophy

Sartre initially opposes Being and nothingness, and he does so in a radical manner. At the end, however, he concluded that Being and nothingness belong together. When should we believe him, at the beginning or at the end? Sartre pretends that his initial and his final position perfectly coincide, but Merleau-Ponty disagrees.[114]

There is a difference, according to Merleau-Ponty, between Sartre's initial and final concepts of Being. At first Being radically excludes nothingness; nothingness, on the contrary, needs Being, because nothingness would not at all be if it were not the affirmation of Being. At the conclusion, however, Being needs nothingness in order to be affirmed, in order to appear "as it is," in order to become true.

Thus there are two movements in Sartre's thought. The first movement, starting from nothingness, views Being; the second one views nothingness, starting from Being. The two movements do not perfectly coincide.[115] In the first movement of thought Sartre sees Being as the negation of negation. Nothingness is the starting-point of this view, and Being seems to be an attribute of knowledge; it is described, as a matter of fact, as the negation of the negation, as the absolute opposite of nothingness. In the second movement, however, nothingness is viewed from the stand-point of Being; by nothingness Being appears as it is; here nothingness is the position of positive Being; nothingness appears to be an attribute of Being, since by nothingness Being is affirmed as Being. In the two cases the movement of thought finds its term in an identity, but the identity seems to be different in each case: in the first case, the identity makes us view nothingness as nothingness, in the light of positive Being; in the second, Being is affirmed as Being, in the light of nothingness which affirms Being.

Is there any meaning in saying that Being is affirmed, that Being is revealed as Being, that Being becomes truth? We must choose. Either this sentence means something—but then how can consciousness which gives this meaning be nothingness—or we maintain that consciousness is nothingness—but then the sentence has no meaning.

---

[114] *V.I.*, p. 95.
[115] "Les deux mouvements, celui par lequel le néant appelle l'être et celui par lequel l'être appelle le néant, ne se confondent pas: ils se croisent." *V.I.*, p. 95.

ii. *The Static Character of Sartre's Basic Concepts*

Being and Nothingness is a massive work. Its purpose cannot be merely to establish the basic concepts of "Being" and "nothingness." As a matter of fact Sartre analyzes many concrete situations. He can do so because there is some differentiation within the massivity of Being: a part of Being, viz., our body, belongs to us in a special manner. The body is our situation which gives us access to Being. An analysis of this situation is essential, and Sartre extensively describes how we are situated in Being through our body. Sartre says that this concrete analysis makes sense, and he promises that, at the end of his book, we will arrive at a larger concept of Being which comprehends both Being and nothingness.[116]

But does Sartre really use his analysis of concrete situations to arrive at his conclusion? This would be the case if his basic concepts had a hypothetical or provisional character, if they could be made richer by the analysis of concrete situations, if they were open to eventual change. But, as a matter of fact, Sartre's basic concepts completely govern his analysis of concrete situations. He analyzes concrete situations in the light of *a priori* concepts. He sometimes seems to make real progress, but in the end he always returns to his basic ideas.[117] When he speaks about the human body, there seems to be density in the human situation, but in the end the body is put back into Being, and man remains radical nothingness. Sometimes a depth and a plurality of levels in Being seems to appear but in the end everything sinks into the density of Being. The Being of Sartre is undifferentiated and univocal. Throughout his entire book Sartre speaks about the same Being and about the same nothingness. They appear in very different situations, which are patiently analyzed by the writer; but the differences in their appearance does not affect their final meaning.

Sartre recognizes that there is a realm where Being-in-itself and Being-for-itself seem to be commingled. There seems to be a realm where consciousness is really engaged in Being and where Being is penetrated by human consciousness. His descriptions of it belong to the classical texts of phenomenological analysis. But at the end the analysis

---

[116] "Sartre dit bien qu'à *la fin de son livre* il sera permis de passer à un sens plus large de l'Être, qui contient l'Être et le néant." *V.I.*, p. 99.

[117] "Même si l'explication renverse apparemment les perspectives, le renversement n'est pas effectif." *V.I.*, p. 98.

appears to be provisional, and is again interpreted in the light of Sartre's basic concepts.[118]

iii. Sartre Does Not Really Transcend Solipsism

Sartre thinks he transcends solipsism. While no one can say that Sartre denies the presence of other persons, he does need a long rational construction in order to explain how we become aware of their presence. Moreover, we cannot experience directly the presence of other persons. Their presence essentially is nothingness. I can experience my own nothingness, but not the nothingness of other persons. There is room for them, because my own body is not the whole of Being, but only a part of it. Insofar as I have a body, I am exposed. One can understand, therefore, that other parts of Being are animated by another nothingness. This appears to be true when I become aware that I am being looked at. I experience the presence of another person in my own exposure.

Sartre says that I am free. I assume my body as a free being. No one can take away my freedom. I am, therefore, exposed to the look of other persons only insofar as I consent to be exposed. I am reduced to passivity only insofar as I choose to be passive. Another person cannot alienate me if I have not alienated myself. Insofar as I am looking I am active and I dominate the scene. The other person's body also is dominated by my vision. And I must cease to dominate my scene in order to be seen. The other person's look does not add something new to my situation. I know that a part of the world belongs to me as my body; I know that I can cease to be actively my body; I know that I can consent to my own passivity; I can freely accept my own weakness. Sartre accepts the other person's presence only insofar as the possibility of his presence can be deduced from my own being, or rather from the way in which I am nothingness.

This is, however, a most inadequate expression of our real experience of other persons.[119] Sartre reduces my experience of the other person to the experience of my own exposure. He accepts the exterior presence of others only insofar as it has been prepared for from within. The other person, according to Sartre's perspective, does not really see and contact *me*. He touches me in my exposure; but I have chosen to be exposed and I do not coincide, therefore, with my exposure. Nevertheless, our

---

[118] "Il n'y a pas progrès ni synthèse, il n'y a pas transformation de l'antithèse initiale; on pousse jusqu'à ses limites l'analyse initiale." *V.I.,* pp. 97-98.

[119] *V.I.,* pp. 100-104.

experience teaches us that the other person sees *me*. He sees me entirely, in my body or my being and in my nothingness. The other person is not only the confirmation of what I expected. He is not only the actualization of a passivity which I have freely accepted. He is not only the catastrophe which confirms my own passivity.[120] He really is another person. He sees me and I see him.

Sartre presupposes what he denies. He says that I, as an embodied nothingness, can be exposed and that my exposure is actualized by the look of the other person.[121] But in this way Sartre only explains that the look of the other person is possible, he does not explain that it is actually there. We can only *experience* that it is actually there. My possible exposure teaches me—at least if Sartre's analysis is right—that another person is possible, but not that he is there. Sartre does not explain the actual presence of other persons. He has to appeal to an experience which he does not explain, an experience which is far more important than Sartre's whole theoretical doctrine. This experience should be the norm of our doctrine, and we do not have the right to subject it to *a priori* concepts, as does Sartre.

According to my experience the presence of the other person is something entirely new, which has not been prepared for from within. He really is another person, and I experience him as such. He is much more than the truth of my exposure. His presence implies many aspects, and not only the ones which are explained by Sartre. According to Sartre I must chose to see or to be seen, to expose the others to my look or to be exposed. I must chose between activity and passivity. This doctrine of intersubjective relationships is extremely poor and it is a most unilateral expression of our relationships to other persons. Let us see how this unilateral expression comes about.

iv. A Philosophy of Panoramic Vision

Sartre's philosophy is certainly not an adequate expression of our experience, but still it must have some basis in experience. Merleau-Ponty thinks that Sartre's philosophy is an expression, or rather a universalization, of our panoramic vision.[122]

My vision gives me the impression of being panoramic. By my vision

---

[120] *V.I.,* p. 109.

[121] "Autrui ne peut s'introduire dans l'univers du voyant que par effraction, comme une douleur et une catastrophe." *Ibid.*

[122] "Elles expriment certainement l'expérience de la vision: la vision est panorama." *V.I.,* p. 105.

I dominate my scene, bring things together into one scene, and am present to the things where they really are.[123] I reach the things themselves and make them co-exist in the manner I want. The person who sees and who makes the world his panorama does not really meet other persons, just because his look dominates the scene.[124] He reduces other persons to statues, just as the photographer does. When I look down from the top of a high building I do not feel myself related with the people who are present on the streets below and who are doing things I cannot experience. People who want to dominate the world with their look are attracted to high places.[125] Panoramic vision has a solipsistic character.

The Solipsism of Panoramic Vision. My vision ceases to be solipsistic when I no longer look at other persons as at a distance or from on high, but rather approach them.[126] Then the other person can turn back upon me the look in which I had captured him. His eyes, which belonged to my scene, begin to look; they begin to capture me in the prison which I had prepared for them.[127] When I experience the other person looking at me, this seems to be a kind of catastrophe. My scene is dissolved. I cease to dominate it because I am seen. The person who lives entirely in his vision does not meet the other person. During a party it can happen that someone does not really participate in the conversation because he is just looking, transforming the room into his scene. He behaves as an outsider and, because his look is dominating, he disturbs the togetherness. He himself is upset when other people start to look closely at him. Then he is threatened in his domination, since other people dominate him with their look.

One who lives entirely in his dominating vision becomes aware of the presence of another person only when he himself is being looked at. The man who dominates the scene with his look is omnipresent and he forgets his particular place. His omnipresence is threatened and denied by the close look of another person. I cannot co-exist with the other person. Either he belongs to my scene or I belong to his; my scene and his scene

---

[123] "Je domine le monde et le rejoins là où il est." *V.I.,* p. 106.

[124] "Pour une philosophie qui s'installe dans la vision pure, le survol du panorama, il ne peut pas y avoir rencontre d'autrui: car le regard domine." *V.I.,* p. 109.

[125] "Les lieux hauts attirent ceux qui veulent jeter sur le monde le regard de l'aigle." *Ibid.*

[126] *Ibid.*

[127] ". . . M'attire dans la prison que j'avais préparé pour lui." *Ibid.*

never coincide. We do not live in a common world, since I try to transform the world into my scene and he tries to do the same. His visual experience is inaccessible to me. The other person is the denial of my dominating presence. The other person is inaccessible to me; he is radically other. If I could enter into his vision, he would no longer be another person. The inaccessibility of the other is the very condition of his existence.[128]

I do not really meet the other. I do not enter into him. But how do I know that he is another person if, in principle, he is inaccessible to me? I only *know* that he is another nothingness which I do not experience. The other, just as other, is an object of thought and not a datum of real experience. In this way the other person finally is an object of abstract thought. This philosophy seems at first to be an affirmation of the other, precisely as the other person, but this affirmation finally appears to be a denial and a destruction. The philosophy of the dominating vision reduces the other to an anonymous *X,* to an object of abstract thought. In this way we fall back into the dogmatism of abstract reason; we do not really escape from solipsism.[129]

This is the approach of Sartrian philosophy. It is based on some aspects of our experience. Sometimes we really are a dominating look. When we live in this experience, we feel strong, we are active and we dominate our world. We see without being seen, or at least without being aware that we are seen. This is a situation of powerful loneliness. Sartre takes up this real moment of our experience. He knows that man can relinquish this situation of strength and that he often does so. But he considers this surrender a sign of weakness. This weakness is perhaps unavoidable, but still it is weakness. Man is not strong enough to remain free. When he no longer dominates, he is dominated.

"Perceiving Nothingness" or *"Perceiving Perceptible."* These reflections make us aware of the basic difference between the philosophical perspectives of Sartre and Merleau-Ponty. *According to Sartre man is a "perceiving nothingness," according to Merleau-Ponty man is a "perceiving perceptible."* Both thinkers stress human intentionality and reluctantly speak of the interior life of man. Man *is* intentional relationship to the world. Both reject radically a causal relationship of man to the world. Their doctrine of intentionality implies the

---

[128] "C'est une expérience interdite." *V.I.,* p. 110.
[129] *V.I.,* p. 111.

transcendence of all physical processes and of causal relationships. We can say, therefore, that they both adhere to the phenomenological tradition. But within this phenomenological tradition they are radically opposed. The "subject" of the intentional relationship is, according to Sartre, nothingness, viz., the opposite of Being—we use quotation marks for the term "subject" because for Sartre this word does not indicate any positive reality; the logical "subject" of intentionality is not a real subject. According to Merleau-Ponty the perceiving subject himself belongs essentially to perceptible reality. He affirms that perceptible reality begins to reflect, that it becomes perceptible to itself. According to Sartre intentionality is possible because there is a term which is opposed to Being; since this term is opposed to Being, it does not belong to Being and it is nothingness. According to Merleau-Ponty the intentional relationship comes into existence within Being itself. Being itself becomes reflective, it begins to see, to perceive itself.

Dualism. In accepting a term which is opposed to Being, Sartre belongs to the dualistic tradition of thinking. This opposition makes the intentional relationship possible. He says, of course, that there is no real dualism, since the term opposed to Being is only nothingness. Still he must say that nothingness *is*. The reality of nothingness makes the intentional relationship possible. Moreover, the real distinction between Being and nothingness is the keystone of Sartre's philosophy. Merleau-Ponty transcends dualism, because for him the intentional relationship is actualized within Being itself. It transcends all physical and causal relationships, but still it is a relationship within Being.

Nothingness and Being. Merleau-Ponty does not completely reject the Sartrian concept of nothingness; he repeatedly says that this idea cannot be rejected. The intentional relationship implies a distance. It transforms perceiving Being into a subject which is confronted with an object. As we have seen, it is a real question for Merleau-Ponty to determine the level of knowledge on which the opposition between subject and object comes into existence. But, nevertheless, on a certain level of knowledge this opposition exists and it implies nothingness. The subject is not the object, nor is the object the subject. Hence there is an aspect of nothingness in perceiving and perceived reality. But Merleau-Ponty refuses to transform nothingness into a term which from the beginning is radically opposed to Being. Merleau-Ponty tries to demonstrate that there is room for nothingness, for the intentional relationship, for knowledge, within Being itself. Being perceives in us, sees in us, speaks in us, thinks in us.

According to Sartre nothingness from its beginning is opposed to Being. It belongs to Being only as its opposite term. It is, therefore, a degradation for nothingness to belong to Being in a positive manner. For the seeing person it is a shame to be seen; when he is seen he ceases to be seeing; when he is seen he is alienated from himself. Our life is a struggle, and the purpose of this struggle is to remain seeing and not to be reduced to an object. We cannot be reduced to an object if we do not consent to it. Man consents to his own alienation.

Two Analyses of Seeing. Sartre interprets seeing as dominating, surveying seeing. This is not merely an expression of experience, it is an *a priori* interpretation of seeing. This interpretation is guided by Sartre's *a priori* concepts of Being and nothingness. Merleau-Ponty rejects this interpretation, because according to him nothingness belongs to Being. Perceiving belongs to perceptible reality itself. It is not a shame, therefore, for the seeing person to be seen. His visibility is an essential aspect of his seeing. He could not see if he were not visible. Our vision is not only a domination, since, precisely as seeing, we are situated in visible reality. We are, precisely as seeing, engaged in the density of Being. Our seeing is, therefore, always partial and it does not dominate the scene. Merleau-Ponty's sentence, *"J'en suis,"* again appears to be the center of his philosophy.

Merleau-Ponty's analysis of vision differs entirely from the one Sartre gives. Merleau-Ponty stresses that the seeing person himself is essentially visible; that there is no conflict between seeing and being visible; that the seeing person is situated in visible reality and sees from a certain point of view; that in order to see we must be at a certain distance from the things we see; that both the seeing person and visible reality are rooted in the density of Being; that the things we see appear within a horizon of Being; that our seeing is essentially partial; and finally that we can endeavor to dominate the scene completely only if we forget our own situation, our own embodiment.

There is a remarkable difference between Sartre's and Merleau-Ponty's descriptions of seeing. The two descriptions are the embodiment of two different ontologies. Merleau-Ponty thinks that his description is much closer to actual experience and that Sartre's description is *a priori*.

I think Merleau-Ponty is right on this point. Sartre's book, *Being and Nothingness,* starts with the definition of his two basic notions of "Being" and "nothingness," and these notions finally dominate and determine all the descriptions of concrete experience that Sartre gives us.

It cannot be denied that Merleau-Ponty's descriptions also imply an ontology. But in Merleau-Ponty's philosophy there is more interchange between experience and ontology; he is willing to make his ontology depend on the description of appearing reality. His description is, thus, not only a verification, but also a test of his ontological concepts. He has the right, therefore, to accuse Sartre of determining his descriptions of appearing reality by his ontological concepts.

Both philosophers are confronted, of course, with difficulties. The main and invincible difficulties of Sartre are caused by his contradictory idea of *nothingness* which *is* and yet is also radically opposed to Being. Merleau-Ponty has to explain how perceptible reality perceives itself, how the light of knowledge comes into existence within the density of Being, how something which belongs to Being begins to see, to perceive, to understand Being. We have seen that Merleau-Ponty struggles with this difficulty in his chapter, *"L'Entrelacs—le Chiasme."* Merleau-Ponty's difficulties, however, are more closely connected with the anbiguities of our own experience.

E. PHILOSOPHY AND DIALECTICS

After a long exposition and discussion of Sartre's philosophy, Merleau-Ponty asks whether a dialectical interpretation could not save Sartre's basic notions. He gives first a description of dialectical thought and then speaks of its value.[130]

Sartre's dichotomy of Being and nothingness can no longer be maintained when we approach the field of real experience. There Being and nothingness are no longer absolutely opposed but penetrate one another. The rational perspective of Sartre, his definition of Being and nothingness, could serve as an abstract introduction to the description of concrete reality, but only if we admit that the concepts themselves are flexible, dynamic, progressive, that their abstract content can be changed in contacting experienced reality. If we accept this, we admit that

---

[130] *V.I.,* pp. 123-130.

dialectical thought must take the place of Sartre's intuition of Being and his "negintuition" of nothingness. Sartre himself does not do so, but perhaps his concepts can be saved in this manner.

Dialectical Thought. According to dialectical thought the relationship between two terms cannot be expressed in one sentence. It must be expressed in many sentences which do not coincide, which are opposed, which logically even contradict one another. The one calls for the other, and in this way the first statement brings about its being surpassed by the following ones. According to this conception, Being must be viewed from different and even opposed angles. It cannot be viewed in one glimpse from an external point of view. Our thought must traverse Being in different directions.

Thought is, therefore, a temporal activity. What we have discovered in one of its phases is surpassed by the following ones, but not in the sense that we leave the earlier phase completely behind. The preceding phase modifies the following one and is also modified by it. Dialectical thought does not go along an established road, but it makes its road as it advances. This thought does not dominate its content, but is rather subjected to it. It is not a reflection or a copy of existing reality; it is neither the testimony of a scene nor the creator of it. Dialectical thought is involved in the reality it discovers. In its progressive discovery it does not pronounce sentences which are maintained in isolation; successive sentences must be understood in relation to one another, so that every new sentence influences all the preceding ones and is influenced by them. There is no real truth in any sentence, but truth comes into existence by the interchange of all of them. The presence of the thinker himself must also be considered; the approach cannot be isolated from the reality which is viewed. There may be opposition between the sentences as they stand in themselves and the sentences in their total context; still, both belong together; for, if a sentence would not have its own meaning, it could not belong to a context. Thus we can say that reality exists in itself and we can also say that reality is an appearance to us; but the dialectical interchange of both sentences will bring us to true knowledge.

Dialectical thought denies the independence of any term, of any sentence, of any judgment which establishes a fact. Each term, sentence, judgment calls for its opposite, and in the interchange with its opposite it reveals truth. In the interchange with its opposite it really becomes itself. It exteriorizes itself in order to return to its own truth. The centrifugal and centripetal movements are but one movement.[131]

Merleau-Ponty asks whether he himself has not submitted Sartre's basic concepts to dialectical thought.[132] He did not say that the idea of Being-in-itself was meaningless, nor did he say that the concept of Being-for-itself should be completely denied. But he stressed that both aspects of Being are commingled, that they are in a continuous and ever changing interaction, and that the truth of the two concepts can be found only in the complete totality.

Merleau-Ponty admits[133] that he himself is searching for the kind of thought he tries to describe here. Why then has he not used the term "dialectical thought" until now? If he adheres to dialectical thought, would it not have been better to say so at the beginning?

He is afraid to propose as a positive thesis that philosophy must be dialectical, that dialectical philosophy is the true philosophy. Several philosophers have done so, but by their statements they have implicitly denied the truth which they explicitly affirmed. Dialectical thought does not admit final truth. It is unstable in the sense in which the chemist uses this word. As soon as dialectical thought calls itself the final truth of philosophy, it contradicts itself, because it is the exclusion of final truth. The thinker who wants to proceed in the attitude of dialectical thought should not speak about it.[134] All the thinkers who maintained that dialectical thought is the final method of philosophy have corrupted dialectical thought itself. This is the reason why Merleau-Ponty has avoided the use of the term "dialectical thought," although he does not deny that his thought is dialectical.

The "Realm of Being" Adapted to Dialectical Thought. Dialectical thought, continues Merleau-Ponty, is adapted to a certain realm of Being. In his description he has tried to indicate the Being to which dialectical thought is adapted. But this Being cannot be properly and positively named.[135]

---

[131] *V.I.*, pp. 123-125.

[132] "Si telle est la pensée dialectique, n'est-ce pas elle que nous avons essayé d'appliquer à la dichotomie de l'Être et du Néant?" *V.I.*, p. 124.

[133] "La dialectique est bien tout cela, et c'est, en ce sens, elle que nous cherchons." *V.I.*, p. 125.

[134] "Si l'on veut en garder l'esprit, il faut peut-être même ne pas la nommer." *V.I.*, p. 126.

[135] "Le genre d'être auquel elle se réfère, et que nous essayions à l'instant d'indiquer, n'est en effet pas susceptible de désignation positive." *Ibid.*

What does Merleau-Ponty mean in these sentences? There are two possible explanations. The term "realm of Being" (*genre d'être*) can indicate either a sector or a level of Being. If the term indicates a sector of Being, Merleau-Ponty means that dialectical thought is adapted to one sector of Being, but not to other sectors. We do not think that this is the meaning he intends, for the preceding description of dialectical thought gives us the impression that it is adapted to all beings. The term "realm of Being" must be understood, consequently, as a level of Being. Human thought is not dialectical as long as it is a superficial approach to Being, but it becomes, or rather it has to become, dialectical as soon as it contacts Being on a deeper level.

What is the level of Being which can be understood only by dialectical thought? There can hardly be any doubt that Merleau-Ponty refers here to what elsewhere in his book he calls "savage Being," viz., Being which underlies the order of reason, the order of language. He does not say so explicitly, but the following sentences make this interpretation quite obvious.

The Being which is adapted to the dialectical approach, he continues, manifests itself in the perceptible world.[136] But it manifests itself only if we take away from it everything that ontological thought has added to it. Ontological thought has covered perceptible reality with all kinds of rational meanings; these meanings pretend to manifest the perceptible world, but as a matter of fact they rather hide it; they pretend to bring clarity, but this clarity is often false. What does Merleau-Ponty mean? We must recall what he said elsewhere of concepts such as "subject," "object," "sensation," "act," "succession of acts" and "perception." These concepts pretend to bring clarity into our perceptive field, but instead they hide its real structure. Through them our perceptive field is analyzed into a rational order of clear meanings, but with this order we forget its real structure.

The Danger of Dialectical Degeneration.   Merleau-Ponty reminds us of the fact that our world of speech is the expression of a silent world, that we have to see the world of speech in relation to the silent world. We are always in danger of forgetting this and of considering our clear concepts as the ultimate norm. Then our thought is not dialectical. It becomes dialectical again only when we consider our concepts as partial expressions of the silent world, when we are willing to transform our

---

[136] *Ibid.*

concepts in an interchange with the silent world, when we accept the relative character of our categories. Our thought becomes dialectical if we do what Merleau-Ponty tried to do in the chapter *"L'Entrelacs—le Chiasme."*

Now we understand why explicit adherence to dialectical thought does not give us any guarantee against the degeneration to which dialectical thought is opposed and exposed. As soon as dialectical thought becomes an established philosophy, it will have its own categories, as for example, in Marxism. There categories, too, will become rootless, divorced from the silent world. Our thought is really dialectical if it assumes a critical attitude, not only toward the notions of past philosophies, but also toward its own notions. Our thought is dialectical only if it is self-critical, and it does not remain self-critical when dialectical thought transforms itself into an established philosophy.

Our thought is really dialectical if it includes its own notions in the dialectical movement of thought, if it allows its own notions to be open also, so that their meaning too will be able to change as soon as a new light enlightens us. But the dialectical thinker cannot remain faithful to this attitude when he proposes his method as the final term of philosophical research. He then closes a road which must remain open in principle.

In this way Hegel and Sartre have denied dialectical thought by affirming it in a false manner.[137] They accepted the profound idea of mediation: each term of the dialectic calls for its opposite and, in the interchange with its opposite, arrives at its own truth. According to Hegel the Absolute Subject, viz., God, denies itself in order to make the world be. Sartre reduces the human subject to a nothingness which affirms the radical positivity of Being. However, Hegel's world becomes an absolute term, since the Divine Subjectivity denied and realized Itself in it. And Sartre's Being becomes absolute, because the subject is nothingness, a parasite of the world. As soon as dialectical thought arrives at final concepts it denies itself. The philosopher is really dialectical only if he recognizes the relativity of his own thought and of his own concepts. Dialectics remains faithful to itself only if it becomes "hyperdialectical," i.e., if it includes itself in the dialectical movement.[138]

Dialectical thought does not remain really dialectical if it arrives at a final thesis, as the Hegelian and Sartrian philosophies do. *Each thesis is*

---

[137] *V.I.*, p. 127.
[138] *V.I.*, p. 129.

an idealization,[139] viz., a sentence which pretends to pronounce the final truth, which transforms real Being into the content of a sentence. But real Being is not a collection of idealizations, and it cannot be reduced to the content of any human sentence. Dialectical thought can remain faithful to itself only if it is and remains a *dialectics without a synthesis.*[140]

Truth. Merleau-Ponty asks whether there is room for real truth in this perspective, whether this perspective does not lead us to a radical scepticism.[141] There is truth in dialectical thought, because it reveals Being. But there is no human thought which ends the revelation of Being. There is no truth which cannot be surpassed. However, truth which is surpassed is not denied. We always can surpass our sentences, but this implies that we make them more true. The revelation of truth is a history which never ends.

It is false to conceive truth as a final and insurpassable statement. Final and insurpassable statements exist only insofar as our judgments are divorced from real Being. Then they have lost the contact with the silent world which they express. When we re-establish this contact, the allegedly final and ultimate truth disappears. But then we lose only a superficial illusion. This is not a real loss. Being liberated from this illusion, we then have access to real truth which, however, is never final and ultimate.

There is no final and ultimate truth for us because our search for truth is involved in Being. If Being could be the object of our search there would be final and ultimate truth. There is, indeed, an objectification of Being. But this objectification is only the expression of an involvement. We cultivate the illusion of final and ultimate truth if we forget that the objectification is but the expression of an underlying involvement. The false idea of truth disappears, however, if we understand our involvement in Being. This does not mean that we renounce all truth and fall into scepticism; it means that we begin to understand what truth is. Sartre separates our nothingness from Being. His philosophy, therefore, is not truly dialectical. There is a radical distance between Merleau-Ponty and Sartre, notwithstanding their common problems and their common terminology. Merleau-Ponty's sentence: *"J'en suis,"* implicitly refutes Sartre's philosophy.

---

[139] "Toute thèse est idéalisation." *Ibid.*
[140] *Ibid.*
[141] *V.I.,* pp. 129-130.

F. CONCLUSIONS

Merleau-Ponty now formulates some conclusions regarding the character of philosophical research.[142]

The fundamental question of philosophy is not whether Being exists. We know already that we are involved in Being. This certainty is one of the essential characteristics of our perception. If we were to really doubt this, we would never find it again.[143]

The real question of the philosopher is the meaning of Being. We should not conclude, however, that philosophy is in search for the meaning of the term "Being." For the exact definition of a word never resolves any philosophical question. Philosophy cannot be reduced to the analysis of language because language is not enclosed in itself. Language, as a matter of fact, is a secondary expression of Being. It is not our primordial involvement in Being, but the expression of an involvement which precedes it. The philosopher speaks, but his speaking does not merely express what is contained in our words; it tries also to say what we do not yet know; it tries to *make* our language more an expression of Being than it had been.[144]

Being is not an object exposed to consciousness which, as nothingness, is separated from Being. We are involved in Being without coinciding perfectly with it. Involved in Being, we are openness toward Being. Involvement and openness express together the reality of our situation.

We are involved in Being as "perceiving perceptibles." By perceptive faith we know that we are involved in Being, but we are not a surveying look which comprehends Being. Our certainty of Being does not exclude, therefore, our being in search of Being. We are involved in Being in such a way that involvement and search imply each other. We not only *have* questions, but we *are* a question.[145] All this is implied in the fact that we are *openness*. Philosophical research is a continuation of our Being.

The questioning of Being implies that we question ourselves, because Being and our involvement in Being cannot be separated. The most

---

[142] *V.I.*, pp. 130-141.

[143] *V.I.*, pp. 130-131.

[144] *V.I.*, pp. 131-133.

[145] "Toute question, même celle de la simple connaissance, fait partie de la question centrale qui est nous-mêmes, de cet appel à la totalité auquel aucun être objectif ne donne réponse et que nous avons maintenant à examiner plus précisément." *V.I.*, p. 141.

simple everyday questions, such as "Where am I?" and "What time is it?" indicate our involvement in Being, at least if we do not content ourselves with superficial answers.

We have briefly summarized these conclusions. In the following chapter we will work out some of them in explaining aspects of Merleau-Ponty's deepened philosophy.

4. *Merleau-Ponty's Criticism of Husserl's Eidetic Reduction*

A. INTRODUCTION

During the period of Merleau-Ponty's life about which we are now writing, he wrote two important texts on Husserl's philosophy. The first, entitled "The Philosopher and His Shadow,"[146] was published in *Signs;* the second is the chapter from *The Visible and the Invisible* that we will now consider, viz., "Interrogation and Intuition."[147] The character of the two texts is quite different. The first is a positive criticism of Husserl's philosophy, while the second tends to be negative.

In "The Philosopher and His Shadow," Merleau-Ponty says that we should make a distinction between the explicit statements of a philosopher and the fundamental light which enabled him to advance those statements.[148] This fundamental light itself is usually not stated; yet it is somehow present in all the statements he makes. According to Merleau-Ponty, Husserl's explicit philosophy is rationalistic, and even idealistic. He brackets Being and seems to be looking for absolute concepts. There are, however, many signs that Husserl was never a complete rationalist and that he never denied the awareness which Merleau-Ponty expressed in the sentence, *"J'en suis."*[149] Merleau-Ponty collects these indications and tries to demonstrate that the fundamental light in which Husserl thought is more acceptable than many of his explicit statements.

In "Interrogation and Intuition" Merleau-Ponty analyzes and rejects

---

[146] *Signs,* pp. 159-181.

[147] *V.I.,* pp. 142-171.

[148] "We should like to try to evoke this unthought-of element in Husserl's thought in the margin of some old pages." *Signs,* p. 160.

[149] "Originally a project to gain intellectual possession of the world, constitution becomes increasingly, as Husserl's thought matures, the means of unveiling a back side of things that we have not constituted." *Signs,* p. 180.

Husserl's eidetic reduction. While in this chapter Merleau-Ponty's judgment of Husserl is more negative than in "The Philosopher and His Shadow," the two texts do not contradict one another at all. In "Interrogation and Intuition" Merleau-Ponty criticizes the explicit statements of Husserl, which he also rejected earlier in "The Philosopher and His Shadow." In the later text Merleau-Ponty demonstrates that there is an implicit ground which is more acceptable than the explicit statements; this, of course, is not excluded in the first text. For our purpose, "Interrogation and Intuition" is more important.

Merleau-Ponty wrote about Husserl's eidetic reduction as early as the Preface of *Phenomenology of Perception*.[150] He denied then the ultimate value of the eidetic reduction, although he attributed a provisional value to it.[151] The phenomenologist tries to find the character, the structure of the experienced world, of the temporal stream of real life. There is no room here for conceptual idealization. But Merleau-Ponty admits that the conceptual idealization, the eidetic reduction, is useful and even necessary as a provisional phase which, however, must be surpassed.[152] We abstract some aspects from the integral unity of concrete experience and transform them into the content of our concepts. We try to define the content of such concepts in a rational manner. We are not allowed, however, to stop at this point. The conceptual fixation serves only to understand better the stream of real experience. The conceptual fixation, therefore, must be provisional and our concepts finally must be reduced to experience.[153]

It is evident that this interpretation of the eidetic reduction differs from Husserl's conception of it, because Husserl did not see his eidetic reduction as a provisional phase of thought. But in his first text Merleau-Ponty tried to leave room for this important element of Husserl's philosophy. In "Interrogation and Intuition," however, Merleau-Ponty radically rejects the eidetic reduction. Here he says that we must finally break with the myths of induction and eidetic reduction.[154] We will now summarize this chapter of Merleau-Ponty's book.

---

[150] *Phenomenology of Perception*, Preface, pp. XIV-XVII.

[151] "Husserl's essences are destined to bring back all the living relationships of experience, as the fisherman's net draws up from the depth of the ocean quivering fish and seaweed." *Phenomenology of Perception*, Preface, p. XV.

[152] "Jean Wahl is therefore wrong in saying that 'Husserl separates essences from existence'. The separated essences are those of language." *Ibid.*

[153] Kwant, *The Phenomenological Philosophy of Merleau-Ponty*, pp. 157-161.

[154] *V.I.*, p. 155.

B. THE FUNCTION OF EIDETIC REDUCTION IN HUSSERL'S PHILOSOPHY

In daily life we often ask questions which can easily be answered.[155] We ask where we are, what time it is. We can answer such questions because we have constructed systems which help us to indicate the time and the place in which we stand. These systems, however, have an artificial character. The answers themselves can be questioned again. We can make the questions themselves radical and so arrive at the question of what it means to be in space and to exist in a temporal manner. Philosophy seems to be a radical asking of the common questions of everyday.[156] But when we radically ask the common questions of everyday, they take on a different meaning.[157] When we simply ask what time it is, we suppose our fundamental awareness of existing in a temporal manner; but we do not question this fundamental awareness itself. Philosophy does so.

No Escape from Perceptive Certainty. Our perceptive awareness teaches us that we live in space, in time, in a world, in a field of colors and sounds. But our perceptive awareness is a perceptive faith. Real perception and illusion are commingled. According to many philosophers our perceptive faith is not reliable; and the method of doubt must help us to arrive at real and undoubtable certainties.

However, the philosophers who say that our perceptive faith is unreliable and who look for another foundation of certainty are always to a certain extent "hypocritical." They deny on the one hand that our perception is reliable; but, on the other, they always select some data of exterior or interior perception and base their certainty on that data. They rely, e.g., on our perception of quantity and quantitative relations, on our perception of the appearance of things, sensations, representations or thought. If they want to avoid radical scepticism—and this attitude of mind ultimately is impossible because the sceptical philosopher is certain at least about his scepticism—they must base their certainty on some data of perceptive faith. Perceptive faith is our primordial contact with Being, and it is, therefore, our final basis of certainty.[158]

---

[155] *V.I.*, pp. 142-143.

[156] "La philosophie, à première vue, généralise seulement ce genre de questions." *V.I.*, p. 142.

[157] "En s'étendant à tout, la question commune change de sens." *V.I.*, p. 144.

[158] "C'est au nom et au profit de ces réalités flottantes que la réalité solide est mise en doute. On ne sort pas du quelque chose, et le doute comme destruction des certitudes n'est pas doute." *V.I.*, p. 143.

Descartes' methodic doubt does not escape this ambiguous attitude.[159] Descartes admits that our perception is certain, because his philosophical doubt is only methodic. But the certainty of perception, he maintains, is commingled with many ambiguous facts; and he wants to arrive at a certainty of pure reason that does not depend on any fact. This desire itself, however, finds its origin in his experience of perceptive certainty. He could not desire to have the certainty of pure reason if he were not living in his perceptive certainty. His experience of ambiguous certainty inspires his desire for absolute certainty.[160] He bases his so-called absolute certainty on the cogito, but this cogito is also commingled with facts. It would not exist in the manner Descartes experiences it if man did not speak. We are certain because we are involved in Being. This involvement is a clarity which is essentially commingled with facts. We cannot arrive at a reasonable certainty that is completely free of all facts.

Husserl's Philosophy of Meaning. Husserl recognizes this. He therefore does not use the method of doubt, whether sceptical or methodic. He does not deny real Being nor does he doubt it; he simply puts the question of Being aside. He does not ask whether Being exists. Whether Being is real or unreal, whether it occasions certainty or doubt, there always remains one fundamental question, viz., *what is Being?* Being appears to us. What does appear to us? Husserl does not affirm that Being transcends us, nor does he say that Being is merely immanent. He simply asks what Being is. This is the fundamental question of Husserl. Being is the intentional object of our human activities. Husserl questions this intentional object without being concerned about its ontological status.[161]

Husserl's philosophy is a philosophy of meaning. However, he is not looking for the meaning which reveals itself as a matter of fact, but for absolute and necessary meaning. Our words always mean something.

---

[159] *V.I.,* pp. 143-144.

[160] "Ainsi le doute methodique, celui qui est conduit dans la zone volontaire de nous-mêmes, se réfère à l'Être, puisqu'il résiste à une évidence de fait, refoule une vérité involontaire dont il avoue qu'elle est déjà là et dont s'inspire le projet même d'une évidence qui soit absolue." *V.I.,* p. 144.

[161] ". . . ne plus nier, ne plus douter même, reculer seulement pour voir le monde et l'Être, ou encore les mettre entre guillemets comme on fait des propos d'un autre, les laisser parler, se mettre à l'écoute.

"Alors, si la question ne peut plus être celle du *an sit,* elle devient celle du *quid sit." Ibid.*

When we say "table" or "world," these words have a meaning. Husserl seeks the conditions which must be fulfilled so that we can speak of "table" and "world." He distinguishes between the accidental and the necessary aspects of meaning. He tries to remove all the accidental aspects in order to penetrate into the necessary ones. It is accidental that this table is brown and small. Which are the essential conditions of any table at all? Husserl looks for the essence of things. This essence is an ideal being. It is neither this nor that appearance. It is the essence which reveals itself in all the appearances.[162] The essences condition the appearance of meaningful things; they condition our language and all our logical operations as well.

Husserl looks for the philosophical grammar of our field of meaning. There must be nuclei of meaning, fundamental points of light which make the whole field of meaning possible. These nuclei of meaning determine the coherence of our whole field of meaning. What makes us say that beings are living, that they are material, that they are spiritual, that they are human? Which are the most fundamental meanings? How do the other meanings derive from them? These are Husserl's questions as he studies the composition of our field of meaning.[163]

Husserl views beings, but he views them solely as meaningful, and it does not interest him whether the meaningful beings do or do not really exist. He transforms Being into meaning. Science does so, but only to a certain extent.[164] As a matter of fact, science sets up many idealizations. Galileo's concept of nature is an idealization because he views only some aspects of appearing nature and abstracts from all others. But in science an interaction between the idealizations and the real experience of facts always remains. Science tries to verify its idealizations and hypotheses in a real contact with real facts.[165]

Husserl's phenomenology goes to the roots of science. His philosophy idealizes everything, reduces everything to meaning; it asks what nature, history, world and Being finally are. Science is often an unconscious idealization because it thinks its idealizations are reality. It confuses

---

[162] "Il sera *ce sans quoi* il n'y aurait ni monde, ni langage, ni quoi que ce soit, il sera l'essence." *V.I.,* p. 145.

[163] ". . . à ce qui fait que le monde est monde, à une grammaire impérieuse de l'Être, à des noyaux de sens indécomposables." *Ibid.*

[164] "Démarche qui est déjà celle de la science." *Ibid.*

[165] "Mais ce travail, elle (la science) ne le termine pas: ses essences, elle ne les dégage pas tout à fait du monde, elle les maintient sous la jurisdiction des faits." *V.I.,* pp. 145-146.

reality and meaning. Husserl reduces everything to meaning and looks for the essential, necessary laws of our field of meaning. The field of necessary meanings is the object of Husserl's research. The eidetic reduction is the method employed to reveal the nuclei of meaning.[166]

C. PHILOSOPHICAL CERTAINTY IS NOT BASED ON THE HUSSERLIAN ESSENCES

If the philosopher is caught in a realm of dubious facts, he will try to penetrate to a deeper realm where he might find certainty. But because philosophy is essentially reflective, the philosopher will have to investigate the character and the ontological status of that new realm. Is Husserl right when he says that the philosopher finds a base for certainty in the realm of essences? Is the essence the final answer to our philosophical questions?[167] The essence is not a real thing but an ideal object. An ideal object demands a subject. Accepting the order of essences, Husserl consequently also accepts an ideal subject which is related to the essences, or rather, to which the essences are related. Is man in his deepest being the contemplator of essences, and are the essences the most profound datum of philosophy?

Merleau-Ponty answers these questions negatively.[168] What is the Husserlian essence? It is the point at which our intellect rests when it searches out the conditions which enable reality to appear. Husserl poses the same kind of questions that we find in the works of Kant. Kant often says: If a world exists it has to fulfill the following conditions . . . ; or, If science exists it must be both synthetic and universal.[169] Husserl proceeds in the same way. He looks for the "conditions of possibility" for reality to appear.

How do we arrive at this kind of questioning? There must first of all be some meaning which reveals itself in appearing reality. This meaning appeals to the intellect, but it has an ambiguous character. It has to say something to the intellect yet does not convince it. It happens, e.g., that

---

[166] "La philosophie serait cette même lecture du sens menée à son terme, science exacte, la seule exacte, parce qu'elle seule va jusqu'au bout de l'effort pour savoir ce que *c'est* la Nature et l'Histoire et le Monde et l'Être." *V.I.,* p. 146.

[167] "La question de l'essence est-elle la question ultime?" *V.I.,* p. 147.

[168] "L'être de l'essence n'est pas premier, ne repose pas sur lui-même, ce n'est pas lui qui peut nous apprendre ce que c'est que l'Être, l'essence n'est pas *la* réponse à la question philosophique." *Ibid.*

[169] *Ibid.*

the same meaning reveals itself in many appearing realities, but in such a way that the meaning differs somewhat in the different phenomena. It also happens that many things reveal themselves as a whole, but we do not immediately know how they belong together, how they constitute a whole. In such cases our intellect grasps the meaning without being satisfied. It tries to formulate what it sees. It constitutes an essence.

The essence, however, is not an original datum. Our experience precedes it. Kant could never have formulated the meaning of the term "world" if a real world had not appeared to him; he could not have formulated the conditions of science if his experience had not taught him that science existed. This also applies to all the essences of Husserl. They are a formulation, an idealization of preceding knowledge.[170]

The essence is not the primordial level of philosophical knowledge. It is not the final source of knowledge which teaches us what Being really is. We do not find there the final answer of our philosophical questions. Hence the subject which views essences is not the primordial subject. We constitute appearing reality as an essence; in the same way, we constitute ourselves as contemplators of essences. Husserl is wrong in considering the essence the primordial object of philosophical thought. It is a secondary expression of experience.[171]

Merleau-Ponty admits that there is some truth in the Husserlian idea of essence. It is true that our experiences are connected. Our field of experience is not a collection of accidental relationships. The coherence of our field of experience, however, is not due to essences; that something like an essence exists is due to the coherence of our field of experience. Essences do not underlie our experience, but our experience underlies essences.

Merleau-Ponty thus rejects the idea that essences comprise something more than our field of experience.[172] Such an idea is not new at all; Plato expressed it when he opposed the necessity of essence to the contingency of our field of perceptive experience. He then rightly

---

[170] "Des essences que nous trouvons, nous n'avons pas le droit de dire qu'elles donnent le sens primitif de l'Être." *Ibid.*

[171] "Les possibilités d'essence peuvent bien envelopper et dominer *les faits,* elles dérivent elles-mêmes d'une autre possibilité, et plus fondamentale: celle qui travaille mon expérience, l'ouvre au monde et à l'Être, et qui, certes, ne les trouve pas devant elle comme *des faits,* mais anime et organise leur facticité." *V.I.,* p. 148.

[172] "(Les essences) sont prélevées par eux sur un être brut où il s'agit de retrouver à l'état sauvage les répondants de nos essences et de nos significations." *V.I.,* p. 149.

concluded that the latter cannot be the cause of the former. The essence must exist, therefore, in another realm and it must have another source. This is why Plato said that the idea, the essence, is innate and that there is a separate world of ideas. Yet, according to Merleau-Ponty we are involved in Being; as "perceiving perceptibles" we are open to the world to which we belong. This original experience is the only source of our idealizations; thus they cannot contain more than their source. The essence is not the basis of knowledge since it is derived from a more original knowledge. If we find some necessity in essences, we must find this necessity in our original experience itself.[173]

It is quite possible that the essence expresses an aspect of original experience which was there only in a latent manner. Were our original experience completely clear, expression would be useless and philosophy superfluous. The idealization unfolds the original experience and manifests what that experience is. But the expression does not open us to a more original realm of reality. It does not ground our experience.

D. THE PURE ESSENCE DOES NOT EXIST

What Husserl calls "essence" is not the ground of our experience, but its expression. As a "perceiving perceptible," I am situated in the world. Many things reveal a common style of Being. It makes sense to use the word "nature," and I can speak of a "world." I can give abstract names to many things which reveal a common style of existence. From this experience, how did Husserl arrive at his "essences"?

He applied the method of eidetic variation, which is an active intervention of the human mind.[174] He analyzed the appearing phenomena and asked whether things would remain the same if this or that element were eliminated. In this way he tried to distinguish between the essential and the accidental aspects of things.

The result of this method he called "essence." But what did he really achieve? He discovered those elements which could not disappear without the thing itself disappearing, e.g., man would not be man if he did not have a human face. Husserl discovered the invariable style of

---

[173] "Les essences, les necessités d'essence, la possibilité interne ou logique, toutes solides et incontestables qu'elle soient sous le regard de l'esprit, n'ont finalement leur force et leur éloquence que parce que toutes mes pensées et les pensées des autres sont prises dans le tissu d'un seul Être." *V.I.*, p. 148.

[174] "La solidité, l'essentialité de l'essence est exactement mesurée par le pouvoir que nous avons de varier la chose." *V.I.*, p. 149.

existence which makes things what they are. His essences are the expression of the fundamental style of existence which constitutes the Being of things.[175]

This is not, however, another and radically different realm of reality.[176] It is an expression of real Being. This expression is always partial because our power of eidetic variation is partial. Our experience measures and limits our power of eidetic variation; and if we could survey all possible experience, our eidetic variation would be perfect and complete.[177] But this is impossible for an experiencing being because of its involvement in Being. Our experience extends over a realm of clarity enclosed in a vague horizon. All our idealizations are rooted in such an experience. In my idealizations I collect many experiences, but I can collect them only because they all belong to one and the same temporal life.[178] The unity of my ideas is supported by the temporal unity of my life and by the connection of my life with the life of the community of men to which I belong. The "flesh of the world," the "flesh of history," supports all our idealizations. Our idealizations can never transcend the density of Being, the density of temporal and spatial experience. If the essence is isolated from this density, it is nothing at all, a mere illusion.

The pure essence does not exist. We have only the provisional expressions of our coherent experience. There is no absolute vision of an essence transcending our experience. There is no absolute essence, no absolute vision of an essence.[179]

Merleau-Ponty also refuses to accept the pure essence as an ideal, a "limit-idea" at which we aim without ever attaining.[180] If we were to accept the absolute essence as an ideal, we would devaluate all our real experiences in the false light of an impossible goal. We would then fall into relativism. Such false ideals are an immense danger. They have often occurred in the history of human thought. Many values in human

---

[175] *V.I.*, pp. 149-150.

[176] "Elle (l'essence) n'est donc pas un être postif. Elle est un in-variant." *V.I.*, p. 149.

[177] "Une essence pure qui ne fût pas du tout contaminée et brouillée par les faits ne pourrait résulter que d'un essai de variation totale." *Ibid.*

[178] "Toute idéation est portée par cet arbre de ma durée et des durées; cette sève ignorée nourrit la transparence de l'idée." *V.I.*, p. 150.

[179] "Il n'y a pas de vision positive qui me donne définitivement l'essentialité de l'essence." *V.I.*, p. 151.

[180] *Ibid.*

life always exist in an ambiguous manner, in an interchange with other values; moreover, real values can to a certain extent be opposed to one another. However, our intellect sometimes abstracts these values from their real context and transforms them into absolute, isolated ideals. The conclusion seems to be that man must aim at such absolute ideals, although they cannot be actualized. But, as a consequence, the real values which exist in actual life, in an interchange with other values, are emptied. The real values are considered shadows of what they should be. We make the real values relative, or even condemn them in the name of false ideal values. This happens when we consider the absolute essence as the ideal of human knowledge. We will never arrive at any absolute essence. When we accept the absolute essence as an ideal, we devalue all our real knowledge in the name of an impossible goal.

The relationship of our knowledge to the order of facts, to the realm of real experience, to "savage Being," is not an imperfection, an impurity to be deplored.[181] I am not an exterior contemplator of Being, a "cosmotheoros," but am involved in Being. It is because of my involvement in Being that there is meaning, light, value. I cannot survey Being, precisely because I am involved in it. The total field of Being will never lie open before my surveying look. We must exclude this, not only as being something which we will never realize, but also as an ideal. God has been conceived as the Absolute Look surveying everything. Such a God emerges out of man's feelings of failure. God becomes the successful man. God is conceived as the actualization of an impossible human ideal.

The Husserlian concept of absolute essence is similarly a false and impossible ideal. It is extremely dangerous because it makes us blind to the light which we do have because of our involvement in Being. Merleau-Ponty does not at all deny that there is coherence in Being, that there are understandable connections, that we can even speak of necessity. He does not even refuse to speak of "essential aspects" of Being. But we find this real light in the Being in which we are involved, in the order of facts. He refuses to separate the "that" and the "what"; the "what" is the connection, the coherence, the interior intelligibility of the "that." Merleau-Ponty does not deny that there is room for idealization. We can abstract the aspect of "what" from the

---

[181] ". . . d'un impossible travail de l'expérience sur l'expérience qui la dépouillerait de sa facticité comme d'une impurité." *Ibid.*

"that." But this abstraction does not allow us to penetrate into an order of absolute essences preceding in some manner the concrete, appearing reality.

The time has come, says Merleau-Ponty, for us to reject the myths of inductive knowledge and of the intuition of essences (*Wesensschau*).[182] Merleau-Ponty calls Husserl's *Wesensschau* a myth, and he compares it with the myth of inductive knowledge. This comparison was alien to Merleau-Ponty when he wrote *Phenomenology of Perception*. At that time he already rejected the value of inductive knowledge, but he tried to save the Husserlian eidetic reduction. Now he rejects both of them and evidently sees some connection between them. The connection is rather obvious. Both the eidetic reduction and the inductive method start from the order of facts and intend to arrive at something different; the eidetic reduction aims at the necessary essence and induction aims at the necessary law. Both methods of thinking start from contingent facts and pretend to arrive at a realm of necessity. For Merleau-Ponty such a transition is a myth. If there is no necessity in the order of facts themselves, there will never be any necessity at all.

In *Sense and Non-Sense* Merleau-Ponty said that not a single induction has ever completely succeeded;[183] in "Interrogation and Intuition" he writes that in Husserl's works there is not one eidetic reduction, not one so-called *Wesensschau,* which Husserl always accepted without any change.[184] Even when Husserl thought he had revealed some essence (*Wesen*) by an eidetic reduction, he always returned to the question and spoke of the same essence in a different manner. This is a clear indication that there is no absolute essence in some mysterious realm, and that the so-called "essence" is the expression of the interior connection of the facts. Facts and essence are two indissoluble aspects of one and the same field of experience.[185]

E. THE UNITY OF ESSENCES AND FACTS

Merleau-Ponty denies the existence of absolute essences, but he does not deny the endeavor of science and philosophy to arrive at general

---

[182] *V.I.,* p. 155.

[183] *Sense and Non-Sense,* p. 98.

[184] *V.I.,* p. 155.

[185] "il serait naïf de chercher la solidité dans un ciel des idées ou dans un *fond* du sens: elle n'est ni au-dessus, ni au-dessous des apparences, mais à leur jointure." *Ibid.*

knowledge.   How, he asks, did psychology, ethnology and sociology advance?   Their progress has not resulted from induction nor from Husserl's eidetic speculation.[186]   We are involved in Being, and each of us has his own experience of psychic life, of social existence, and of the life of the people to whom he belongs.   If we ourselves were not involved in Being we would not have access to the experiences which are expressed by science.   Moreover, we can also contact one another and exchange our experiences.   We do so by speaking with one another and also by reading and by penetrating into civilizations of the past. Involved in Being, we can share the involvement of other people.   In this way we can enrich our own experience and see more coherence, more connections of the Being in which we are involved.

We can use the term "eidetic variation" in this context.   For it is a fact that we compare our experiences with the experiences of others; we correct and amplify our own ideas.   We practice together the "eidetic variation" which Husserl reserved for the solitary imagination and thought of the individual philosopher.   He was wrong on this point. The real "eidetic variation" takes place in the encounter of scientists and philosophers.[187]   The "cosmotheoros," the thinker who surveys the world, has no need for encounter, at least not in principle.   But the thinker who knows that his involvement in Being is the source of his thought, who recognizes that he is essentially a local and temporal involvement in Being, understands that he needs other people in order to think for himself, understands that the enrichment of his own thought depends on the encounter with other "involvements" in Being.   Merleau-Ponty calls science a "common opinion."   He does not mean, of course, that science has no real insight into Being but that this insight is conditioned by the mutual contact between scientists and philosophers.

In this way there is an increasing objectivity of knowledge.   This must not be explained by some mysterious reflection of a "Being-in-itself," nor by an equally mysterious contact with absolute essences or ideas.   It is simply explained by the enrichment of our access to Being

---

[186] "Nulle recherche féconde n'est inductivité pure, pur recensement des constantes en soi." *V.I.,* p. 156.

[187] ". . . en organisant l'*Ineinander,* et, finalement, en pratiquant cette variation eidétique que Husserl a eu le seul tort de réserver d'abord à l'imagination et à la vision solitaires du philosophe, alors qu'elle est le support et le lieu même de cette *opinio communis* qu'on appelle la science." *Ibid.*

which is the result of encounter with other people.[188]   This encounter makes possible the "eidetic variation" which deepens our involvement in Being and helps us to correct and enrich our concepts.

It is in this way that we discover an authentic generality in the facts themselves.   There is intelligibility in the facts and in their coherence; we can discover essences in the facts and in their interconnection.   It is not necessary to appeal to some heaven of ideas in order to have access to essences.   If we separate facts and essences we are confronted with two idle abstractions: the facts have become unintelligible since they are separated from their intelligibility, and essences have lost the density of reality since they are exterior to the real facts.   The primary realm in which we are involved is the world which is a unity of essences and facts. In this world everything is related to everything else.   Being placed in it is the same as being related to other things.   Without relationships to other things and to the whole, nothing could be itself.   This totality is not strange to us who live in it.[189]   All the basic concepts of philosophy and science imply our experience of the total Being in which we are involved.   Merleau-Ponty promises to analyze time, space, and the relationship between time and space, the bilaterality of our body—its visible and invisible aspects—in the light of this basic truth.[190]   For the moment he stresses the fact that the intrinsic unity of Being transcends the classical distinction of essence and existence, of essence and fact.

Because we are involved in Being, Being reveals itself to us.   It does not reveal itself as an object which is distinguished from us.   Being penetrates us.   Our body is a "perceiving perceptible."   The reality it perceives is both in the body itself and outside it.   One and the same reality penetrates the body and extends beyond it.   Our experience of Being is the same.   Being penetrates us and extends beyond us, and yet it remains the same Being.   Being becomes aware of itself in us.   All the aspects of our existence are an access to Being.   We usually forget this fundamental unity which precedes and supports all the distinctions.   It is not useless to make distinctions.   Merleau-Ponty makes many distinctions himself.   But it is dangerous to forget that all the distinctions we

---

[188] "Il est bien sûr qu'on accède à l'objectivité. . . . en tant que nous sommes intérieurs à la vie, à l'être-humain et à l'Être, aussi bien que lui en nous." *Ibid.*

[189] "Ce milieu de l'existence et de l'essence brutes n'est pas mystérieux: nous n'en sortons pas, nous n'avons pas d'autre.   Les faits et les essences sont des abstractions." *Ibid.*

[190] *V.I.*, p. 157.

make are distinctions within a fundamental unity.[191]   All authentic metaphysicians have known this. Merleau-Ponty stresses here points which are really metaphysical. Our existence itself *is* access to Being; and it is, therefore, our "natural light." Being obtains an "interiority" in man. Man is the self-revelation of Being. In Being facts and essence are not at all opposed.

F. ESSENCES AND LANGUAGE

It is quite understandable that Merleau-Ponty, after having criticized the essences of Husserl, speaks of language. For there is a close connection between essences and language. "Essence" is a most analogous concept and it is almost impossible to list the definitions which have been proposed for it throughout the long history of philosophy. There is, however, one element which always appears in the definitions of essence, viz., that there is generality and universality in it. This element indicates a connection between essences and language, because there is generality and universality in language also. Several philosophers have said, therefore, that language is at the origin of generality and universality. The reality which appears here and now is concrete and individual; the essence begins to exist when we indicate many appearing realities with a common name.

In a note of February, 1960,[192] Merleau-Ponty writes that nominalism is correct in saying that there is no positive vision of any essence.[193] There is no general object which corresponds to our general words. Merleau-Ponty said the same in his criticism of the essences of Husserl. Does this imply that generality and universality come into existence only with our common names?

"Deflections" of Being. In the note we have just cited Merleau-Ponty says that concept and meaning refer to the singular phenomenon insofar as it is considered within the dimensions of its existence.[194] He

---

[191] "Il suffit de faire voir, pour le moment, que l'Être unique, la dimensionnalité à laquelle appartiennent ces moments, ces feuillets et ces dimensions, est par-delà l'essence et l'existence classiques et rend compréhensible leur rapport." *Ibid.*

[192] *V.I.*, pp. 290-291.

[193] "Le nominalisme a raison: les significations ne sont que des *écarts définis.*" *V.I.*, p. 291.

[194] "Le concept, la signification sont le singulier *dimensionnalisé,* la structure formulée, et il n' y a pas de vision de cette charnière invisible." *Ibid.*

denies that any singular phenomenon has an isolated existence. It exists in connection with other things, within a structure. The general concept, he says, is the formulation of the structure in which the singular phenomenon exists. He ends his note with a sentence that is difficult to understand: "General meanings are nothing but deflections which have been defined" (*des écarts définis*).[195] The notion "deflection" (*écart*) returns several times in *The Visible and the Invisible*. This notion is connected with Merleau-Ponty's central point of view expressed in the sentence *"J'en suis,"* I belong to it, I belong to Being. This sentence, however, is still too particular; Merleau-Ponty does not intend to say that I alone belong to Being. Everything belongs to Being—the other person, the things I perceive. Everything belongs to Being, not because the general concept "being" can be applied to everything, but because everything is penetrated by Being which at the same time exceeds it.

Two things are simultaneously true: first, everything belongs to Being, everything is penetrated by the common reality of Being; second, everything is a being in its own way. Everything is a "deflection" (*écart*) of Being. We have seen this same idea already in our study of the chapter *"L'Entrelacs—le Chiasme."* Studying the visibility of things, Merleau-Ponty says that every visible thing is a *contraction of the general visibility*. A concrete phenomenon is visible, but it does not coincide with visibility as such. Visibility permeates it, but at the same time exceeds it. General visibility is contracted in a special manner in each thing. Therefore every visible thing appears within a horizon of visibility. It is a "deflection" (*écart*) of the general visibility.

Positive thought disengages concrete phenomena from the context in which they exist. We have become so accustomed to analytic thought that we are almost blind to the context, the structure, in which things exist. Merleau-Ponty's philosophy protests against this blindness of analytic thought. This is why he speaks of the "clutter" of concepts which must be removed. By isolating things, we have projected a false clarity which denies the complex structures of existence. This is also the reason why he speaks of "savage Being"; he wants to return to the original structures in which things reveal themselves as interwoven with other things; in which appears the central truth, viz., "it belongs to it" (*il en est*), in which things are a "deflection" (*écart*) of a common reality which exceeds them.

---

[195] *Ibid.*

No "Ideal" Reality.   Merleau-Ponty denies the "ideal" reality of essences. There is no heaven of ideas. The eye of our mind does not see an ideal reality of essences in some mysterious realm. The perceptive reality in which we live and to which we belong is the final source of all knowledge, including our general concepts. This does not imply, however, that our general words are the origin of the phenomenon of generality, that generality begins only with our words. Merleau-Ponty certainly does not accept such a superficial nominalism, for it does not explain the phenomenon of generality at all. *J'en suis;* I belong to Being. So, too, my speaking belongs to Being. If the generality of our words had no foundation in Being, it would be an idle and meaningless phenomenon.

According to Merleau-Ponty, essences are not above us, but below us, in the structure of appearing Being itself.[196] The reality of the essence does not belong to the heaven of ideas but to the structure of Being. This essence is common to our expressive language and to the reality expressed by it.

Our body is a "perceiving perceptible." It is a being which becomes aware of itself. Being is in me, but it exceeds me. The body is at the same time awareness of itself and of the surrounding world. This is not strange, since both the body and the surrounding world belong to the same Being. We have seen that Merleau-Ponty applies this general truth to all the forms of our perceptive knowledge. Our vision is co-extensive with all visible reality.

Being and Language.   In the same way our speaking is a particular manner of being which is co-extensive with all reality.[197] In language Being becomes aware of itself in a new manner. The word "awareness" can be used to express what happens in vision and what happens in speech, but in both cases the same word has a different meaning. Both in vision and in speech Being finds an access to itself, but on a different level. Our vision is the actualization of the visibility of Being; our speech embodies the actualization of the intelligibility of Being.[198] In our vision Being sees itself; in our language Being understands itself.

---

[196] "Il y a une essence au-dessous de nous, nervure commune du signifiant et du signifié." *V.I.,* p. 158.

[197] "La parole . . . est donc une certaine région dans l'univers de significations, aussi organe ou résonateur de toutes les autres, et, par là, coextensive au pensable." *Ibid.*

[198] Language is "l'asile du monde intelligible." *Ibid.*

Our vision presupposes the visibility of Being and our language presupposes its intelligibility. Visibility is both presupposed and actualized by vision; intelligibility likewise is both presupposed and actualized by human speech.

Being is intelligible because it has a structure which penetrates all particular beings. All particular beings are "deflections" (*écarts*) of Being in general. Being in general is not separated, of course, from particular beings. The visible in general is not separated from concrete visible things, but it reveals itself in all of them and makes them cohere. Similarly, Being reveals itself in all particular beings, in all its "deflections" (*écarts*). There is an "essence" in the things themselves. Their essence is the interior coherence of the things, their intrinsic togetherness. This coherence is just as real as their distinction. Their distinction could not exist without their coherence. For their coherence constitutes their visibility and their intelligibility.

To enclose the world of speech within itself is a serious error. This is the mistake made by linguistic analysis and all positivism of language. Philosophers and scientists who approach language this way seek the exact meaning of our words; they try to get a perfect grasp of the meanings of their words. But, according to Merleau-Ponty, those ideas which I possess in a complete way are no longer real ideas.[199] They have lost contact with the essence they must express. They are cut off from Being. If we make the meaning of our words too precise we lose their real meaning.

What is the essence of which Merleau-Ponty speaks? It is the coherence of different beings, the unity which reveals itself within the plurality of things. We saw some examples of this in our commentary on the chapter *"L'Entrelacs—le Chiasme."* The world is essentially visible, and visibility connects the body and all worldly things. The reversibility of all forms of perception is another "essence." Our perception is essentially reflective, because we are "perceiving perceptibles." Essences belong to the silent world, to "savage Being."

We can make use of language and still not speak in the full sense of the word. This happens when we use the "spoken word." We are then repeating and making precise what has already been really said. We place ourselves within the world of speech and of constituted meanings.

---

[199] "Les idées trop possedées ne sont plus des idées." *V.I.,* p. 159.

We take the world of speech and the field of meanings for granted.   In this case we speak about meanings without knowing that meanings are really the translation of the silent world into speech.   The "speaking word" embodies the deepest reality of speech.   In the "speaking word" we presuppose, of course, the world of words and the field of meanings; but we approach them as the expression of the silent world, and we live in the act of expression.   We try to transform the essence into meaning. This is the definition of philosophy: our endeavor to transform "essence" into meaning.[200]

There is no immediate vision of essences.   Sometimes philosophers are under the illusion that immediate knowledge is possible, that the philosopher can withdraw from the world of speech and immediately view the silent world.[201]   This is absolutely impossible.   It is through language that the philosopher must view the ultimate reality, the silent world, the essences.   The philosopher can, consequently, make two mistakes.   He can have the illusion of immediate contact with the silent world, or he can enclose himself within meanings which have already been constituted by speech.[202]   According to Merleau-Ponty, these are two forms of positivism.[203]   In both cases we ignore the essential function of language.   Language is the mediation between the silent world and the field of meanings.[204]   There is an essential coherence between them; the silent world becomes meaningful to the philosopher in the mediation of language.

Thus philosophical truth is embodied in language.   Truth, consequently, cannot be immediate and cannot coincide with Being.   Language mediates between Being and truth.   In language we contact

---

[200] "Comme le monde est derrière mon corps, l'essence opérante est derrière la parole opérante aussi, celle qui possède moins la signification qu'elle n'est possédée par elle, qui n'*en* parle pas, mais *la* parle, ou parle *selon* elle ou la laisse parler et se parler en moi, perce mon présent." *V.I.*, p. 158.

[201] "Ce que nous proposons là et opposons à la recherche de l'essence n'est pas le retour à l'immédiat, la coïncidence, la fusion effective avec l'existant, la recherche d'une intégrité originelle, d'un secret perdu." *V.I.*, p. 162.

[202] "On se tromperait autant à définir la philosophie comme recherche des essences et comme fusion avec les choses, et les deux erreurs ne sont pas si différentes." *V.I.*, pp. 168–169.

[203] "Ce sont là deux positivismes." *V.I.*, p. 169.

[204] "Soit qu'on s'installe au niveau des énoncés, qui sont l'ordre propre des essences, ou dans le silence des choses, soit qu'on se fie absolument à la parole, ou qu'au contraire on s'en défie absolument,—l'ignorance du problème de la parole est ici celle de toute médiation." *Ibid.*

Being, but always at a certain distance.[205]   The immediate involvement in Being is dissolved as soon as we speak about it, and yet we are still in contact with it.   We transform essence into meaning, and yet essence and meaning will never be identical.   Meaning is *expressed Being*.   Because we are involved in Being, Being always exceeds us; Being is never perfectly captured in our meanings although our meanings express Being.[206]   If we really speak, viz., if we speak in contact with Being, we always say more than we know.   What we say exceeds our words, for in what we say there are lateral aspects which are not said.   The essence is revealed in such a way that it is hidden at the same time.   Philosophy, therefore, can never come to an end.   Being will never be completely translated into the world of speech.   There would be nothing more to say if we could translate the world of silence completely into the world of speech.   The mistake of some analytic philosophers is that they enclose the world of speech within itself, as if it spoke only of itself.   It speaks of the silent world of Being.[207]

[205] "Il faudrait revenir à cette idée de la proximité par distance." *V.I.*, p. 170.

[206] "Le dévoilement d'un Être qui n'est pas posé, parce qu'il n'a pas besoin de l'être, parce qu'il est silencieusement derrière toutes nos affirmations, négations, et même derrière toutes nos questions formulées." *V.I.*, p. 171.

[207] "La philosophie est la reconversion du silence et de la parole l'un dans l'autre." *Ibid.*

CHAPTER FOUR

LANGUAGE, PHILOSOPHY, BEING

Introduction

In the first chapter we examined the self-criticism of Merleau-Ponty in order to get an idea of the changes in his philosophical approach. It became clear that during the last years of his life he denied the original character of the subject-object relationship, and he rejected the "silent cogito" insofar as it implies such a relationship. In our second chapter we examined *"L'Entrelacs—le Chiasme,"* the main part of *The Visible and the Invisible.* If the book had been finished, other parts might perhaps have been more important, but it makes no sense to measure the existing text against a non-existing criterion. Consequently, we inquired into *"L'Entrelacs—le Chiasme"* to give us some idea of Merleau-Ponty's new philosophy. Furthermore, he criticized science and some philosophical trends of thought in the light of his new awareness, and we examined this criticism in our third chapter.

In the Introduction we promised a final chapter that would explain some of the important aspects of Merleau-Ponty's new philosophy. The themes we have chosen are stated in the title of the present chapter: language, philosophy, Being. It would have been possible, of course, to chose other themes, but we have selected those which occur most frequently in Merleau-Ponty's text.[1] The coherence of these three themes can be expressed in one brief sentence: the philosopher speaks of Being.

It will be quite difficult to write a commentary on language, philosophy and Being in the new perspective of Merleau-Ponty. He planned to write a separate chapter on language, and in a note he expressed the hope that toward the end of his book he might be able to say what philosophy is. We cannot, therefore, give a complete synthesis

---

[1] The body is another obvious theme. Merleau-Ponty developed this theme in *"L'Entrelacs—le Chiasme."* We have explained his new approach to the human body in our commentary on this chapter.

of Merleau-Ponty's new conception of language, philosophy and Being, simply because this conception does not exist. There is, however, a large number of texts which give us some idea of Merleau-Ponty's thought. Although these texts embody one fundamental attitude of mind, they are spread throughout the book and do not constitute a whole. The same points are often stressed in different contexts. We will try to formulate the ideas presented in these texts.

1. Language

A. MERLEAU-PONTY AND "POSITIVISM OF LANGUAGE"

Three currents of thought, at this moment of history, dominate Western philosophy, namely, linguistic analysis, Marxism and phenomenology. It is dangerous, of course, to make such a statement, because any enumeration of philosophical currents is always simplistic and never complete. It can hardly be denied, however, that the three currents we have indicated are important on today's philosophical scene. Merleau-Ponty explicitly and repeatedly confronted Marxism, although in his last book he seldom mentions it. What was his attitude toward linguistic analysis? Shortly before his death he attended a congress treating the relationship between linguistic analysis and phenomenology, and he was pressed to give his opinion on this topic. He refused to do so.[2] But in his last book he repeatedly, though vaguely, speaks of the approach of analytic philosophy.

We think that there are two reasons why Merleau-Ponty hesitated to make a public statement on the relationship between linguistic analysis and phenomenology. First of all, there are no indications that he made an intensive and detailed study of linguistic analysis.[3] Secondly, he was in the process of revising his own philosophy of language and he had not yet achieved this revision. He probably felt himself insufficiently prepared to make a public statement.

It is not possible, therefore, to exactly describe Merleau-Ponty's attitude toward linguistic analysis, but the available texts enable us to suggest the direction of his thought in this matter. In *The Visible and the Invisible* he often speaks of language, and he consistently sets himself

---

[2] We received this information from a person who was present at this congress.

[3] In his notes he often mentioned the books he was currently reading. There is no mention of his reading the actual texts of analytic philosophers.

in opposition to a philosophy of language which he indicates with terms such as "positivism of language," "linguistic analysis" or "analytic thought." The inconsistency of his terminology is another indication that he did not thoroughly examine linguistic analysis but opposed a general style of thinking. His rejection—insofar as there is a rejection —is not the result of a patient analysis of the current of thought he opposes, but arises out of his own positive position.

The Realm of Significations. Merleau-Ponty recognizes that language constitutes a realm of ideal objects.[4] Although he sometimes speaks of "pre-linguistic significations,"[5] he usually reserves the term "signification" for the ideal objects constituted by language. Language, and especially the abstract language of science, transforms perceptive meaning into an ideal object; this ideal object is a "signification." One of Merleau-Ponty's main problems is the possibility of this transformation.

The "ideal object" is not an original datum precisely because it is constituted by language. This is one reason why Merleau-Ponty rejects the eidetic reduction of Husserl. For this reduction pretends to arrive at an original datum, but in fact it arrives at something constituted. Merleau-Ponty does not give a description of the ideal object, of the signification. He says only that it is situated in a realm of "pure ideality" (*idéalité pure*). And he opposes the "ideality of horizon" (*idéalité d'horizon*) to "pure ideality." Visible reality has, as we have seen, an invisible aspect. There are "ideas" which are and will always remain connected with perceptible reality, for example, musical ideas. But there also are ideas freed from the horizon of perceptible reality. They are "ideas of intelligence" (*idées de l'intelligence*), i.e., the objects of our abstract intellection. These ideas are general in another way. There is a "natural generality" in our body which as a perceiving perceptible, is co-extensive with all perceptible reality. The "natural generality" of our body does not imply, however, that it surveys all perceptible reality. This is impossible, because our body is involved in perceptible reality. Our ideas have a "created generality"—a term

---

[4] "Certes, c'est une question de savoir comment s'instaurent par là-dessus les 'idées de l'intelligence', comment de l'idéalité d'horizon on passe à l'idéalité pure." *V.I.,* p. 200. "L'idéalité pure n'est pas elle-même sans chair . . . La visibilité . . . changeait de chair, abandonnant celle du corps pour celle du langage." *V.I.,* p. 200.

[5] *V.I.,* p. 225.

Merleau-Ponty uses in the text just quoted.[6] He probably means a
constituted generality which is not given by our involvement in Being,
but by the abstraction of our intellect. Merleau-Ponty recognizes the
existence of general ideas which have been freed from the horizon of
perceptible reality.

Merleau-Ponty speaks of that philosophy which focuses its attention
on ideal objects, on the signification of words, on the verbal substitute of
the perceived world.[7] According to this philosophy our primary task
would be to define the significations of words. All important philosophical words would have their own significations, and the philosopher
would be speaking vaguely as long as he failed to define them.

Philosophy and Ideal Significations. Although Merleau-Ponty accepts the existence of ideal significations, he refuses the thesis that the
primary task of philosophy is to define them.[8] This seems rather strange.
If one admits the existence of abstract significations and if the
philosopher uses them, it seems obvious that they are to be defined.
Their definition seems to be the first task of the philosopher. All
through philosophy's history, those who recognized the existence of ideal
objects always were inclined to focus their attention on them. Merleau-
Ponty takes a most remarkable and exceptional stand; he recognizes the
existence of ideal objects, but refuses to give them central importance.

The ideal signification is, for Merleau-Ponty, the expression of a
preceding meaning situated within the perceptive field. Although
Merleau-Ponty calls the eidetic reduction a myth and although he rejects
Husserl's phenomenological reduction which brackets Being, his own
philosophy has remained reductive. Philosophy is, according to him,
awareness of the source or the origin of all meaning. The mathematician and the scientist who think within the field of ideal meanings may

---

[6] *V.I.,* p. 200.

[7] "Mais la philosophie n'est pas un lexique, elle ne s'intéresse pas aux
'significations des mots', elle ne cherche pas un substitut verbal du monde." *V.I.,*
p. 18.

[8] "La question sur le sens d'être est si peu soluble par une définition des mots,
—que l'on tirerait de l'étude du langage, de ses pouvoirs et des conditions
effectives de son fonctionnement—, qu' au contraire elle reparaît dans l'étude du
langage, qui n'en est qu'une forme particulière; on ne peut ramener la
philosophie à une analyse linguistique qu'en supposant que le langage a son
évidence en lui-même, que la signification du mot 'monde' ou 'chose' n'offre en
principe aucune difficulté, que les règles de l'emploi legitime du mot sont lisibles
en toute clarté dans une signification univoque." *V.I.,* p. 131.

forget the source of those meanings; the philosopher may not forget. As we will see, philosophy is an expression, even a creative expression—Merleau-Ponty calls philosophy an art—but the philosopher is not allowed to forget the source of his own creative expression. Philosophy *is* awareness of its own origin.[9]

This explanation, however, seems to be insufficient. There is an obvious objection: if the philosopher has any hope of revealing the source and the origin of all meaning, he must do so by speaking of that source. But he then transforms the source into an ideal meaning. There is, consequently, no opposition between the process of idealization and the awareness of the origin of thought. In the idealization itself the philosopher becomes aware of the origin of thought.

There must be a deeper reason why Merleau-Ponty rejects the analysis of ideal meanings as the proper method of philosophy. Although he did not live long enough to clearly answer the question implied here in his philosophy, we find in his works some points which allow us to construct at least a possible answer.

We can speak of everything. Language is *partie totale,* a "total part," precisely because we can express everything in words. Nevertheless, we cannot express everything equally well in words. Mathematics and the natural sciences are very successful in the verbal expression of their objects. They are, therefore, easily inclined to idealization. But we have seen in our second chapter that there are also ideas which cannot be adequately expressed in words, for example, artistic ideas. Real ideas exist in music, in painting. We speak of those ideas; e.g., Proust speaks of the *petite mélodie.* But here our words are highly inadequate. Words do not mean anything at all to those who do not first grasp these ideas in their fleshy existence. These ideas cannot be freed from perceptible matter; we contact them in our perception. We can speak of them only if we have already experienced them in their fleshy existence. We cannot transform these ideas into ideal objects, into "pure ideality."

It is evident that language functions differently in mathematics and in natural sciences than in the realm of artistic ideas. Language does not transform appearing reality into ideal objects equally well in all fields. But how does language function in philosophy?

---

[9] ". . . d'en parler non pas selon la loi des significations inhérentes au langage donné, mais par un effort, peut-être difficile, qui les emploie à exprimer, au-delà d'elles-mêmes, notre contact muet avec les choses, quand elles ne sont pas encore des choses dites." *V.I.,* p. 61.

The Function of Language in Philosophy. We noted already Merleau-Ponty's distinction between frontal and marginal aspects of appearing reality. The frontal aspect can be called "figure" and the marginal aspects the "field" in which the figure appears. (The distinction between "figure" and "field" was made by Edgar Rubin.) Philosophy inquires into the marginal aspects of appearing reality. Its object does not appear directly but co-appears in everything that appears. We will elaborate on this point in the next section. The final object of philosophy is Being. Being appears in everything, but we are never directly confronted with Being. Philosophy is interested in our access to Being. But we *are* this access. We cannot capture our access to Being in an abstract idea, at least not adequately.

The object of philosophical research not only precedes our language, but also exceeds it. The philosopher can create ideal meanings and idealizations; but the reality which he intends to express in such idealizations always exceeds them. Philosophical speech is more adequate than the verbal expression of artistic ideas, but not as successful as the language of mathematics and natural science. When we speak of music and painting our words mean *nothing* if we have not already perceived these realities. Here our words express a contact which has been already effected and which does not depend upon words. On the other hand, the idealizations of mathematics and natural science constitute the object of these sciences. Without idealizations their object simply does not exist; thus the immense importance of idealization in the fields of mathematics and natural science. The function of philosophical language is situated between these two extremes.

Merleau-Ponty is convinced that the philosopher can speak, and even must speak, in order to illuminate his object. The philosopher constructs his own idealizations, his own ideal objects. But Merleau-Ponty is also convinced that philosophical idealizations are highly inadequate and do not comprehend what they want to express. The philosopher will never find Being *in* his idealizations, at least not adequately and completely. His idealizations do express something of the reality which interests the philosopher; otherwise philosophical speech would be useless. But his concepts will never capture his object, which is more than just an object. The philosopher views Being, and Being cannot be reduced to a number of verbal significations.[10]

This is why Merleau-Ponty rejects "positivism of language" and "analytic philosophy." Philosophy has its own ideal objects, its own

---

[10] "L'Être n'est pas fait d'idéalisations ou de choses dites." *V.I.,* p. 129.

idealizations. But if the philosopher considers the analysis and clarification of these idealizations as his main task, he will miss the reality which should attract him.[11]

Philosophical language does not fully capture what it expresses. While it certainly makes possible communication between philosophers, it also presupposes the communication which it develops.[12] Philosophers speak, not only of what they know, but also of what they do not know and continue not to know, even as they are speaking.[13] On this point we can compare the vision of our mind with the vision of our eyes. Remarkably enough, philosophers have always used the word "vision" in this double sense,[14] and furthermore, the expression "the eye of the mind" is quite common.[15] We must see with our eyes in order to see with our mind.[16] Just as visible reality is greater than our scene, so too Being exceeds our idealizations. In both cases we must confess: I belong to it. Our seeing participates in the visible world; and the philosopher, likewise, is involved in the object of his inquiry.[17] Philosophical speech is an inadequate translation of a reality which is already there.[18] It relates us to something to which we are already related.[19]

---

[11] "L'examen des significations en elles-mêmes nous donnerait le monde réduit à nos idéalisations et à notre syntaxe. Mais, par ailleurs, ce qu'elle trouve en revenant ainsi aux sources, elle (la philosophie) le dit." *V.I.,* pp. 138–139.

[12] *V.I.,* p. 229.

[13] ". . . on ne parle pas seulement de ce qu'on sait, comme pour en faire étalage,—mais aussi de ce qu' on ne sait pas, pour le savoir—, et que le langage se faisant exprime, au moins latéralement, une ontogénèse dont il fait partie." *V.I.,* p. 139.

[14] *V.I.,* p. 195.

[15] *V.I.,* p. 203.

[16] *V.I.,* p. 191.

[17] "Mais de quelque façon que nous ayons finalement à la (l'idéalité) comprendre, elle fuse déjà aux articulations du corps esthésiologique, aux contours des choses sensibles, et, si neuve qu'elle soit, elle se glisse par des voies qu'elle n'a pas frayées, transfigure des horizons qu'elle n'a pas ouverts." *V.I.,* p. 200.

[18] "Comprendre, c'est traduire en significations disponibles un sens d'abord captif dans la chose et dans le monde même. Mais cette traduction vise à rendre le texte; ou plutôt le visible et l'explicitation philosophique ne sont pas coté à coté comme deux ensembles de signes, comme un texte et sa version dans une autre langue. . . . La philosophie de son coté est plus et moins qu'une traduction, plus, puisqu'elle seule nous dit ce qu'il veut dire, moins, puisqu'elle est inutilisable si l'on ne dispose pas du texte." *V.I.,* p. 58.

Elsewhere Merleau-Ponty warns us against taking language to be a type of literal translation: "Si nous chassons de notre esprit l'idée d'un *texte original* dont notre langage serait la traduction ou la version chiffrée. . . ." *Signes,* p. 54.

[19] *V.I.,* p. 158.

Being exceeds philosophical speech just as the world exceeds my body.[20]

In the light of the foregoing, it is easier to see why for Merleau-Ponty the analysis of philosophical meanings is not the primary task of the philosopher.[21] Such analysis encloses us within the realm of inadequate meanings and makes us forget their inadequacy. It makes the ideal signification absolute; and we forget that the meaning (*sens*) is the source of the "signification."[22] Merleau-Ponty does not deny that philosophical speech brings some clarity into the philosophical field;[23] otherwise, he would not be writing. Philosophy creates its own idealizations.[24] But we must not forget the inadequacy of such philosophical clarity.

The Question: "What Do You Mean?" We can illustrate Merleau-Ponty's point by analyzing the simple question usually posed by representatives of analytic philosophy: "What do you mean?" They

---

[20] "Comme le monde est derrière mon corps, l'essence opérante est derrière la parole opérante." *V.I.*, p. 158.

[21] "Philosopher, ce n'est pas révoquer en doute les choses au nom des mots, comme si l'univers des choses dites était plus clair que celui des choses brutes, comme si le monde effectif était un canton du langage, la perception, une parole confuse et mutilée, la signification des mots, une sphère de positivité parfaitement rassurante. Or, la remarque ne porte pas seulement contre un positivisme du langage: elle atteint toute tentative pour chercher la source du sens dans les pures significations, même quand aucune mention n'est faite du langage." *V.I.*, p. 132.

[22] Cf. *Ibid.*

[23] "La Parole opérante est la région obscure d'où vient la lumière instituée." *V.I.*, p. 202.

"Le langage réalise en brisant le silence ce que le silence voulait et n'obtenait pas." *V.I.*, p. 230. Language gives a clarity which the silent world does not give.

"Sa description même du silence repose entièrement sur les vertus du langage." *V.I.*, p. 233.

Language is "prise de possession du monde du silence." *Ibid.*

". . . quand elle veut se saisir, non plus à travers un horizon et en vertu d'une institution de nature, mais directement et sans reste, alors tout ce qu'elle peut faire est de se sublimer en verbalisation." *V.I.*, p. 257. Verbalization brings about a clearer understanding.

"Elucidation des choses que nous savons." *V.I.*, p. 170.

There is no doubt that language brings a new clarity. Why, then, does Merleau-Ponty write: ". . . comme si l'univers des choses dites était plus clair que celui des choses brutes . . ." (*V.I.*, p. 132)? He wants to say that what is revealed by speech is already there in the "silent world," that there is no more evidence in the world of speech than in the "silent world." He does not deny, however, that the evidence exists in the world of speech in a new manner.

[24] "De l'idéalité d'horizon on passe à l'idéalité 'pure'." *V.I.*, p. 200.

claim that everyone who speaks, either as a scientist or as a philosopher, places himself in the clarity of ideal objects; they maintain that the density of Being is translated into the clarity of a "signification." They often forget, however, that, although it seems simple, their question is not simple at all. *Another person* asks me what *I* mean. This supposes two fundamental things: that I *mean* something, and that we both live in *the same field of meaning*.

How do I mean something? "To mean" is a transitive verb; whoever means, means something. What does my meaning refer to? Does it refer to my own interior life, to the real world, to an ideal object? All the fundamental questions of intentionality are present in the simple "what" of the question: "What do you mean?" It is precisely the mystery of man that he means. He does not exist as a stone which cannot mean. He is a worldly being which means, viz., which is not enclosed in itself. He means because he is the self-awareness of the world.[25] One could work out a phenomenological philosophy starting from the basic fact that man means.

The question: "What do you mean?" supposes, moreover, that the person who asks the question and the one who is interrogated live in the same field of meaning. *He* could not ask what *I* mean if both of us did not live in the same field of meaning. We both exist as beings who mean. It is supposed that we mean the same reality or, at least, that we should mean the same reality. As long as we do not mean the same reality we cannot really speak with one another. The basic fact of communication is supposed by the simple question: "What do you mean?" According to Merleau-Ponty, one of the aspects of perceptive faith is that we are convinced that we live in a real world which is also accessible to other persons.[26] This certainty of our perceptive faith is presupposed likewise by the linguistic analysts who ask: "What do you mean?" They presuppose this perceptive evidence but do not demonstrate it. In truth, it cannot be demonstrated because it is presupposed in every demonstration. The representatives of linguistic analysis try to situate themselves in the realm of the ideal objects. The fact, however, that ideal objects are common to many persons is—also for them—an hypothesis supported by perceptive faith. Our basic communication, our real togetherness in a world which is accessible to all of us is certainly

---

[25] "Il y a vision, toucher, quand un certain visible, un certain tangible, se retourne sur tout le visible, tout le tangible dont il fait partie." *V.I.,* p. 183.

[26] *V.I.,* pp. 25-27.

not an ideal object.[27] The realm of ideal objects does not explain the two basic aspects of the simple question, "What do you mean?", viz., that we are beings who mean and that we live in the same field of meanings.

B. LANGUAGE AND SILENCE

The attentive reader of *The Visible and the Invisible* will observe that Merleau-Ponty seldom speaks of language without speaking of silence and of the silent world.[28] His stress on the relationship between language and the world of silence is an important difference between his philosophy and the "positivism of language." It is very difficult, if not impossible, to say what the silent world is. By our very speaking of silence we break silence. How can the philosopher speak of the silent world in a meaningful way? Merleau-Ponty knows very well that the philosopher, as a philosopher, contacts the silent world through the mediation of language.[29] How can philosophical speech give us access to the silent world if speech breaks that silence?

We have seen how Merleau-Ponty answers this question: the philosopher must recognize the inadequacy of philosophical speech. The proper theme of philosophical speech is not the "figure" which stands out from the field, but the field itself; not the particular beings, but Being itself; not that which directly appears, but that which only co-appears. The philosopher transforms his theme into an object, because by speaking of something he transforms it into a reality spoken about, i.e., into an object. But the philosopher must know that his essential themes resist this objectification. They are and will always remain pre-objective. Still the philosopher has access to his themes through the mediation of language. How does philosophical speech make us aware of the silent world?

Saying the Ineffable. There is only one solution, viz., that philosophical speech has the paradoxical power to go beyond itself and preserve

---

[27] *V.I.*, p. 229.

[28] "We shall see that the idea of *complete* expression is nonsensical, and that all language is indirect or allusive—that it is, if you wish, silence." *Signs*, p. 43.

Merleau-Ponty's article, "Indirect Language and the Voices of Silence," (*Signs*, pp. 39-83) deals, however, with painting more than language.

[29] "Mais naïveté aussi d'un cogito silencieux qui se croirait adéquation à la conscience silencieuse alors que sa description même du silence repose entièrement sur les vertus du langage." *V.I.*, pp. 232-233.

silence. Notwithstanding the sound of speech, speech makes us aware of silence.[30]   One might object that it seems quite easy to contact the silent world.   Since speaking is a free human act, we can abstain from it, both exteriorly and interiorly.   I can look out of my window and see the buildings on the other side of the street and beyond them the South Hills of Pittsburgh, without saying even one word.   This objection is, however, very superficial and underestimates the influence of language.[31] It is true that I can see buildings, streets, cars, passengers, the river and hills without actually using words.   But language continues to influence me even when I do not actually use it.   I see something because my visual field is structured; and the structuring of my visual field is deeply influenced by language.   The fact that some things stand out in my field as figures and that other things do not depends on the way in which I have learned to speak.   Merleau-Ponty would not be aware of the silent world in the way he is if he did not speak of Being as he does.   How can the awareness of the silent world be actualized by speaking?

Reflection on the phenomenon of "ineffability" can help us to understand what Merleau-Ponty means.   Both philosophers and theologians have often spoken of "ineffability."   The Bible calls God ineffable. Philosophers who reflect on man often come to the awareness that man, too, cannot be fully expressed.   However, he who has scarcely learned to express himself has no right to say that some realities are ineffable.   The ineffability of reality becomes evident to those who have earnestly tried to express it.   We become aware of the ineffability of reality only in our endeavor to express it.   In our attempts at expression we become aware of the expressive power of language, and also of its inadequacy.

This experience is important for us.   By speaking we transform meanings into significations, make reality accessible in a new manner, transform the silent world into a world of speech.   The speaking person, however, does not contact only the realm of significations, of ideal objects, the world of speech; he also contacts the silent world.   He is aware of the fact that this silent world is expressed, but he also knows that it is not completely expressed because he knows the inadequacy of his own expressions.   We are often dissatisfied with our expressions and

---

[30] "Language is much more like a sort of being than a means, and that is why it can present something to us so well." *Signs*, p. 43.

[31] "Tout le paysage est envahi par les mots comme par une invasion, n'est plus à nos yeux qu'une variante de la parole, et parler de son 'style', c'est à nos yeux faire une métaphore." *V.I.*, p. 203.

look for new ones.   How can we do so if we do not know the inadequate character of our expressions?   We evidently are aware of reality, not only as it is expressed, but also as it is not yet expressed.   We come to this awareness in our expression itself.   We use mediating language, but we transcend the means, because we are aware of its limits.

The person who tries to express the silent world certainly views this silent world through the mediation of his expression; nevertheless, this mediation reveals the silent world as both expressed and as not yet expressed.   We must go even further: only the person who tries to express the silent world can know the silent world, precisely as silent. The awareness of the silent world is not diminished but increased by expression.   Those who best express reality know best its ineffability. Awareness of ineffability is not the opposite of expression but rather an essential aspect of it.

The awareness of ineffability is not the same in all forms of expression.   Mathematicians do not complain of the ineffability of their object.   They are not confronted with that density of Being which exceeds expression.   They construct their object almost entirely; mathematical entities are what mathematicians make them to be.   How then could they exceed the power of mathematical diction?   The artistic "ideas" of music and painting, on the contrary, are to the highest degree inexpressible.[32]   These few examples make it clear that the expressive force of our diction is not the same in different realms.

Philosophical expression is, according to Merleau-Ponty, highly inadequate.[33]   We have already seen the reasons for this inadequacy: philosophy speaks of that which only co-appears, the marginal aspects of appearing reality, the "field" in which all the "figures" appear.

---

[32] "L'explicitation ne nous donne pas l'idée même, elle n'en est qu'une version seconde, un dérivé plus maniable.   Swann peut bien serrer la 'petite melodie' entre les repères de la notation musicale, rapporter au faible écart entre les cinq notes qui la composent et au rappel constant de deux d'entre elles la 'douceur rétractée et frileuse' qui en fait l'essence ou le sens; au moment où il pense ces signes et ce sens, il n'a plus la 'petite phrase' elle-même, il n'a que 'de simples valeurs', substituées pour la commodité de son intelligence à la mysterieuse entité qu'il avait perçue." *V.I.,* p. 197.

[33] "C'est donc une question de savoir si la philosophie comme reconquête de l'être brut ou sauvage peut s'accomplir par les moyens du langage éloquent, ou s'il ne lui faudrait pas en faire un usage qui lui ôte sa puissance de signification immédiate ou directe pour l'égaler à ce qu'elle veut tout de même dire." *V.I.,* p. 139.

Philosophy speaks of Being which co-appears in all particular beings.[34] We cannot adequately grasp Being in the orderly world of speech.[35] Being remains silent even when we speak of it. Precisely in speaking of Being we become aware of its silence. The philosopher, as a philosopher, becomes aware of the silence of Being. This is why Merleau-Ponty uses the expression "savage Being." The philosopher adequately tries to grasp Being in his words, and he must do so; but in this endeavor he becomes aware of the inadequacy of his expression. Being cannot be completely grasped in the orderly world of speech. It remains silent and "savage."

The Inadequacy of Philosophical Speech. Here again Merleau-Ponty opposes "positivism of language" and analytic philosophy. The analytic philosopher says that the inadequacy of philosophical language is the fault of philosophers who have not yet learned to speak. Mathematicians and scientists have learned to speak, and therefore they do not complain of any inadequacy of their expressions. The philosopher's way of speaking, however, is still pre-scientific. He has not yet defined the meaning of his terms. His way of speaking is incoherent and often metaphorical. He does not sufficiently respect the iron laws of strict logic. If only the philosopher too would adapt himself to scientific speaking, he would no longer complain of such inadequacy. The silence of the philosophical field is due to the immaturity of philosophical speech.

Merleau-Ponty opposes this point of view. According to him philosophical speech is inadequate *in principle.* Philosophy cannot achieve the adequacy of mathematical speech. If it pretends to do so it denies its own essence.[36] Still the philosopher must speak, and he must do so in the best possible manner. His very speech is the awareness of silence, and he

---

[34] "Monde et Être."
"Leur rapport est celui du visible et de l'invisible (la latence), l'invisible n'est pas un autre visible ('possible' au sens logique) un positif seulement *absent.*"
"Il est *Verborgenheit* de principe, *i.e.,* invisible *du visible." V.I.,* p. 305.

[35] "L'idée du *chiasme,* c'est-à-dire: tout rapport à l'être est simultanement prendre et être pris, la prise est prise, elle est *inscrite* et inscrite au même être qu'elle prend."
"A partir de là, élaborer une idée de la philosophie: elle ne peut être prise totale et active, possession intellectuelle, puisque ce qu'il y a à saisir est une dépossession." *V.I.,* p. 319.

[36] "L'idée du chiasme et de *l'Ineinander,* c'est au contraire l'idée que toute analyse qui *démêle* rend inintelligible—Ceci lié au sens même de la *question* qui n'est pas d'appeler réponse à l'indicatif." *V.I.,* p. 322.

arrives at this awareness in his endeavor to speak. The improvement of his expression will not eliminate silence.

Merleau-Ponty does not place the silent world in the past.[37] One might well think that our world was silent before we began to speak, but that its silence has been progressively eliminated by speaking. The increase of speaking would be the diminution of silence. This view totally misses the point. What Merleau-Ponty calls "silence" is not simply the situation in which we are not yet speaking. Silence is much more than just the absence of speech; it is in speech that real silence comes to birth.[38] Silence belongs to the positive awareness which we achieve in expression. It implies that man transcends his expression, for he understands not only its expressive power but also its inadequacy. There is silence because man is not the victim of his expression. In positivism of language man does make himself the victim of his expression. Awareness of the inadequacy of language, awareness of silence, is a gain. Positivism impoverishes language. To confess that our language is inadequate is to see that Being exceeds us.

The philosopher is caught in a paradox. On the one hand, he recognizes that the inadequacy of his expression has a positive character; on the other, he continuously struggles to overcome this inadequacy. He tries to express Being, knowing that he will continue to fail. But his failure is not really a failure.[39] The philosopher would fail if he forgot the inadequacy of his expression. His awareness of this inadequacy is the most convincing proof that he really contacts Being.

The Essential Relationship of Language and Silence. Language and silence are not like two rivals struggling to occupy the same space. If they were, the increase of the one would mean the decrease of the other. Rather than being competitors, they develop together.[40] The philoso-

---

[37] This denial is implied in the fact that there is *réversibilité* between the world of speech and the world of silence. See *V.I.*, pp. 202-203.

[38] "Il n'y a pas à chercher des choses spirituelles, il n'y a que des structures du vide—Simplement je veux planter ce vide dans l'Être visible, montrer qu'il en est *l'envers*,—en particulier l'envers du langage." *V.I.*, p. 289. If "silence" is the "other side" of language, it supposes language and develops with language.

[39] "L'Être dont le langage est la maison ne peut se fixer, regarder, il n'est que de loin." *V.I.*, p. 267.

[40] "La philosophie, précisément comme 'Être parlant en nous', expression de l'expérience muette par soi, est création. Création qui est au même temps réintégration de l'Être." *V.I.*, p. 230.

pher is aware of the silence of Being to the degree that he succeeds in expressing Being. Expression does not reduce silence, but rather nourishes it. Silence is not the result of the failure, but of the success, of the expression. Our speaking is, indeed, *une partie totale,* a "total part." For it influences the way in which we are situated in our whole field of existence, even in those realms which seem to be quite independent of speech. There is, therefore, an essential interchange between silence and language; they actualize one another.[41]

This is the reason why Merleau-Ponty stresses his former distinction between "spoken word" and "speaking word."[42] If the philosopher reduces philosophical speaking to the "spoken word," he is no longer a real philosopher. He situates himself in the field of established meanings and by doing so reduces Being to the poverty and inadequacy of the "spoken word." This is also why Merleau-Ponty is afraid of any established terminology, of the "clutter" of concepts. As soon as we limit ourselves to an established terminology we forget "savage Being." Philosophy must be a "speaking word." Inadequate speaking must continually renew itself. The real wisdom of the philosopher implies the awareness of his ignorance. The philosopher is a person who cannot be satisfied. What he has said must always be said anew. Philosophical expression cannot be finally accomplished, because it can never overcome its inherent inadequacy.

Does philosophical speaking make sense if it never can be fully or finally accomplished? Philosophy is the developed awareness of our situation. We are situated; we "belong to Being," *j'en suis.* We will never be able to create a complete expression of the reality to which we belong and which, consequently, exceeds us. The awareness of this fundamental situation makes sense. We are the awareness of Being. Philosophy actualizes man, precisely as the awareness of Being.

We have developed a few aspects of the philosophy of language implied in *The Visible and the Invisible.* In the book as we have it, we find only incidental texts; the chapter on language was never written. Yet it has been possible to see the trend of thought. This trend of thought poses several questions, however. Possibly these questions

---

[41] This is implied in Merleau-Ponty's idea of *réversibilité.*
[42] Kwant, *The Phenomenological Philosophy of Merleau-Ponty,* pp. 53-54. Merleau-Ponty maintains this distinction, but he sometimes uses different terms to express it. He speaks, for example, of *"langage opérant et constitué."* (*V.I.,* pp. 201-202).

would have been answered had Merleau-Ponty completed the book. It is also quite possible that they would have remained unanswered. In his article, "The Philosopher and His Shadow," Merleau-Ponty says that every philosopher writes within a fundamental awareness which rules his expressions, but which is not itself expressed. This must be applied to Merleau-Ponty as well. Each philosophy implies some unanswered questions.

Critical Remarks. The essential relationship between language and silence is one of the basic insights of Merleau-Ponty. But he presupposes it and does not sufficiently explain it. While he explains to some extent why many forms of expression do not eliminate silence, he does not explain the essential interaction between them. He usually identifies "silent Being" and "savage Being." Since the term "savage Being" makes us think of something primitive which precedes the development of civilization, the identification of "silent Being" and "savage Being" could lead to a serious misunderstanding. One could think that "silent Being" is there before man begins to speak, that it is the primitive situation of man. Merleau-Ponty's rejection of current philosophical and scientific terminology favors the same misunderstanding. Does philosophical wisdom consist in returning to a primitive past in which Being has not yet been expressed?

This is certainly not the intention of Merleau-Ponty, although his terminology favors such a misunderstanding. He should have distinguished between the poverty of primitive silence and the richness of developed silence. Primitive silence precedes human expression, while developed silence is one of its most mature fruits. Merleau-Ponty often says that silence is the source of expression. This statement is too broad. Primitive silence is certainly not the source of philosophical expression. There are still some parts of the world where people live in a rather primitive silence. We cannot reasonably expect that they will publish important philosophical works. There is a most important distinction between the ignorance of primitive people and the *docta ignorantia* of learned and wise men. We must make the same distinction between primitive and developed silence. Merleau-Ponty does not do so and his statements, therefore, lose clarity and sharpness.

To distinguish primitive from developed silence is not sufficient either; we must also describe the nature and the origin of developed silence. Developed silence is one of the mature fruits of the labor of expression.

Merleau-Ponty calls silence the source of expression. His statement is correct, but he should have added that the expression nourishes its own source.

Merleau-Ponty does not explain, therefore, *how* human thought renews itself. He indicates the source of every renewal, namely, the silent world; but he does not explain how this renewal takes place. It would have been very significant had Merleau-Ponty elaborated this difficult problem. On every level of expression man continually renews himself. He does so on the level of science. At a certain moment in history man invents a scientific method and for some time develops it. But then he returns to the source and renews the fundamental line of his inquiry. Man does the same in art, in philosophy, in practice. How does man renew his access to Being? How does he become aware of the inadequacy of his former access? Merleau-Ponty says that the silent world is the source of every renewal but he does not explain how it is so. History teaches us that man renews his access to Being as he develops his expression. As long as man's expression was primitive it was also rather static. But there were also highly developed forms of expression which were equally static; we find many examples of this in the Eastern world. What is the origin of the rapid evolution of expressive life characteristic of the Western world? Is the silent world really the source of the rapid changes of the Western world? Does the silent world make modern man restless?

These questions Merleau-Ponty does not answer. His book is, as we have often said, incomplete. He could have answered in the chapters which have not been written. In his notes he sometimes anticipates what he intended to write, but even there we do not find the beginning of an answer.

Merleau-Ponty's notions of the silent world and of "savage Being" are certainly important, but they are not developed. They remain undefined. His last book *The Visible and the Invisible* seems to be a new start rather than the continuation of an established philosophy.

C. THE ONE-SIDEDNESS OF MERLEAU-PONTY'S APPROACH

We have written that there is a marked one-sidedness in Merleau-Ponty's approach.[43] His trend of thought is, and has remained, reductive. Convinced of the constituted character of our "lived" reality,

---

[43] Kwant, *op. cit.*, pp. 231-238.

he tries to return to our original awareness. We should not understand this in an historical sense. Merleau-Ponty is interested in the history of philosophy, but certainly not excessively; and, insofar as he pays attention to philosophers of the past, he is inclined to view their doctrine from the vantage point of today's problems. He has in view an origin which is still present.

An "Explosion" of Being. In a note of November, 1960, he wrote on evolution.[44] I doubt the perspective of evolution, he says. I want to replace it by a cosmology of visible reality. I place myself within time and space as they actually appear to me, and I do not raise the question of origin, of limits, of a series of events leading to a first cause. I am the witness of an enlightening explosion (*éclatement*) of Being which appears now, but which is always there. I must describe the world which is composed of "worldly beams" appearing everywhere. I try to overcome the choice between a temporal series, eternity and timeless ideality. I accept an existential eternity (the here and now as a contraction of space and time); I must stress the eternal body.[45]

We have given here a free translation of this remarkable text. Merleau-Ponty sees a source, an origin, working here and now, but which at the same time reveals something eternal. He is interested neither in a series of events extended in time, nor in timeless eternity or ideality. He is a witness of the "explosion" of Being, and this event is enlightening. Yes, it takes place here and now, but it does not reveal only what is happening here and now.[46] Merleau-Ponty is interested in

---

[44] *V.I.*, pp. 318-319.

[45] "Je révoque en doute la perspective évolutioniste; je la remplace par une cosmologie du visible en ce sens que, considérant l'endotemps et l'endoespace, il n'y a plus pour moi question des origines, ni de limites, ni de séries d'événements allant vers cause première, mais un seul éclatement d'Être qui est à jamais. Décrire le monde des 'rayons de monde' par delà toute alternative sérial-éternitaire ou idéal—Poser l'éternité existentielle—le corps éternel." *V.I.*, p. 318.

[46] He stresses the same point in a later note: "La nature est au premier jour: elle y est aujourd'hui. Cela ne veut pas dire: mythe de l'indivision originaire et coïncidence comme *retour*."
"*L'Urtümlich*, l'*Ursprünglich* n'est pas d'autrefois."
"Il s'agit de trouver dans le présent, la chair du monde (et non dans le passé) un 'toujours neuf' et 'toujours le même'—Une sorte de temps de sommeil (qui est la durée naissante de Bergson, toujours neuve et toujours la même). Le sensible, la Nature, transcendent la distinction passé présent, réalisent un passage par le dedans de l'un dans l'autre Eternité existentielle."
"L'indéstructible, le Principe barbare." *V.I.*, pp. 320-321.

the development of Being as it takes place in us, before our eyes, so that we can actually witness it.

This development of Being should not be understood teleologically.[47] Continuing to reflect upon his own philosophy, Merleau-Ponty explicitly says this. I am not a teleological thinker, he says, *"parce qu'il y a déhiscence, et non production positive."* By the term *production positive* Merleau-Ponty means a type of development in which the preceding reality makes us absolutely sure of what follows. One who understands the antecedent knows the consequent. There is a causal process which excludes all surprise. The development of Being is not such a production. Being does not produce the human body in this way, nor does the human body thus produce perception and thought. There is, on the contrary, *déhiscence,* i.e., blossoming, burgeoning, efflorescence. Being unfolds its potentialities, its hidden possibilities. We do not know and we can not know what will be. There is an element of surprise in the development of Being as there is an element of surprise in the awakening of nature in the springtime.

Man is not the result of the body, continues Merleau-Ponty, nor is the organized body the result of its components. That which is lower develops of itself, but this development is not isolated; it is poised in the emptiness of the new future which is coming into existence. The inferior and the superior level of Being gravitate around each other. They cohere with each other, and yet we cannot say that the former causes the latter. In this note Merleau-Ponty points out a relationship between two distinctions which he regularly uses separately. We have often mentioned the one distinction between the "two sides" of corporal reality; the invisible is the "other side" of the visible. He frequently makes another distinction between lower and higher levels of Being. Now he relates these two distinctions.[48] He seems to mean that the "other side" of visible Being reveals itself on the higher level of Being.

---

[47] "Je ne suis pas finaliste parce qu'il y a déhiscence, et non production positive,—à travers finalité du corps,—d'un homme dont notre perception et notre pensée prolongeraient l'organisation téléologique." *V.I.,* p. 319.

[48] "L'homme n'est pas la *fin* du corps, ni le corps organisé la *fin* des composants: mais plutôt le subordonné chaque fois bascule dans le vide d'une nouvelle dimension ouverte, l'inférieur et le supérieur gravitent autour l'un de l'autre, comme *le haut et le bas* (variantes du rapport coté-autre coté)—Au fond j'entraîne la distinction haut-bas dans le tourbillon où elle rejoint la distinction coté-autre coté où les deux distinctions s'intègrent à une *dimensionnalité universelle* qui est l'Être (Heidegger)." *Ibid.*

The invisibility of corporal Being reveals itself in human perception and human thought, and this "other side" of corporal Being bears a promise of a higher level of existence, which promise is fulfilled as Being develops itself.

Our explanation is not well defined. But we are commenting upon a text which itself is condensed and undefined. In this text Merleau-Ponty meditates on the structure of his own thought. He establishes three fundamental facts. First, he is interested in a development of Being that does not belong to the past but takes place here and now. Second, this development is not a causal process. The lower level does not completely *explain* the higher level. There is an essential element of surprise in the development of Being. Third, the higher level of Being announces itself in the "other side," in the "invisible aspect" of the lower level. Being, concludes Merleau-Ponty, has many dimensions. The development of Being is a revelation of the many dimensions of Being. It is not accidental that Merleau-Ponty mentions Bergson in several notes. His trend of thought is reminiscent of Bergson's philosophy, although the continuity of Being is stronger in Merleau-Ponty's philosophy than in the perspective of Bergson.

Now we can better understand the relationship of the silent world to the world of speech. The world of speech, the realm of ideal objects, is a revelation of the silent world.[49] The world of speech is new and on a higher level. But at the same time it reveals the silent world.

Metaphysical Self-Transcendence. The vision Merleau-Ponty explains in this note of 1960 does not belong exclusively to the last period of his life. It is implicit in one of the basic notions of his first period, the notion of the "movement of transcendence" (*mouvement de transcendance*). Merleau-Ponty conceived man as a movement which continually transcends itself. There is, however, a new element in the perspective of *The Visible and the Invisible.* Merleau-Ponty at first considered the "movement of transcendence" to be characteristic of *human life.* The world is involved, of course, in this movement, but only insofar as it is the field of human existence. Man cannot develop without the world. But the "movement of transcendence" had its center in man. Now, however, *the "movement of transcendence" belongs to*

---

[49] "La philosophie. . . . non pas comme recherche d'un invariant du langage, d'un essence lexicale, mais comme recherche d'un invariant du silence. . . ." *V.I.,* p. 314.

Being. Being transcends itself in man, and man transcends himself in the thinking person. Being sees in man, perceives in man, thinks in man, speaks in man.[50] The "movement of transcendence" now has a metaphysical character. Merleau-Ponty's philosophy has become a dynamic metaphysics.

In our first book on Merleau-Ponty we emphasized the unilateral character of his philosophy. Man is a "movement of transcendence." Man's potentialities are revealed on the higher levels of human existence. If this is true, the obvious thing to do is to analyze these higher levels. We must stress, as Merleau-Ponty does, that they develop out of the lower levels. We must approach the higher levels of human existence as the fruits of the "movement of transcendence." Merleau-Ponty's reductive approach, though necessitated by the "movement of transcendence," is not sufficient. On its lower level the "movement of transcendence" is loaded with potentialities, virtualities which cannot be understood on the lower level itself, precisely because they are hidden there. They are revealed only on the higher level of human existence. Thus the base of man's self-transcending movement reveals something of the higher levels, but the higher levels, too, reveal more of the lower ones.

It is strange that Merleau-Ponty does not analyze the intrinsic character of the higher levels of human existence. He speaks of them, but only in order to stress that they are the fruit of man's self-transcending movement. When Merleau-Ponty speaks of thought in *Phenomenology of Perception,* he does not analyze its inner nature, he always stresses that thought is rooted in perception. He does not analyze what freedom is in itself either. This method is unilateral and, as such, is alien to the deepest insight of Merleau-Ponty himself. The highest fruits of man's self-transcending movement are the clearest revelations of what this movement finally is.

Reduction of Light to Darkness. We stressed that Merleau-Ponty's approach shares in a general trend of thought which tends to reduce light to darkness. One of the most important realizations of the last century is the rootedness of man's spiritual life in the darkness of body and matter. Descartes considered the human spirit an absolute "substance,"

---

[50] "Que c'est l'être qui parle en nous et non nous qui parlons de l'être." *V.I.,* p. 247. Merleau-Ponty adds in a note: "Finalement il y a quelque chose de profond chez Ruyer quand il dit que l'en soi et le pour soi sont même chose. Mais à ne pas comprendre comme: les choses sont des âmes." *Ibid.,* note.

and he wondered about its relationship to the body. Descartes represented that type of spiritual thinking which opposed the corporal and spiritual orders. Modern thought has realized that our spiritual life is rooted in body and matter, and that it cannot be completely understood in itself. This awareness is implied in Marx's infrastructural style of thinking. Marx did not deny that man thinks, but he stressed that human thought is rooted in the infrastructure of human life. Taking a different approach, Freud came to the same awareness. He analyzed man's spiritual life, his attitude toward other persons, and the manner in which the person situates himself; he discovered that man is less spiritual than he often thinks himself to be, that the so-called light of human life is rooted in the darkness of instincts. Although the philosophy of Marx and the psychoanalysis of Freud were indignantly rejected by many Western thinkers, their influence has been extremely strong. Another style of thinking, evolutionary thought, also fostered the development of modern thought. When Darwin published his *Origin of Species,* the book became a scandal. Now the awareness that man is the result of evolution has become quite common. We have become aware of the fact that man's spirit is not a datum which is absolutely independent of matter. We do not deny the spirit of man, but we refuse to affirm that it is a reality completely alien to matter. There is a general tendency to stress the continuity of Being.

Merleau-Ponty shares in this general movement of thought. He denies the independence of human spirit. He does not deny the spirit itself but considers the spirit rooted in body and matter. He always stresses this continuity. He emphasizes that human thought is rooted in perception, that freedom is not absolute, that language is rooted in silence. For him the light of spiritual life is rooted in the darkness of matter. The human spirit is not an absolute light, nor is matter absolute darkness, for matter too has "another side," a "spiritual side."

The human spirit is, at once, both rooted in body and matter—in Being—and, at the same time, the most remarkable revelation of Being, body and matter. There is no other reality which reveals more of the self-transcending movement of Being. It seems obvious, therefore, that we should analyze first of all the inner character of man's spiritual life, of thinking, of human language. By such analysis we could become aware of the richest character of Being.

It seems that in his philosophy of language, Merleau-Ponty should first of all have analyzed language. In language the ideal aspect of reality, he says, does not leave the body and the world, but receives a new body. What is this body? The fact that meaning obtains a new body implies, of course, that meaning begins to exist in a new manner. What is this new existence of meaning? The general style of Being is expressed in universal concepts. What is a concept, what is universality? We do not yet know what universality is if we know only that it is the expression of the general style of Being. Language presupposes human communication but, at the same time, it renews this communication. It is necessary to examine this renewal. Merleau-Ponty always maintains that language is rooted in something which precedes it, but he does not analyze the positive essence of language.

Merleau-Ponty makes a valuable contribution to the philosophy of language both in his earlier works and in *The Visible and the Invisible*. But his philosophy was and remains reductive. Perhaps this criticism is unjust, because we do not know how Merleau-Ponty would have developed if he had finished his work. However, in his earlier writings and in the published part of his last book, he always follows the reductive method. His notes give us some hints as to how he would have continued *The Visible and the Invisible*. They predict no profound change in Merleau-Ponty's philosophical approach.

We repeat that this one-sidedness does not agree with some fundamental viewpoints of Merleau-Ponty himself. The "enlightening explosion" of Being is a progressive revelation of Being. What Being really is becomes more manifest in the higher self-revelations of Being. The source enlightens that which proceeds from it, but the results of the self-transcending movement of Being more thoroughly enlighten the source.

2. *Philosophy*

A. PHILOSOPHY AS QUESTIONING

Saint Augustine characterized philosophy in his famous remark about time: when someone asks me whether I know what time is, I answer in the affirmative; but when he continues and asks me to say what time is, I do not know.[51] Philosophy reflects on the most common realities, such as time, space, world, Being and knowledge. They are taken for granted in ordinary life, and to a certain extent in science as well. When I arrive in a strange city without knowing where I am or what time it is, almost every citizen can tell me where I am and what time it is. The

---

[51] *V.I.*, p. 17.

philosopher, however, does not take these basic certainties for granted, but asks what it means to be in space, in time, in the world, in Being.[52] In doing so, he discovers that the so-called clarity is not clarity at all. Thus he tries to redefine our most basic notions and invents new words in order to understand them.[53] In the philosopher's reflection on the most basic aspects of human life, those which generally seem to be clear appear to be most mysterious. The philosopher is expected to transform darkness into light, but in fact he often transforms light into darkness. Hence philosophy has always been distrusted.[54] Socrates, who dethroned the "gods of the city," remains the prototype of the philosopher. Socrates did not simply deny the idols of the city but claimed to understand them better than most people. By not taking them for granted he indeed destroyed their absolute character.[55]

The World. Our perception reveals the world and in this world we do not observe only isolated facts. Everywhere we see coherence and connections. Thus our perception occasions our faith in that coherent Nature which is present in everything. The basic words of Greek philosophy, such as *Physis* and *Kosmos,* embodied this certainty. We easily believe that our perception is also assumed into this coherent Nature;[56] we are also inclined to explain our human life starting from Nature. Coherence is taken for granted, and we wonder only when incoherence appears. We presume that the incoherence is only apparent and that it will eventually be dissolved into the coherence of Nature. Today we have broken with this blind belief, and we wonder how it is possible that the things we perceive constitute a world, and how we belong to this world. We ask, What does the word "world" mean?[57]

---

[52] *V.I.,* pp. 142-144.

[53] "Revoir et redéfinir les notions les mieux fondées, d'en créer de nouvelles, avec des mots nouveaux pour les désigner." *V.I.,* p. 17.

[54] ". . . qui viennent ranimer la mauvaise humeur séculaire contre la philosophie, le grief qu'on lui a toujours fait de renverser les rôles du clair et de l'obscur." *V.I.,* p. 18.

[55] Kwant, *The Phenomenological Philosophy of Merleau-Ponty,* pp. 81-82.

[56] "Parce que la perception nous donne foi en un monde, en un système de faits naturels rigoureusement lié et continu, nous avons cru que ce système pourrait s'incorporer toutes choses et jusqu'à la perception qui nous y a initiés." *V.I.,* pp. 46-47.

[57] "La tâche s'impose donc à nous de comprendre si, et en quel sens, ce qui n'est pas nature forme un 'monde' et d'abord ce que c'est qu'un 'monde' et enfin, si monde il y a, quels peuvent être les rapports du monde visible et du monde invisible." *V.I.,* p. 47.

The world is not something *a priori,* preceding and even explaining our perception, our openness to it. Our openness is not an effect of Nature. It is an original fact which brings about the "Nature" and "world" of things. Our body appears to be a mysterious reality, the wonder of all wonders, because it is that part of Nature by which Nature is Nature; it is a worldly being upon which the world, as world, depends. The body is not a mere object, but is the reality which makes the existence of objects possible.[58] The body makes the "that" become a "what",[59] it is the condition for the existence of meaning. The philosopher does not take for granted the existence of Nature, world, objects, essence, "what" and meaning. He asks how they are possible. The philosopher's questioning involves the philosopher himself, for he wonders that he himself is an access to Being.[60]

Our involvement in Being implies freedom. There is already freedom in seeing, for I can move my eyes and my body toward the object to be seen. But the freedom of seeing is always limited since I always see things from some vantage point. Man's freedom increases when he creates a new and more subtle body by which he has access to the world, viz., language. Language also is a worldly reality, but its subtlety enhances the freedom and mobility of our access to the world. Still we never survey the world, because we are an embodied access to the world; we belong to it. Merleau-Ponty compares our situation with that of animals in a zoo: they seem to be free because there are no cages; but their freedom ends in a softly fading manner, i.e., at a ditch which is too large to be crossed.[61]

The philosopher, therefore, cannot reconstruct our relationship to Being entirely in an intellectual manner, but neither does he simply accept it without reflection. He exists within his relationship to the world, wonders at it and questions it. Wondering and questioning, he is present at the very formation of the world. This formation to a certain extent has already taken place, but it continues to take place, because the world is not an accomplished fact. We can be present, therefore, at the formation of the world. It really is a *world* which is formed, and not a

---

[58] "Réexaminer la définition du corps comme objet pur pour comprendre comment il peut être notre lien vivant avec la nature." *Ibid.*

[59] *Ibid.*

[60] "La philosophie est l'ensemble des questions où celui qui questionne est lui-même mis en cause par la question." *Ibid.*

[61] *V.I.,* p. 136.

collection of incoherent facts.   There is a structure, and this structure
has its own laws.   The world which arises in front of us corresponds
with our look, with our perception, and even with our language.   There
is a mysterious connection between the appearing world and ourselves as
an access to the world.   The philosopher constitutes neither the world
nor himself as an access to that world, but rather he wonders at both,
and especially at their interconnection.

There is a kind of logic which reveals itself both in the world and in
ourselves, and likewise in the interconnection of both.[62]   It is a logic
which the philosopher does not construct, but which he becomes aware
of.   It is the task of the philosopher to express this logic and to stress its
philosophical importance.   Notions which are the result of an analysis,
such as "subject" and "object," are dangerous for the philosopher.[63]   For
he might conceive them as absolute and isolated entities, and he might try
to deduce their interconnection from their individual contents.   If so, he
would break down the intrinsic coherence of the world to which he
belongs into isolated elements, and he would try to understand the
structure of the whole by starting from these elements.   Neither isolated
elements nor ideal objects are the starting-point of philosophy.   The real
starting-point is the world and man himself as an access to that world;
these two must be taken together because *j'en suis,* because "I belong to
it."   The philosopher tries to see in a new manner what is already there
and what is already accessible to him.   He prepossesses the result of his
philosophical reflection.[64]   The logic of the philosopher is the expression
of the hidden logic of Being itself.   He awakens a sleeping vision.   He
wonders at what is already there.   He constitutes the expression of this
wonder, but not the wonder itself.

Negative Descriptions of Philosophical Questioning.   Merleau-Ponty
gives some negative descriptions of philosophical questioning.   Philos-

---

[62] *V.I.,* pp. 136-137.

[63] "Selon une logique en action, et dont il faut définir le statut philosophique si
nous voulons sortir des embarras où nous jettent les notions toutes faites de
pensée, de sujet et d'objet et savoir enfin ce que c'est que le monde et ce que c'est
que l'être." *V.I.,* p. 137.

[64] "La philosophie ne décompose pas notre relation avec le monde en éléments
réels, ou même en références idéales qui feraient de lui un objet idéal, mais elle
y discerne des articulations, elle y réveille des rapports réglés de prépossession,
de récapitulation, d'enjambement, qui sont comme endormis dans notre paysage
ontologique, qui n'y subsistent plus que sous forme de traces, et qui, pourtant,
continuent d'y fonctionner, d'y instituer du nouveau." *Ibid.*

ophy does not follow the procedure of the sciences which try to reduce the unknown to what is known, supposing that both the known and the unknown belong to the same order.[65] Philosophy reflects on man, world and Being. We know them from the beginning and cannot reduce them to something with which we are more familiar. The most familiar aspects of reality are the content of philosophical reflection.

We might well be led to believe that philosophy is the growth of human awareness.[66] We know the deepest features of appearing reality, but somehow we are not aware of what we know. There is a hidden knowledge which must be uncovered. Merleau-Ponty rejects this conception of philosophy, because he is afraid that thus we would only fall back into reflective philosophy. We have no hidden ideas in our mind which contain the essence of man, world and Being. We are familiar with them, not because we have ideas of them, but because we are an access to the world and to Being.

Philosophy is not an analysis of the meaning of words, of ideal significations. Merleau-Ponty does not deny that there are ideal significations; but if there is any light in our ideal significations, this light is the expression of "savage Being."[67] Philosophy turns toward the final source and it is interested, therefore, in our involvement in Being and in the Being in which we are involved.

Philosophy cannot be described as objective knowledge, because the reality in which philosophy is interested is not an object. An object would be opposed to a subject, but the philosopher is not opposed to the world, man and Being. Merleau-Ponty does not deny that the philosopher objectifies, but philosophical objectification means that we express what is not an object in objective terms. To conclude that the philosopher's field of thought is originally an objective one would be a serious error.[68]

The philosopher will never arrive at solutions which solve the

---

[65] *Ibid.*

[66] "La philosophie n'est pas davantage *prise de conscience:* il ne s'agit pas pour elle de retrouver dans une conscience législatrice la signification qu'elle aurait donnée au monde et à l'être par définition nominale." *Ibid.*

[67] "La signification lexicale, et même les significations pures, reconstruites à dessein, comme celles de la géometrie, visent un univers d'être brut et de coexistence auquel nous étions déjà jetés." *Ibid.*

[68] "L' 'objet' de la philosophie ne viendra jamais remplir la question philosophique, puisque cette obturation lui ôterait la profondeur et la distance qui lui sont essentielles." *V.I.,* p. 138.

fundamental philosophical questions. Solutions make some of our questions disappear; but we will never solve the questions concerning world, man and Being. The philosopher will find some answers, but they only point to that depth which underlies them. Answers do not satisfy philosophical wonder, but strengthen it.[69] We will never survey Being, for we are involved in Being. We are openness to a wonder which reveals itself to us but which at the same time exceeds us. It would not reveal itself to us if we were not involved in it. Yet our involvement itself is never fully accomplished; we can always be more fully involved in Being. However fully we are involved in Being, Being continues to exceed us. An adequate concept of Being is, therefore, impossible. Whoever desires to have an adequate concept of Being has lost sight of real Being.

This is the reason why Merleau-Ponty always stresses the silent character of Being. As philosophers we speak of a reality which is already there before we speak, and it continues its silent existence even when we speak of it.[70] We are involved in silent Being in a silent manner. We can believe that we have broken the silence of Being by our words, but then we have lost contact with real Being and our thought has situated itself in a realm of unreal significations.[71]

Merleau-Ponty's negative description of philosophy is impressive. Philosophy does not survey its field as science does, nor does it appeal to ideas. It does not analyze meanings, nor is it interested in objects, as objects. It questions without expecting final solutions. There is one common reason for all these negations: philosophy questions that in which we are involved as well as the involvement itself.[72] We cannot place at a distance the reality into which philosophy inquires because it is the field of our being. Should we then conclude that philosophy is an immediate experience, a knowledge which perfectly coincides with that which is known?[73]

Merleau-Ponty refuses to accept this conclusion for the simple reason that the philosopher speaks. Philosophy is not an immediate knowledge

---

[69] "Elle n'obtient pas *réponse,* mais confirmation de son étonnement." *Ibid.*

[70] "Elle est aussi question posée à ce qui ne parle pas." *Ibid.*

[71] *V.I.,* pp. 138-139.

[72] ". . . le profond mouvement par lequel nous nous sommes installés dans le monde et qui se recommence encore un peu de temps." *V.I.,* p. 141.

[73] *V.I.,* p. 162.

because it depends on the mediation of language.[74]   The philosopher's work is a cultural creation, a human construction. When it has been written it takes its place among all other cultural accomplishments.

The Paradox of Philosophy.   Merleau-Ponty is well aware of the fact that he has arrived at a paradox.   On the one hand, he indicates that the silent world, "savage Being," is the final source of philosophical knowledge; nobody is a genuine philosopher unless he contacts the silent world and "savage Being."[75]   On the other hand philosophy cannot exist without the mediation of language.[76]   However, Merleau-Ponty does not feel that this is an impossible paradox.   He thinks that the very nature of language enables him to escape contradiction.   Language is not just the depository of constituted meanings, because the "spoken word" is not the only manner of speaking.   There is also the "speaking word" which is, as we have seen, the origin of the "spoken word."   In the "speaking word" we speak of that which we do not know in order to come to know it.   When we speak the "speaking word" we constitute, while speaking, language itself.   For, we make our words express what they have never before expressed.   While doing so we translate the silent world into meaning.   The "speaking word" *is* the contact with the silent world; it *is* the translation of the silent world into the world of speech. When speaking the "speaking word," we make meaning exist in a new manner, and our speaking is itself involved in this creative process.[77]

In this way the paradox is not at all a contradiction.   The "speaking word" is essentially a contact with the silent world, and yet there is still the mediation of language.   But this mediation does not take away our contact with the immediate.   The mediation itself implies our contact with the immediate, with silent Being.   Merleau-Ponty concludes that the clearest philosophical terms, viz., the determined concepts which have a constituted meaning, are not the most important ones for the philosopher.   If the philosopher always uses such terms he does not really contact silent Being.   If he contacts silent Being he will have to go

---

[74] *V.I.*, pp. 162-163.

[75] "Le philosophe parle, mais c'est une faiblesse en lui, et une faiblesse inexplicable: il devrait se taire, coïncider en silence, et rejoindre dans l'Être une philosophie qui y est déjà faite." *V.I.*, p. 166.

[76] "Tout se passe au contraire comme s'il voulait mettre en mots un certain silence en lui qu'il écoute.   Son 'oeuvre' entière est cet effort absurde." *Ibid.*

[77] *V.I.*, pp. 169-170.

beyond current and constituted philosophical language.[78]   The philosopher's contact with silent Being is in inverse proportion to the established
clarity of constituted language.   Merleau-Ponty mistrusts clear philosophical language.   Language which is an access to silent Being cannot be
clear.   The words we use in our "speaking word" must be deprived of
the clarity which they have in the realm of the spoken word."

Until now we have closely followed Merleau-Ponty's exposition.
What does he mean in these pages, which will most likely scandalize
some people?   It is clear that according to him genuine philosophy can
never become an institutionalized doctrine.   As soon as it does, it is no
longer real philosophy.   We try to survey our present culture, as well as
the culture of the past, and try to amass all important cultural
phenomena in our encyclopedias.   In the same manner we have collected
the doctrines of important philosophers in manuals of the history of
philosophy.   We juxtapose and compare different doctrines.   As soon as
a philosopher seems to be important, books appear which offer us a
synthesis of his doctrine.   Readers of such books appreciate the clarity of
the exposition.   We "educate" young people in philosophy by making
them survey philosophy's history.   When they prepare their examina-
tions, they summarize the summaries which they have been taught.
They look for coherent systems of ideas.

All this belongs, according to Merleau-Ponty, to the institutional
philosophy which is not genuine philosophy.   Such doctrine is but the
poor and lifeless skeleton of genuine philosophy.   There is genuine
philosophy only at the moment when a thinker contacts silent Being and
when he *expresses* it.   Philosophy is expression in the integral sense of
this word.   It is an expression which takes place here and now.
Merleau-Ponty knows very well that the genuine philosopher is supported also by the past.   If Merleau-Ponty had been born in a world
where no philosophy existed, he himself would not have been a
philosopher.   But although the philosopher is supported by the past, he
does not take it for granted; he speaks as if what he were saying were
being said for the first time.   He expresses silent Being; and, even
though he makes use of expressions of the past, he gives birth to them
again.   Genuine philosophy cannot, strictly speaking, be repeated.
Many people use philosophical language without being real philosophers.
Probably a majority of those who call themselves philosophers are not

---

[78] *V.I.,* p. 139.

philosophers. The genuine philosopher is at the origin of light. Even if the light already exists, he must make it come to life again. The philosopher must contact the silent world.[79]

Critical Remarks. Here we again find the same one-sidedness which we noted in speaking of Merleau-Ponty's philosophy of language. Merleau-Ponty insists that philosophy is the expression of the silent world, and that there is genuine philosophy only when this silent world is actually expressed by a thinker. There exist current expressions of the silent world, but the philosopher is not allowed to take them for granted. In order to make use of the current terminology, he must test it; he must examine whether the alleged expression is really an expression. The silent world is the final norm of philosophical expression. It is in this attitude that Merleau-Ponty speaks of the "clutter of concepts" which should not be taken for granted.[80] Real philosophical questioning lives only when we confront current expressions with their norm, viz., with the silent world.

This, undoubtedly, is a fundamental aspect of philosophy, but it is not the only one. Expression actualizes our accessibility to the silent world. It is true, we *are* an access to the silent world. As a "perceiving perceptible" we contact the silent world and are aware of that contact. But this access is not the one the philosopher is looking for. Merleau-Ponty says that our being *is* questioning of Being. What does this mean? There is no actual question in our silent access to the silent world. This access is the source of many questions, even of all questions; but the virtual questions must be actualized, and this is done by expression. By expression our very access to Being becomes accessible. Merleau-Ponty would not have been the philosopher he was if preceding philosophers had not nourished his philosophical reflection. Of course, there must have been a first philosopher. But the first philosopher would not have existed if he had not been enlightened by pre-scientific expression, e.g., the myth.

Undoubtedly the silent world is the norm of philosophical expression;

---

[79] "Elle-même (la philosophie) est langage, repose sur le langage; mais cela ne la disqualifie pas ni pour parler du langage, ni pour parler du pré-langage et du monde muet qui les double: au contraire, elle est langage opérant, ce langage-là qui ne peut se savoir que du dedans, par la pratique, est ouvert vers les choses, appelé par les voix du silence, et continue un essai d'articulation qui est l'Être de tout être." *V.I.,* p. 168.

[80] See Chapter One.

nevertheless, the norm itself becomes accessible only by expression. The philosopher cannot avoid asking whether the expression is an expression. But he cannot ask this question merely by turning toward the silent world. Expression itself must urge him to question the expression. The essential point is that the current philosophical expression urges us to question it. Merleau-Ponty rightly stresses our turning to the silent world, but he does not explain the genesis of this attitude. We are confronted once again with the question raised by our section on Merleau-Ponty's philosophy of language: how does the light of expression prompt us to correct it? The history of philosophy is the history of the self-correction of philosophical expression.

Merleau-Ponty's analysis is not wrong, but incomplete. He rightly insists that the silent world is the final source of philosophical self-correction, but he does not explain the genesis of this self-correction. The one-sidedness of his approach appears clearly in his sentence: "Philosophy is perceptive faith questioning itself."[81] In this description the mediation of expression is omitted. Our perceptive faith does not question itself. Rather should we say that the philosophical expression of our perceptive faith continually questions itself. We then ask how expression is prompted to question itself. Had Merleau-Ponty asked this question, he would have met many traditional viewpoints, for the question of self-correction has haunted philosophical speech for centuries.

B. PHILOSOPHY AS CREATIVE ACTIVITY

Although we stressed the one-sidedness of Merleau-Ponty's description of philosophy, it cannot at all be denied that he brings to light a true and valuable aspect of philosophy. Man is a being which continually expresses itself. Man expresses himself in behavior, in work and play, in art and science, in philosophy and religion. Man's self-expression is a development of his original involvement in Being. Man cannot express himself, therefore, without expressing Being. Man belongs to Being, and there is no separation between man's self-expression and his expression of Being. Philosophy is a particular kind of expression. The particularity of philosophy, however, consists precisely in its return to the final source of all expression.[82] Philosophy is a radical reflection on

---

[81] "La philosophie, c'est la foi perceptive s'interrogeant sur elle-même." *V.I.*, p. 139.

[82] "La fin d'une philosophie est le récit de son commencement." *V.I.*, p. 231.

expressive life as such.[83]   It makes us aware of the fact that our existence
is an expressive power.

Philosophy too is expression.   It uses, or rather constructs, a coherent
terminology.   Philosophy, therefore, is creative.[84]   On this point we can
compare philosophy with a work of art.   Philosophy, however, differs
from other creative actions in its awareness of the final source of all
creative activity.[85]   It is an expression which consciously returns to the
source of all expression.   Philosophy is a *Gebilde,* a construction, and it
acknowledges itself to be a construction.   It desires to surpass its
constructed character, because this is only the expression of silent Being.
Philosophy is a construction which joins its origin and this origin, at the
same time, is the origin of all possible constructions.

Philosophy is, therefore, a radically creative activity.   Its creativity
consists in the creative revelation of the source of all creativity.
Philosophy is a *creative expression of Being*.   The essential ambiguity of
philosophy is contained in the simple words: creative expression.   Insofar
as philosophy is creative it moves away from its source; insofar as it is
expression which is aware of itself, it returns to its source.   Here we
have two movements which seem to be opposed, but which together
constitute the essence of philosophy.[86]

Philosophy and Art.   Philosophy is a creation which is at the same
time adequation.[87]   By this expression Merleau-Ponty means that
philosophy's creative effort intends to penetrate into Being.   His use of
the term "adequation" here is confusing, because in other contexts he has
avoided it.   We belong to Being which exceeds us.   An adequate
knowledge of Being is, therefore, impossible.   In this note Merleau-
Ponty conveys by the term "adequation" the sense of the *reality* of our
knowledge of Being, and not that we know it adequately.   At the end of
his note Merleau-Ponty writes that Being *requires that we be creative,*
because this is the only manner in which experience of Being becomes

---

[83] Philosophy is *"ascension sur place." Ibid.*

[84] "La philosophie, précisement comme 'Être parlant en nous', expression de
l'expérience muette par soi, est création.   Création qui est en même temps
réintégration de l'Être." *V.I.,* p. 250.

[85] "Elle se sait *Gebilde* et veut se dépasser comme pur Gebilde, retrouver son
origine.   Elle est donc création dans un sens radical: création qui en même
temps est adéquation, la seule manière d'obtenir une adéquation." *V.I.,* pp.
250-251.   See also *V.I.,* pp. 227-228.

[86] *V.I.,* pp. 231-233.

[87] *V.I.,* p. 251.

possible.[88] This is a remarkable and profound idea, i.e., that by creative activity we become aware of Being. The endeavor of philosophy and science has often been thought to be opposed to the creativity of art. According to this view, philosophy and science would reflect upon Being while art would realize new forms of Being. Merleau-Ponty denies this opposition. Man cannot arrive at the awareness of Being except in creative activity.

Merleau-Ponty quotes Souriau, who says that philosophy is the supreme art.[89] He accepts this idea and intended to deepen it in his new book; in this note he only makes a few remarks. Both art and philosophy, he says, should not be considered artificial constructions within the realm of mind or of culture. They are creative activities which contact Being. It is remarkable that for Merleau-Ponty, not only philosophy, but also art contacts Being. On the one hand, he distinguishes them, because he holds that philosophy is creative in the most radical sense, for it is a creation which is also an adequation with Being. There is no contradiction between the two expressions. Both philosophy and art contact Being, but philosophy alone is aware of contacting Being. This awareness is not an essential aspect of art.

Now we understand why Merleau-Ponty's writings from the last period of his life often dealt with painting.[90] He finds in painting what he tries to bring about in his philosophy, viz., contact with silent Being. He prefers to consider painting rather than literature and music, because the painter expresses himself in the order of visible reality, the central interest of Merleau-Ponty's philosophy. It is quite understandable that the writer of *The Visible and the Invisible* is vitally interested in painting.

Descartes' Concept of Vision and Painting. Merleau-Ponty opposes Descartes' theory of vision and painting. While Descartes did not often speak of painting, the few remarks he made were entirely determined by his philosophy of human vision. This philosophy Descartes explains in

---

[88] "L'Être est *ce qui exige de nous création* pour que nous en ayons l'expérience." *Ibid.*

[89] *Ibid.*

[90] E.g., "Indirect Language and the Voices of Silence," *Signs,* pp. 39-83; "*L'Oeil et l'Esprit,*" *Les Temps Modernes,* Vol. 17, no. 184-185, pp. 193-227, and often in the notes.

[91] Merleau-Ponty summarizes and criticizes Descartes' description in "*L'Oeil et l'Esprit,*" *op. cit.,* pp. 204-214.

his *Dioptrics*.[91] Descartes did not think of real light as that which we see all around us, but he approached light as something that acts on our eyes. Light acts by contacting our eyes. Light touches our eyes in the same way that things touch the stick of a blind person.[92]

In this interpretation, one of the most essential problems of human vision disappears. That we see things where they are, at a distance, was not a real problem for Descartes.[93] Things are where they are, all right, but between them and us there is the mediating action of light which touches us and which provokes in us impressions. For Descartes impressions in us are signs of the thing rather than its resemblance; the real thing has three dimensions, while its impressions in us have only two. The qualitative aspects of our impressions, e.g., color, have only subjective value. Our impressions, therefore, do not bring us into contact with real things. Our thought does contact things, although only by interpreting the signs caused by the action of things on our bodies.[94]

According to this understanding of vision, painting cannot have much value. Naturally, color does not have great importance, since it is among the subjective impressions. Design is more important; hence Descartes spoke only of the design of the painting. Yet this design which we know is not a real resemblance.[95] Precisely because it is not like things themselves, precisely because it is not a resemblance, it helps us to have an idea of real things: there must be deformations in our designs, otherwise they could not give us an impression of reality. If, for example, I want to create the impression of a cube, my sketch must not *be* a square or a cube—the sketch could not be one, for it has only two dimensions. The deformations of the design are the conditions for their effectivity. Painting does not make us *see* the world, because it is not a resemblance of it. It provokes our thought as do other signs such as our words, which do not resemble the things either. The painting is a design which helps our understanding. Descartes opposed the traditional doctrine that images of things exist in our mind. This absurd idea arises

---

[92] "Les aveugles, dit Descartes, 'voient des mains'. Le modèle cartésien de la vision, c'est le toucher." *"L'Oeil et l'Esprit,"* *op. cit.,* p. 204.

[93] "Il nous débarasse aussitôt de l'action à distance et de cette ubiquité qui fait toute la difficulté de la vision (et aussi toute sa vertu)." *Ibid.*

[94] *"L'Oeil et l'Esprit,"* *op. cit.,* pp. 205-206.

[95] "Elle n'en est l''image' qu'à condition de 'ne lui pas rassembler'." *"L'Oeil et l'Esprit,"* *op. cit.,* p. 205.

from mirrors and paintings. He therefore interprets painting in an entirely new manner.

Our vision of the world and of painting needs the interpretation of our intellect in order to be understood. Descartes knew very well that our understanding intellect needs such signs.[96] There is no vision without thought, but thought alone is not sufficient for vision. A blind person thinks, but he does not see. There is no vision if the intellect does not interpret the signs offered to the body. But our intellect does not construct these signs. Our interpreting thought is subjected to the intrinsic law of the signs themselves. Human thought is subject to something which it does not constitute.[97] The word "vision" has, therefore, for Descartes a double meaning. Vision is first of all that which has become the clear object of thought; this vision is a form of thought, an inspecting activity of the mind. Vision is also an obscure activity of the body functioning according to its own laws; this bodily activity does not depend on the activity of the intellect.[98]

Vision in the second sense is inaccessible to our understanding. Here we confront the mysterious realm of the union of body and soul. This realm is inaccessible to pure thought. We find this realm in us, although we cannot set out to understand it; it is an order of existence which for our intellect is *terra incognita*.[99] How is it possible that this obscure realm does not prevent us from thinking at all? Both the light of our intellect and the obscure realm of existence proceed from one and the same source of light, viz., from God. In this way Descartes explains how the obscure realm of corporal existence gives us signs which can be interpreted by our intellect. Descartes appeals to metaphysics in order to dispense us from metaphysical reflection on the obscure realm of corporal existence.[100]

Descartes' few written pages on painting have a very profound metaphysical background,[101] which makes us aware of the fact that

---

[96] "Descartes cependant ne serait pas Descartes s'il avait pensé d'*éliminer* l'énigme de la vision." *"L'Oeil et l'Esprit," op. cit.*, p. 210.

[97] "La pensée de la vision fonctionne selon un programme et une loi qu'elle ne s'est pas donnés." *Ibid.*

[98] *"L'Oeil et l'Esprit," op. cit.*, p. 211.

[99] "Ce sont les indices d'un ordre de l'existence—de l'homme existant, du monde existant—que nous ne sommes pas chargés de penser." *"L'Oeil et l'Esprit," op. cit.*, p. 212.

[100] *Ibid.*

[101] *"L'Oeil et l'Esprit," op. cit.*, p. 214.

reflection on painting finally has a metaphysical character. Merleau-Ponty objects to the Cartesian opposition between the obscure realm of corporal existence and the clarity of thought. The union of body and soul is not an obscure realm which is transcended by clear thinking. This union, on the contrary, is the real realm of our existence and the real field of human thought. In this realm world and Being are accessible to us, and all our thoughts are rooted in it. Our corporal vision does not present us with signs which must be interpreted by the intellect; our vision itself is a real access to Being.

The Creative Character of Vision. Metaphysical reflection on painting can help us understand the creative character of our vision itself. The painting is not an image of real things. Someone who visits a beautiful place can take a picture of it in order to recall the scene when he is no longer there. The painting is not such an image, substituting for our real presence to things. It does not refer to something other than itself. It is a world in itself and must be understood—seen—in itself. The painting is a contraction of the visible world and expresses its essence.[102] The painter can paint because he sees. But his vision itself is creative. He places himself within the enlightened scene and, by the manner in which he situated himself, constitutes the play of light and shadow. He chooses the way in which the colors reveal themselves to him; he makes things relate to each other within his vision. Vision and visible things are not constituted by thought, but by the seeing body. The painter questions Being in and through his body. His seeing and his painting almost coincide. His expression is dominated by his vision. For his expression is creative because his vision is creative. The world comes into existence both in his vision and in his painting. The painter tries to express the essence of things, but their essence is not separated from their existence. He has a vivid imagination, but in his imagination he expresses the existing essence of things. He speaks in his painting of the invisible aspects of things, but the invisible appears to be the "other side" of the visible itself and is embodied in it.

The painter does not conceive depth as a third dimension which is not really present in his two dimensional, flat surfaced painting and which is

---

[102] "Le monde n'est plus devant lui par représentation: c'est plutôt le peintre qui naît dans les choses comme par concentration et venue à soi du visible, et le tableau finalement ne se rapporte à quoi que ce soit parmi les choses empiriques qu'à condition d'être d'abord 'autofiguratif', il n'est spectacle de quelque chose qu'en étant 'spectacle de rien'." *"L'Oeil et l'Esprit,"* *op. cit.,* p. 217.

accessible only to the intellect interpreting some ambiguous signs.[103]
The painter knows that the things he sees have depth, that this depth
constitutes their visible essence.   Each thing has its own individuality, but
this individuality cannot be abstracted from the thing's involvement in
depth and from its connection with other things.   The painter,
therefore, does not paint isolated things, leaving empty space between
them.   He paints things as they are involved in space and with one
another.   Things have their identity in their space and in their mutual
connection.   This involvement, this connection, is not a "being-in-itself";
it is the scene in which the seeing person is also involved, because he
constitutes it.

A thing has a surface, but this surface is not separated from the Being
of the thing.   Although the surface is expressed on a flat canvas, the
surface itself is not flat.   The surface of a painted object does not stop at
the line drawn as its outline; the apples of Césanne disappear into depth.

The painter expresses animals and men in movement, but the painted
movement is not the expression of any particular instant of movement.
There is an immense difference between the photograph and the painting
of a movement.   When an athlete is photographed during his jump, a
static picture of a dynamic event is preserved.   The movement seems to
be frozen like the movement conceived by Zeno.[104]   The painter, on the
contrary, expresses moving men in a way which we never observe in
reality because it does not exist.   The way in which Géricault gives
expression to galloping horses no one has ever observed in galloping
horses.[105]   The artist gathers the duration of the movement, and
therefore he can express the movement itself.   The artist does not make
an instantaneous photograph of the movement but expresses the whole of
it.   He does so because he expresses the visible essence of the movement.
Our eyes also perform this miracle, because we see real movement, not a
succession of instants.

When man contacts Being it is not possible to say where Nature ends
and expression begins.[106]   We contact Being, expressing it in a visible

---

[103] "On ne peut plus dire qu'elle (la profondeur) est 'troisième dimension'.
D'abord, si elle en était une, ce serait plutôt la première." *"L'Oeil et l'Esprit,"*
op. cit., p. 216.

[104] "Elles donnent une rêverie zénonienne sur le mouvement." *"L'Oeil et*
l'Esprit," *op. cit.,* p. 221.

[105] *"L'Oeil et l'Esprit,"* *op. cit.,* p. 222.

[106] "Dans ce circuit, nulle rupture, impossible de dire qu'ici finit la nature et
commence l'homme ou l'expression." *"L'Oeil et l'Esprit,"* *op. cit.,* p. 225.

field. We contact Being by expression. Vision is already expression, and the painter assumes a creative activity which is performed by everyone of us when he really sees. This creation takes place within the silent world. True, man does not paint as long as he does not speak; but when he paints he expresses Being in a silent and creative manner.

Creativity as Access to Truth. This reflection on painting makes us understand that our creative expression is our access to truth. In the past intellectual adequation with Being was overemphasized.[107] Being was thought of as an existing, fully accomplished light, already there. The ideal of knowledge was to appropriate that light. Man tried to coincide with it; and, insofar as he was still removed from it, he was removed from truth. Then there was no place for creative expression in the search for truth because all the means, all the signs we would create, would only prevent us from coinciding with the light we were looking for.

Being, however, is to be revealed by man. Man makes it visible by seeing, and perceptible by perceiving. Man is, as we stressed in the second chapter, the self-awareness of Being. But he raises Being to its self-awareness by his own activity, and this activitity is creative. When man becomes the self-awareness of Being, he also becomes the self-actualization of Being. Merleau-Ponty calls painting the "in-spiration and 'expiration' of Being." By his own self-actualization man appropriates Being, namely, by expressing it. His appropriation is expression, and the expression is appropriation. Man "in-spires" Being by "expiring" it.

Now we understand why Merleau-Ponty insists that philosophy is a creative activity. The philosopher makes use of words, but these words are not a screen between the philosopher and Being. The original philosopher uses words in an original way, because he makes those words express what they have never before expressed. In this sense philosophy can be compared to art. This creation is, however, a real revelation of Being. We can better understand now why Merleau-Ponty dislikes that positivism of language which focuses our attention on ideal meanings. He does not want to isolate ideal meanings from Being; he does not deny the existence of ideal meanings; but he considers them the revelation of silent Being and demands that we view them as such. They make no sense philosophically unless they are taken as the expression of Being.

---

[107] *"L'Oeil et l'Esprit,"* p. 226.

It remains strange, however, that Merleau-Ponty always points toward the dark origin of our creative expressions. One can easily understand his insistence not to forget their source for, if we lose our contact with silent Being, we no longer understand our own expressions. But one would expect that Merleau-Ponty would also point to the other direction. The dark origin is brought to light precisely by our creative expressions. Not only are they our access to the silent world, they are even the actualization of the silent world. The world becomes visible, perceptible, intelligible by our expressive presence. This does not mean, of course, that we place some realm of light above another realm of original darkness. By our expression we bring the darkness itself into the light. Expression is at the same time appropriation. We become aware of what Being really is. Our awareness of Being will never be finally or fully accomplished. The idea itself of a completed awareness is false, since Being is not a positive datum which can be completely appropriated. Truth is not the appropriation of a positive datum, but neither is it a creation in the emptiness of a contingent future. It is the appropriation of something which we actualize by expressing it.

C. PHILOSOPHY AND HISTORY

Until now our discussion has centered on Merleau-Ponty's conception of philosophy as such. Yet, according to him, what is the relationship between the philosopher and the history of philosophy? He does not describe this relationship in the chapters prepared for publication, but the fact that the largest part of this text is a confrontation with other philosophers clearly implies that he felt the need to relate to the history of philosophy. In several notes the problem of the relationship between the individual philosopher and the history of philosophy is explicitly posed.

Philosophy or History of Philosophy? Merleau-Ponty is interested in a problem raised by Henri Gouhier: we must make a distinction between the questions posed by a certain philosopher, e.g., by Descartes, and the questions we pose now; do we have the right to ask a philosopher of the past our questions?[108] If we answer in the negative, we recognize the unique character of each philosophy; but then we reduce the different philosophies to isolated cultural works. Each philosopher poses his own

---

[108] *V.I.,* p. 239; pp. 252-253.

questions and gives his own answers. If, however, we answer in the affirmative, we tend to deny the unique character of each philosophy and reduce the history of philosophy to philosophy. In the first case there is a history of philosophy, but not philosophy; in the second case there is philosophy, but the real history of philosophy seems to disappear.[109]

Merleau-Ponty answers that a philosophy, like an artistic product, can provoke more thoughts than are explicitly contained in it.[110] We must recall Merleau-Ponty's article "The Philosopher and His Shadow." There he explains that the philosopher's expositions are usually supported and made possible by a fundamental light of which he does not speak. In seeing our eyes are guided by a light at which we do not look; we look at the illuminated things. In the same way the philosopher is usually guided by a spiritual vision which is not the explicit theme of his exposition. We must make a distinction, therefore, between the problems which philosophers explicitly pose and the underlying problems which move them but which they do not formulate. Their explicit problems belong to a certain historical context and can become unimportant when this context has disappeared. Historical research is necessary in order to understand them. We must restore the historical context to enable the explicit problems to come to life again. The deeper, underlying problems, however, do not disappear with the historical context. They can remain actual; they can well be the problems raised by us today.[111]

In this way a philosophy of the past remains meaningful even after its historical context has disappeared. Merleau-Ponty goes further, stating that a philosophy has full meaning only outside its historical context. He does not deny, of course, what he has just affirmed, viz., that a philosophy poses its problems within an historical context and has its meaning within this context. Merleau-Ponty wants to say that the ultimate and deepest meaning of a philosophy becomes manifest only when its more superficial historical meaning has become unimportant.

---

[109] "La philosophie. Pour définir son milieu, partir de la question de Gouhier: peut-on poser à une philosophie des questions qu'elle ne s'est pas posées? Répondre non, c'est faire d'elles des oeuvres séparées, c'est nier *la* philosophie. Répondre oui, c'est reduire l'histoire à la philosophie." *V.I.,* pp. 252-253.

[110] *V.I.,* p. 253.

[111] "Mon point de vue: une philosophie, comme une oeuvre d'art, c'est un objet qui peut susciter plus de pensées que celles qui y sont 'contenues' (peut-on les énumerer? Peut-on dénombrer un langage?) qui garde un sens hors de son contexte historique, qui *n'a* même de sens que hors de ce contexte." *Ibid.*

We must remember what he says in the introduction to *Signs,* viz., that a thinker becomes classical when his influence can be observed almost everywhere and when, at the same time, nobody repeats him literally.[112] Plato lives among us and influences every real philosopher, but nobody follows the literal text of Plato. In this sense Merleau-Ponty says that the real meaning of a philosopher becomes manifest when the historical context of his works belongs to the past.

This vision of the history of philosophy seems to imply, however, a danger of relativism. If the real meaning of a philosophy is related, not to the questions it explicitly raises, but to the underlying questions which later become manifest and which perhaps are raised by us, then its final meaning can never be established. We read the works of a philosopher in the light of the underlying questions which we think to be important, but after some decades others will think they must read these same works in the light of other underlying questions. The attempt to save the philosopher of the past from his contingent historical context seems to deny the existence of any final meaning.

Merleau-Ponty's answer is not clear. He says that all philosophies embody the same fundamental question which is implied in our existence itself.[113] The interrogation which prompts the philosophers to speak will, therefore, never be surpassed. We find these sentences at the end of one note. In another note, however, Merleau-Ponty explains his point of view in more detail. All the different philosophies, he says, cannot simply be reduced to a single level.[114] As situated in history they are exterior to one another. Yet this exteriority is not the last word. They meet one another on a deeper level, because they are all rooted in the same Being of which they speak.[115]

We must recall here the central point of Merleau-Ponty: *j'en suis,* "I belong to it." We are involved in Being and we are all involved in the

---

[112] *Signs,* p. 10-11.

[113] "Ceci conduit-il à des conclusions toujours relativistes? à savoir, qui seront bouleversées par un autre temps? Non, si les philosophies dans leur intégralité sont *question,* la pensée interrogative qui les fait parler n'est pas dépassée par ce qui viendra ensuite (Lefort sur Machiavel)." *V.I.,* p. 253. As Claude Lefort explains in a note, the last words are an allusion to a book which Lefort at that time was writing on Machiavelli.

[114] "Chercher à définir une histoire de la philosophie qui ne soit pas aplatissement de l'histoire dans 'ma' philosophie." *V.I.,* p. 251.

[115] "Les suivre dans leur problèmes (Guérould),—mais leur problèmes sont intérieurs à celui de l'Être." *Ibid.*

same Being. Although on the surface different philosophers seem to speak of different things, they ultimately speak of one and the same reality, because all are involved in the same Being. There is a unity between philosophers as there is a unity between different "perceiving perceptibles." I live in my perceptive field, and other persons live in their own. But this is a superficial statement. Radically speaking, we all belong to the same world which comes to awareness of itself in each of us. There is an inner connection between the different "perceiving perceptibles," and their unity is not just the result of a contingent common history. In the same way there is an intrinsic connection between different philosophers. I speak, but ultimately Being itself speaks in me. The same Being speaks about itself in all philosophers. Merleau-Ponty says that there is a "perceptive relationship" between philosophers,[116] and that philosophers transcend themselves to one another. As "perceiving perceptibles" we are accessible to one another. In the same way philosophers are accessible to one another.

"Objective" and "Vertical" History of Philosophy. Merleau-Ponty opposes an "objective" and a "vertical" history of philosophy, and says that both have the right to exist.[117] It is rather clear what he means by "objective" history. An "objective" historian tries to understand each philosopher within the horizon of the man's own period. He tries to become aware of the attitude of mind of that period in which the philosopher lived, of the problems which were then raised, of the meaning words currently had. There is, however, another kind of history of philosophy, viz., the "vertical" kind. There is continuity, not only between the philosopher and his actual field of existence, but also between the philosopher and his past and future. Man is involved in Being as a being which questions Being. The philosopher, like the artist, is creative; he builds a construction (*Gebilde*) of words. This construction is an answer to the fundamental question implied in man's being. The construction is, as we have seen, an expression of Being. "Vertical" history views all philosophical constructions as expressions of the same Being. *My* Being is expressed in all the constructions of the

---

[116] "Histoire de la philosophie comme *perception* des autres philosophes, empiètement intentionnel sur eux, pensée propre qui ne les tue pas, soit en les dépassant, soit en les copiant." *V.I.*, p. 251.

[117] "Donc histoire verticale, qui a ses droits à côté de l'histoire de la philosophie 'objective'." *V.I.*, p. 240.

past. In this sense the past is no longer just the past.[118] The past remains actual. I become aware that *my* questions are answered in the philosophical constructions of the past and that my construction is an answer to the questions which underly the philosophies of former periods. These philosophies become simultaneous in the perspective of "vertical" history.

Although he knows that he is a particular person and that he speaks the language of his period, the philosopher of the twentieth century can presume to express Being. He has no exclusive right to this privilege, though; he must admit that other philosophers of his own period and philosophers of the past also express Being. Radically, insofar as we touch Being, we form a community which transcends the distinction of persons and the diversity of periods. The realm of diversity and the realm of community are not separated. Both "objective" and "vertical" history have, therefore, the right to exist. We are different *in* our community and we are connected *in* our diversity. It is difficult to understand these relationships. But this problem is implied already in our perceptive faith, that faith which teaches us that we are different persons who have, or rather, are an access to one and the same world. All these facets are implied in the basic sentence of Merleau-Ponty: *J'en suis.*

We must avoid two extremes. We should not dissolve all the philosophies of the present and of the past into our own philosophical perspective. For then we would make the history of philosophy extremely flat and impoverished. But we must also avoid what Merleau-Ponty calls "idolatry."[119] He means by this our tendency to reduce the past to something absolute, to think we can fully understand, for example, Descartes by placing his works into their historical context. The two extremes are not really opposed. In the first case we view our own perspective as something absolute; in the second case, we isolate the perspective of the philosopher of the past. In both cases we forget that each philosophical perspective is an expression of Being.[120] No philoso-

---

[118] "Ce que je propose n'est pas une 'vue' d'histoire de la philosophie. Ou c'est de l'histoire, mais structurale: i.e. non pas l'événement de telle philosophie comme *création* et *solution* de 'problèmes', mais cette philosophie située dans l'ensemble hiératique de l'Être et l'éternité existentielle, i.e. dans un ensemble *interrogatif* qui, comme le *Machiavel* de Lefort, n'est pas un dogmatisme." *V.I.*, p. 241.

[119] *V.I.*, p. 251.

[120] *V.I.*, p. 239.

pher belongs entirely to the past, nor do we belong entirely to the present. No philosopher has been completely surpassed, but neither is there any philosopher whose works can simply be repeated.

Something Absolute. Merleau-Ponty goes still further. He says that there is something absolute, viz., a philosophy which is somehow immanent in the whole history of philosophy.[121] This does not mean that the differences of philosophies are denied and that all are absorbed in one single philosophy. The differences of the many philosophies are real, but so also are their intrinsic coherence and their communication. We become aware of this, says Merleau-Ponty, if we view philosophy as a perception and the history of philosophy as a perception of the past. What does he mean by these mysterious sentences? Unfortunately, he writes them in a note but does not explain them. This note refers to a chapter which he intended to write.

Philosophy, as we have seen, is "our perceptive faith questioning itself."[122] Perceptive faith is the origin of philosophy. Perception is the self-awareness of Being. Philosophy finally is an expression of Being. The perception of other people is accessible to us because their perception is the awareness of Being of which we, too, are aware. For the same reason the philosophy of other thinkers is accessible to us; the same Being we express is expressed by them also. There is, therefore, a "perception" of other philosophers, even of philosophers of the past. When Merleau-Ponty says that there is something absolute, that there is a philosophy in all philosophies, he means that in all philosophers Being speaks of itself. But he does not deny that different philosophers speak of the same Being in different ways. There is something absolute, but this is always conceived in a relative manner.

Merleau-Ponty concludes that our intellectual comprehension is not the immanent possession of an object.[123] Our perception is openness to the

---

[121] "Montrer qu'il y a un absolu, une philosophie, qui est immanente à l'histoire de la philosophie, et qui n'est pourtant résorption de toutes les philosophies dans une seule, ni d'ailleurs éclecticisme et scepticisme. On le voit si l'on arrive à faire de la philosophie une perception, et de l'histoire de la philosophie une perception de l'histoire—Tout revient à ceci: faire une théorie de la perception et de la compréhension qui montre que comprendre n'est pas constituer dans l'immanence intellectuelle, que comprendre est saisir par coexistence, latéralement, *en style,* et par là atteindre d'un coup les lointains de ce style et de cet appareil culturel." *V.I.,* p. 242.

[122] *V.I.,* p. 139.

[123] *V.I.,* p. 242.

world and our comprehension is openness to Being. Our openness arises from our involvement in Being. Because we exist in Being we have access to it. We have a hold on it because we coexist with it, because we belong to it. Nevertheless, we never understand it entirely; we understand it "laterally," i.e., as a field, not as a figure; and we are sensitive to its style. This, moreover, is the reason why we are sensitive to other persons who are likewise an access to Being. We are open to one another because we are all open to Being.

It is regrettable that Merleau-Ponty was not able to work out these interesting points which imply a new notion of *philosophia perennis*. He insists that there is an intrinsic connection between different philosophies, but this connection does not deny their diversity. The connection is not made possible by some mysterious human nature, nor by some transcendental mind, nor by a direct influence of God. Merleau-Ponty opposes naturalistic, humanistic or theological philosophies.[124] The connection between different persons and between philosophers is the result of their common involvement in Being. The notion of Being— often capitalized by Merleau-Ponty—has become extremely important in his philosophy. We will complete this book, therefore, with a section on Being.

3. Being

A. MERLEAU-PONTY'S NOTION OF "EN-ÊTRE"

The phrase *"j'en suis"* has been repeated again and again in this book. It was often quoted as Merleau-Ponty's final argument. This was unavoidable for this sentence expresses Merleau-Ponty's deepest point of view.

We explained the meaning of this sentence in the preceding chapters. The intentional relationship, although not denied by Merleau-Ponty, is nevertheless, not the final truth of human existence. When man has reached a certain level of self-actualization, he finds himself to be a subject opposed to an object. But the intentional relationship appears only at this level of self-actualization. According to Merleau-Ponty the

---

[124] "Mon plan: I le visible
           II la Nature
           III le logos
doit être présenté sans aucun compromis avec l'humanisme, ni d'ailleurs avec le *naturalisme,* ni enfin avec la *théologie.*" *V.I.,* p. 328.

intentional level is preceded by a pre-intentional level, and the intentional level is, therefore, not understandable in itself. In order to understand the intentional relationship we must reduce it to the pre-intentional level.

We must go even further. According to Merleau-Ponty the pre-intentional level not only precedes the intentional relationship, but it continues to exist *in it*. The term "pre-intentional" is, therefore, not adequate. We could also use the term "super-intentional." The intentional relationship is not the first aspect of our human being, nor is it its ultimate truth. The intentional relationship, wherever it exists, is permeated by a "super-intentional" aspect. We are never completely absorbed in the opposition implied in the intentional relationship.[125]

"Frontal" and "Lateral" Aspects of Reality. To become aware of the above mentioned problem is understandably difficult. Insofar as our being has become intentional, we are a subject, opposed to an object. Our attention is focused on the object. We pay attention to the frontal aspect of the appearing reality and can hardly avoid stressing its opposition to us. This opposition is the truth of the intentional relationship. The opposition, however, always appears within an intrinsic connection. But because this intrinsic connection between subject and object, the fact that they are intrinsically permeated by one and the same reality, cannot be directly observed, we are inclined to stress the opposition and to forget the intrinsic connection.

For this reason Merleau-Ponty often uses the word "lateral." With the focus of our attention only on the frontal aspects of appearing reality, we only see the opposition between subject and object. Our eyes thus close to what Merleau-Ponty considers the most essential truth, viz., the

---

[125] "Toute l'analyse husserlienne est bloquée par le cadre des *actes* que lui impose la philosophie de la *conscience*. Il faut reprendre et développer l'intentionnalité *fungierende ou latente* qui est l'intentionnalité intérieure à l'être. Cela n'est pas compatible avec la 'phénoménologie', c'est-à-dire avec une ontologie qui assujettit tout ce qui n'est pas rien à se *présenter* à la *conscience* à travers des *Abschattungen* et comme dérivant d'une donation originaire qui est un *acte, i.e.* un *Erlebnis* parmi d'autres (*cf.* critique de Husserl par Fink dans l'article ancien du colloque de la phénoménologie). Il faut prendre comme premier, non la conscience et son *Ablaufsphänomen* avec ses fils intentionnels distincts, mais le tourbillon que cet *Ablaufsphänomen* schématise, le tourbillon spatialisant-temporalisant (qui est chair et non conscience en face d'un noème)." *V.I.*, pp. 297-298. Merleau-Ponty refers here to the article of Eugen Fink, *"L'Analyse Intentionnelle," Problèmes actuels de la Phénoménologie*, Desclée de Brouwer, 1952.

intrinsic connection between subject and object. The term "connection" is ambiguous, since every philosopher who accepts a doctrine of intentionality will admit that subject and object are connected. Merleu-Ponty means something more. According to him the connection consists mainly in the fact that the opposed terms belong to one and the same reality. The opposition is not just a kind of unity, of togetherness, but takes place within a unity which precedes and exceeds the opposition.[126] This unity cannot be directly observed. It is not an object itself, since it involves the subject also. It is not a phenomenon, but it co-appears in all phenomena and makes phenomena possible. It is the "quasi-object" of a lateral awareness.

This is the source of the difficultness of Merleau-Ponty's new philosophy. The ultimate subject of his entire book is something which does not appear to us, but only co-appears in everything which appears. The proper subject of his book is not a phenomenon, but is the essential horizon involving both the phenomena and he to whom the phenomena appear. According to Edgar Rubin's classical distinction between "figure" and "field," when we perceive something, our attention is focused on a "figure," viz., on what appears. But it always appears within a "field." We do not and we cannot observe the field, because it is essential that the field be only co-observed. Merleau-Ponty is interested in that which co-appears, which is co-observed. But the privilege of clarity belongs to what is observed, and it is contradictory to try to make the co-appearing field also clear. For this reason *The Visible and the Invisible* is an obscure book. It must be obscure. We are convinced that it would have remained obscure until its very end; for its obscurity does not arise from the unfinished state in which it was left.

It is easy to see now why Merleau-Ponty is afraid of clear words and clear concepts. Clear words order the appearing "figures." Words which try to express the field must be obscure. It is impossible to give a clear exposition of that which does not directly appear but which only co-appears. Attending only to the clarity of what appears may well blind us to the essential theme of Merleau-Ponty's philosophy. Paradoxical as it seems, our book can be valuable only if it is obscure.

The meaning of Merleau-Ponty's notion *en-être* now becomes under-

---

[126] "Découverte du *Wesen* (verbal): première expression de l'être qui n'est ni l'être-objet ni l'être-subjet, ni essence ni existence: ce qui *west* (l'être-rose de la rose, l'être-société de la société, l'être-histoire de l'histoire) répond à la question *was* comme à la question *dass.*" *V.I.,* p. 228.

standable. The subject and the object belong together, not only and not mainly because they need one another in order to be opposed terms, but because they are permeated by one and the same reality. This reality supports the opposition. It is not possible for us to abstract from the opposition and to focus our attention on the reality which permeates the opposed terms. This reality is the final truth of philosophical research, but the philosopher can never directly grasp it. What the philosopher must bring to light is always there, but always escapes him.

The *en-être* reveals itself in two ways: the subject belongs to that which appears as an object, and the object, of course, belongs as well to the subject. We find, therefore, two expressions of the same truth in Merleau-Ponty's book. He says first that "I belong to it," that the subject belongs to the world, that it is essentially worldly. The seeing person belongs to the visible world, and the perceiving subject is itself perceptible. Merleau-Ponty says secondly that the world belongs to me. He speaks, therefore, of the "flesh of the world." My flesh is not a substance alien to the world. It is the world itself which becomes flesh in me, and my flesh is therefore a revelation of an essential possibility of things themselves. My self-actualization implies an actualization of things themselves. When man becomes flesh he does not leave the world; he remains related to it; he takes the world along with him in his own self-actualization.

The *en-être* is why Merleau-Ponty uses terms which belong to the world in order to indicate man, and words which belong to man in order to indicate the world. Man is worldly and the world is human; man is matter and the world is flesh; man is spatial and space is human. Merleau-Ponty often uses terms which seem to be metaphorical, but they are not metaphors to him. The *en-être* brings about an interchange between man and world which is the final truth of both. We can say that the world humanizes itself by becoming man, and that man is the humanization of the world. Man is not a being alien to the world, a being which raises the world to its own level. In man the world itself reaches a new level, but this level is not alien to the world. The world comes to itself in man. Man's presence does not bring a strange element into the world.

Hence Merleau-Ponty often says that the world has "an invisible aspect," or even "a spiritual side." Merleau-Ponty is not at all a materialist. He recognizes wholeheartedly what has been called "mind" or "spirit" by thinkers of the past, and he does not deny any phenomenon of human existence. His notion of *en-être,* however, implies that everything which is in man is a revelation of a fundamental possibility of the world. If man is a spiritual being, the world itself must be virtually spiritual and must have its "spiritual side."

Merleau-Ponty's notion of *en-être* does not imply simply a return to realism. He denies that we are able to directly understand the fundamental reality which permeates both man and world. We cannot focus our attention on that which precedes man in order to make man himself understandable from that point of view. Man is the actualization of the visibility, the perceptibility and the intelligibility of the world; briefly, man himself actualizes the accessibility of the world. Man cannot abstract from his own presence and understand that which precedes his presence. His presence *is* access and it conditions, and even brings about, every form of the world's accessibility. Man recognizes, of course, that something precedes him, that his presence is the actualization of a preceding possibility. But he can recognize this only within the actualization of the world's accessibility.

Merleau-Ponty's notion of *en-être* does imply, however, that we are not enclosed within the realm of human meaning.[127] Man recognizes the ontological density of what appears to him and of his own being, since the latter belongs to the former. Nothing is more alien to Merleau-Ponty than the "subjectivism of meaning." Any separation between "phenomenon" and "noumenon" would be the destruction of Merleau-Ponty's most essential insights. He has never accepted such a separation and, during the last years of his life, was further removed from it than ever. He rejects positivism of language and the Husserlian essences precisely because they embody the danger of separating "phenomenon" and "Being." He hesitates to stress the frontal aspects of appearing reality and emphasizes that we must pay attention to its lateral aspects, precisely because the lateral aspects make us aware of the density of Being.

B. IS MERLEAU-PONTY STILL A PHENOMENOLOGIST?

In our first book on Merleau-Ponty we pointed out that Merleau-Ponty is not primarily an adherent of any philosophical "school." He thinks for himself. He recognizes that he is influenced by the phenomenological trend of thought, but he takes it up in his own

---

[127] "En réalité il n'y a ni moi ni autrui comme positifs, subjectivités positives. Ce sont deux antres, deux ouvertures, deux scènes où il va se passer quelque chose,—et qui appartiennent toutes deux au même monde, à la scène de l'Être." *V.I.*, p. 317.

manner. We cannot describe phenomenology and then proceed to deduce from that what Merleau-Ponty thinks. We must consider how he works out the traditional phenomenological themes, and it is possible that they have an entirely new meaning in his works. We will therefore briefly examine the meaning which the traditional phenomenological themes obtain in Merleau-Ponty's last book.

Intentionality. He does not deny intentionality, because man is indeed a subject confronted with an object. But this is not the final truth of human existence. The phenomenon which appears to us as an object is a frontal datum which easily leads us to forget the more important lateral aspects. He writes: "If Being reveals itself, it does so to a subject which transcends itself, and not to an intentional subject. Being which reveals itself is the savage Being which is hidden in darkness. It comes to itself in man. It is perceptible Being which perceives itself in man."[128] The intentional relationship is only an aspect of human life, and not even the most important one. The intentional relationship implies opposition between the subject and the object. Merleau-Ponty does not deny that this opposition exists. But if we focus our attention on this opposition, on the intentional relationship, we will never be open to the revelation of Being. Exclusive attention to the intentional relationship narrows our view down to the frontal aspects of appearing reality and blinds us to Being. We become aware of Being when we pay attention to the lateral aspects of the intentional relationship itself. Then we transcend ourselves. Transcendence means more, however, than viewing an object. The object, precisely as an object, is essentially related to the subject. We do not transcend ourselves just because we recognize the object; we transcend ourselves when we recognize the common density of Being which involves both the subject and the object, when we become aware that this density of Being exceeds both the subject and the object. Then we reduce the clarity of the intentional relationship to an underlying darkness, to "savage Being."[129]

---

[128] "Si l'être doit se dévoiler, ce sera devant une transcendance, et non devant une intentionnalité, ce sera l'être brut enlisé qui revient à lui-même, ce sera le *sensible* qui se creuse." *V.I.*, p. 263. We give here our own free translation.

[129] "L'être et l'imaginaire sont pour Sartre des 'objets', des 'étants'."
"Pour moi ils sont des 'éléments' (au sens de Bachelard), c'est-à-dire non pas des objets, mais des champs, être doux, non-thétique, être avant l'être,—et d'ailleurs comportant leur auto-inscription leur 'corrélat subjectif' fait partie d'eux. La *Rotempfindung* fait partie du Rotempfundene—ceci n'est pas *coïncidence,* mais déhiscence qui se sait telle." *V.I.*, p. 320.

This implies a most remarkable re-evaluation of the intentional relationship; it is no longer the first nor the ultimate truth of philosophical knowledge. This does not mean that Merleau-Ponty denies the intentional relationship, for the *en-être* reveals itself only within the intentional relationship, thus we cannot delete it in order to consider the *en-être*. But, the *en-être* has become more important than the intentional relationship.

Reduction. Consequently, the phenomenological reduction, according to Merleau-Ponty, is the awareness of the *en-être* in any intentional relationship. Husserl bracketed real Being in order to penetrate into the most basic intentional relationships. Nothing is more alien to Merleau-Ponty. According to him the philosopher discovers the truth of the intentional relationship only if he becomes aware of the density of Being which supports the intentional relationship.

We have already seen that Merleau-Ponty considers the eidetic reduction a myth with which we must break. The philosopher is interested in Being. Being, however, does not have an essence which can be expressed in an idea. In Being there is a fundamental style, which style is more than a fact but less than an essence. Husserl's eidetic reduction is of no use, therefore, to the philosopher.

Merleau-Ponty no longer accepts the simple intentional relationship, the phenomenological reduction or the eidetic reduction in their traditional meanings. He focuses his attention on that which Husserl bracketed. Can we still call Merleau-Ponty a phenomenologist? In our first book we hesitated to call Merleau-Ponty either a phenomenologist or the philosopher of the "body-subject." Now we propose to call him the philosopher of *en-être*.

Merleau-Ponty and Phenomenology. In May, 1960, however, Merleau-Ponty wrote a note in which he defends phenomenology, and the manner in which he writes implies that he still considers himself a phenomenologist.[130] François Bresson attacked phenomenology, saying that this philosophy tries to describe the qualitative aspects of reality, and that such a description expresses an experience which cannot be expressed objectively. Real scientific communication, he concluded, is impossible in this realm. Merleau-Ponty first answers *ad hominem*. What do scientific psychologists speak of if they try to avoid speaking of

---

[130] *V.I.,* pp. 305-306.

phenomena? Their "facts" make no sense if they do not make us aware of phenomena which we have forgotten. Qualitative aspects of reality, Merleau-Ponty continues, seem to be obscure and inaccessible to those who are not writers. Writers, on the contrary, speak of the qualitative aspects of reality; readers understand them and feel that their experiences have been expressed. In the same way perceptible reality is a source of inspiration to the philosopher (who is also a writer). Perceptible reality is an inexhaustible source of philosophical expression. The phenomenologists utilize this source, and they are understood and utilized even by those thinkers who say that phenomenology is an impossible endeavor. The basic aspect of reality, viz., the perceptible, is inexpressible for those thinkers who are not philosophers or writers. The reason for this is not that there is nothing to say about perceptible reality, but that many people are not able to say it.[131]

It is clear that shortly before his death Merleau-Ponty still considered himself a phenomenologist. How is this possible since he interprets all the essential themes of phenomenology in a way that is alien to Husserl's interpretation? In his article, "The Philosopher and His Shadow," Merleau-Ponty establishes that behind the explicit statements of Husserl there is an obscure awareness of a deeper realm of reality. Yet Husserl only implicitly expressed this deeper awareness. Merleau-Ponty admits that there is an immense difference between Husserl's explicit philosophy and his own. How then does he consider himself as a phenomenologist?

The answer is not difficult. Merleau-Ponty feels that he is entirely supported by the phenomenological tradition. Without this tradition his own philosophy would simply not have existed. This tradition prompted him to think of the intentional relationship. Thinking of it, he penetrated to the *en-être* which supports our intentional life. The *en-être* exceeds and transcends intentionality, but Merleau-Ponty discovered his basic point of view with the help of the phenomenological tradition. Merleau-Ponty does not wonder at the fact that he is supported by the phenomenological tradition and yet transcends it. When the real philosopher is supported by some tradition, he utilizes it in order to say what has not yet been said. To use a tradition is likewise to transcend it. The thinker who merely repeats a tradition is not a real

---

[131] "Le fond des choses est qu'en effet le sensible n'offre rien qu'on puisse dire si l'on n'est pas philosophe ou écrivain, mais cela ne tient pas à ce qu'il serait un en Soi ineffable, mais à ce qu'on ne sait pas dire." *V.I.*, p. 306.

philosopher. Real philosophy is not a "spoken word" but a "speaking word." A philosophy exists in a static way only after the philosopher has died or when he ceases to be a real philosopher. Merleau-Ponty is convinced that he does not deny phenomenology but contributes to the revelation of its real meaning. His last work demonstrates the metaphysical impact of the phenomenological tradition. And for this reason *The Visible and the Invisible* is an important contribution to the actual discussion of the relationship between phenomenology and metaphysics.

C. CONTINUITY AND EVOLUTION IN
MERLEAU-PONTY'S PHILOSOPHY

We have gradually become aware of the metaphysical implications of Merleau-Ponty's new philosophical perspective. He criticizes his former works because they stressed too much the relationship between subject and object. When he called the realm of silence a "silent cogito," he implicitly introduced even there a distance between subject and object. In the last period of his life he refuses to regard this distance as the most original datum. In commenting on the only positive chapter of his final work—the other chapters were either introductory or a criticism of other philosophers—it has become clear to us why Merleau-Ponty refuses to accept the subject-object relationship as the most original datum. The basic truth of Merleau-Ponty's matured philosophy is expressed in the sentence "I belong to it," *J'en suis*.

One sentence cannot express, of course, a basic philosophical truth. To the sentence "I belong to it," another must be added: "It belongs to me." These two sentences embody Merleau-Ponty's basic awareness of *en-être*. The perceiving subject is a perceptible reality and perceptible reality is the "flesh of the world." The subject and the object are opposed, but the opposed terms are permeated with one and the same Being. They belong essentially together. Their unity precedes their opposition, and the opposition is possible only because it is an opposition within a unity. The unity continues to exist even when there is opposition. The "seeing visible" can transform the visible world into a field which surrounds it because it belongs to visible reality itself.

The basic awareness of the *en-être* determines Merleau-Ponty's criticism of other trends of thought and of other philosophical systems. He criticizes science because it approaches both physical and psychic reality as objects, because it forgets that the subject of science belongs to its object—that the object, therefore, is originally not an object. Science forgets the *en-être*. Reflective philosophy also forgets the *en-être*. Removing the reflecting subject from its worldly density and obscurity, and reducing the worldly datum to an ideal object, it forgets that both the subject and the object are originally involved in one and the same density of Being. Sartre makes the same mistake by defining human consciousness as "nothingness." The *en-être* is denied as soon as human consciousness is considered to be "nothingness." Husserl focuses his attention on essences and considers them ideal objects. The ideal object, however, has been shaken loose from the density of the *en-être*.

The *en-être* expresses the basic viewpoint of Merleau-Ponty. Yet the reader of *The Visible and the Invisible* does not easily notice this. Merleau-Ponty neither sets forth his basic awareness at the beginning of his book, nor does he treat all its chapters clearly in the light of this basic awareness. It emerges from the book as a whole rather than as a clear principle stated at the beginning. This harmonizes well with Merleau-Ponty's general style of writing. He does not write after having clearly achieved his own thought. Kant wrote his *Critique of Pure Reason* after he had fully worked out his insight, or at least, after he thought he had done so. The conclusion of Kant's book is clearly there from the very beginning. This is certainly not the way in which Merleau-Ponty writes. He is in search of his own thought. When he starts to write he does not know yet, at least not clearly, where he will arrive. When we read Merleau-Ponty's works we are allowed to witness the birth of a philosophy.

Why does Merleau-Ponty do this? Would it not be better to follow Kant's method, namely, to write only after one's thought has been achieved? Merleau-Ponty does not do so because he is convinced that philosophical thought is never fully accomplished.[132] Not even Kant's philosophy was fully accomplished. The relationship between phenomenon and noumenon was its central theme, and here Kant certainly did not achieve his thought. He proposed his interpretation of the relationship between phenomenon and noumenon as final, but it was by no means final. Merleau-Ponty is sensitive to the fact that there is no final interpretation of any basic aspect of reality, that all interpretations

---

[132] "La philosophie 'reste question', elle interroge le monde et la chose, elle reprend, répète ou imite leur cristallisation devant nous." *V.I.*, p. 136.

must be interpreted again.[133] He wants to leave his own interpretations open. No matter how much or how clearly he knows, he is still searching, and he writes with this attitude. He does not say that we cannot arrive at some knowledge, but he knows that all knowledge is open toward a future. No wonder, then, that a basic awareness emerges from Merleau-Ponty's books, an awareness that becomes clearer toward the end than it was at the beginning. This, needless to say, makes the reading of Merleau-Ponty's books rather difficult.

We now see the *en-être* as Merleau-Ponty's basic awareness. Does this imply a radical rupture with his former works? Does the passage from phenomenology to metaphysics imply a radical break with his initial phenomenology? We do not think so. Merleau-Ponty never considered the opposition between subject and object the ultimate truth. He never felt himself completely at ease with this opposition. In *Phenomenology of Perception* he stressed that man is originally a body-subject. The body-subject is a dialectical interchange with the world on a pre-objective level. In *Sense and Non-Sense* he wrote explicitly that intentionality is at root, not a relationship of knowledge, but a relationship of Being.[134] He always felt that the opposition between subject and object was not the most original datum, that it was preceded by something else, by something deeper. Yet he did not succeed in expressing this deeper reality, since he continued to conceive it as a dialectical relationship, as an interchange. He was too much caught by the phenomenological notion of "intentionality" and could not free himself from the dualism implied in it. He felt that he should transcend this dualism, and at times succeeded; but when he raised objections he would fall back into dualism. He could not turn sufficiently toward the lateral aspects of appearing reality, because he was caught up too much by the frontal aspects.

There is continuity in Merleau-Ponty's philosophy. According to *Phenomenology of Perception* the body-subject is a "logic of the world," and it knows more about the world than I do as a conscious subject. The body is intrinsically adapted to the world and the world to the body. Meaning is constituted within the dialectical interchange between the body-subject and the world, and this constitution of meaning seems to be the fulfillment postulated both by the body and by the world. The

---

[133] "A partir de là, élaborer un idée de la philosophie: elle ne peut être prise totale et active, possession intellectuelle." *V.I.,* p. 319.

[134] *Sense and Non-Sense,* p. 72.

dialectical relationship between the body-subject and the world seems to imply, therefore, an intrinsic affinity between both. In our earlier criticism of Merleau-Ponty we raised the objection that he presupposed this affinity, but at the same time did not explain it. Nevertheless, the implicit affirmation of the affinity was there. If he had denied it he would have undermined his essential positions. But he did not explicitly reflect on this affinity. He does so in *The Visible and the Invisible*. The continuity, then, consists in making explicit what was implicit in his former works. This kind of continuity, however, implies a rupture. Merleau-Ponty now stresses that the same Being penetrates both man and world, and that the dialectical relationship, the intentional opposition, takes place within common Being. Emphasizing this viewpoint gives new meaning to all his former positions. Far from denying his former positions, he now speaks of them in a new manner.

D. APPLICATIONS OF THE *"EN-ÊTRE"*

We have seen that the *en-être* has become a basic notion of Merleau-Ponty's new philosophy, and we have asked whether this fact compelled him to change his attitude toward phenomenology, to break with his former positions. Having found rather a continuity of thought, we will now examine some applications of this basic notion.

We saw in the second chapter that Merleau-Ponty comes to realize the importance of the *en-être* in his analysis of seeing. "He who sees belongs to the visible and is situated in it."[135] Sartre inaccurately describes the visible as Being and the seeing person as nothingness. There is a pre-established harmony between our look and visible reality. In and through our look Being actualizes its own visibility. The preceding chapters described this and we will no longer labor the point.

Merleau-Ponty extends this awareness to all experiences. We *are* experiences which feel behind them the weight of space, time and Being.[136] We think of space, time and Being, and at the same time we feel their weight behind us. Merleau-Ponty wants to say that space, time and Being are not just objects in front of us but are also behind us as aspects of our own being. The variety of spatial and temporal beings

---

[135] "Celui qui voit en est et y est." *V.I.*, p. 136.
[136] "Nous sommes des expériences, c'est-à-dire des pensées, qui éprouvent la pesée derrière elles de l'espace, du temps, de l'Être même qu'elles pensent." *V.I.*, p. 155.

that we experience is real, and so is the serial aspect that the world takes on. The serial variety of things, however, is supported by a deeper unity of Being.

Distance. Merleau-Ponty explains that in this way we know reality which is distant from us. The philosopher is often led astray by the ideal of perfect coincidence. Reflective philosophy considers the matter of knowledge to be an ideal object; the ideal object can be absorbed by the interiority of thought. The Sartrian consiousness is nothingness; nothing separates us, therefore, from things; we can be entirely present to them, without any distance. The awareness of the *en-être,* on the contrary, makes us realize that we are at a distance from surrounding things without being separated from them.[137] We emerge from the world and are surrounded by it, but we belong to it and are permeated with it.

The Body. Merleau-Ponty tries to understand the enigma of our body in the light of the *en-être.* The human body is, indeed, a most remarkable reality. It is a thing among all other things, and yet it is openness to all things. If we use the notions of subject and object we must say that our body is at once both object and subject. This simple fact, however, implies unexpected relationships between the subjective and the objective orders.[138] It cannot be accidental that our body is both subject and object. The fact that they coincide in the one reality of our body demonstrates that the two orders belong essentially together, that the two orders are fundamentally one. A particular being actualizes the perceptibility of all Being. Both the subjective and the objective orders arise at the same time from the intrinsic unity of Being. Being unfolds itself in the subjective and the objective orders without losing its intrinsic unity. Our body is the fulfillment of this event. Our body manifests the unity of Being and reveals that Being can be dual without ceasing to be one.

Time. We must understand time also in the light of the *en-être.*[139] Time must not be conceived as a discontinuous series in which each new moment reduces all former moments to the past. In so doing we deny the unity of time. We do not save the unity of time by posing a

---

[137] "L'immédiat est à l'horizon, et doit être pensé à ce titre, ce n'est qu'en restant à distance qu'il reste lui-même." *V.I.* p. 164.

[138] *V.I.,* p. 181.

[139] "Il faut que le temps se *constitue,*—soit toujours vu du point de vue de quelqu'un qui *en est.*" *V.I.,* p. 237.

transcendental subject which surveys all time. Such a transcendental subject does not explain the intrinsic unity of time. Time does exist, of course, for a subject, for otherwise we could not explain the coexistence of its dimensions within the present. But the subject which constitutes time must belong to it (*qui en est*). The temporal subject *is* the unity of time. Being is transformed into an appearing world because a particular being transforms itself into the awareness of Being. In the same way Being becomes temporal because a particular being temporalizes itself and assumes everything into its own temporalization.

Figure and Field. In a very interesting but rather difficult note of May, 1959,[140] Merleau-Ponty again raises the problem of the subject-object relationship. His reflection is occasioned by the words of Bergson: "A consciousness which is at the same time spontaneous and reflective."[141] According to Merleau-Ponty, Bergson is looking for the notion of *en-être* without finding it, because he is too strongly attached to the ideal of immediate knowledge, knowledge without any distance. It would take too much space to adequately discuss this long and involved note, but we must mention its last lines. To be aware of something, Merleau-Ponty says, means that something appears as a "figure" within a "field." Our awareness disappears as soon as the field is no longer articulated, viz., as soon as the "figure-field" structure dissolves.[142]

Merleau-Ponty gives a most remarkable interpretation of this structure. The distinction between figure and field, he says, calls for a third term between subject and object. The figure arises from the field—it stands out. The term Merleau-Ponty uses here is *s'écarter,* which often occurs in *The Visible and the Invisible.* This "standing out" originally constitutes perceptive meaning. Merleau-Ponty's meaning is not obvious. He does not say that the "standing out" is a third term between figure and field, but between subject and object. What is the relationship between the "standing out" of the figure from the field and the distinction of subject and object? Merleau-Ponty probably wants to say that the subject stands out from Being just as the figure stands out

---

[140] *V.I.,* pp. 247-250.

[141] *V.I.,* p. 247. This sentence of Henri Bergson is found in *La Pensée et le Mouvant,* Paris, 1934, p. 10.

[142] "Comprendre que le 'avoir conscience'—avoir une figure sur un fond, et qu'il disparaît par désarticulation—la distinction figure-fond introduit un troisième terme entre le 'sujet' et l' 'objet'. C'est cet *écart-là* d'abord qui est le *sens* perceptif." *V.I.,* p. 250.

from the field. The figure comes into existence because it stands out from the field in which it remains. In the same way the subject comes into existence in its standing out from Being. The entire note deals with the articulation of Being. The subject is the result of an articulation of Being to which the subject continues to belong.

"Standing Out" from Being. It would be interesting to continue this metaphysical reflection on the figure-field structure for Merleau-Ponty's note is not at all exhaustive. What is the field from which the figure stands out? The figure can stand out from a particular field, but ultimately it stands out from Being, our final field of existence. We could distinguish objective and subjective "standing out"; the "standing out" of the figure from the field corresponds to the "standing out" of the subject from Being. The more a subject becomes a subject the more outstanding becomes the figure. Merleau-Ponty's text inspires such comments, but this is not the place to make them.

We "stand out" from Being, and we do so first of all in our corporal existence. Merleau-Ponty obviously concludes that we are sensitive to the meaning of Being through our "carnal participation" in Being.[143] Being is the original silent Being, and our primordial participation in it is also silent. We first participate in the meaning of Being because our body adapts itself to it. When we lose contact with our body, we also lose contact with Being.

Body and World. Our body, Merleau-Ponty writes in a note of May, 1960, is entirely worldly, while the world participates in the being of our body. The perceived world is, therefore, thoroughly subjective, and at the same time thoroughly material. Man is worldly and the world is human. Our body is not just a particular perceptible datum, but is the perceptible datum which measures all perceptible data.[144] Our

---

[143] "Il s'agit de ce 'logos' qui se prononce silencieusement dans chaque chose sensible, en tant qu'elle varie autour d'un certain type de message, dont nous ne pouvons avoir idée que par notre participation charnelle à son sens, qu'en épousant par notre corps sa manière de 'signifier'." *V.I.,* p. 261.

[144] ". . . nous sommes déjà *dans* l'être ainsi décrit, que nous *en sommes,* qu'entre lui et nous, il y a *Einfühlung.*"
"Cela veut dire que mon corps est fait de la même chair que le monde (c'est un perçu), et que de plus cette chair de mon corps est participée par le monde, il la *reflète,* il empiète sur elle et elle empiète sur lui (le senti à la fois comble de subjectivité et comble de matérialité), ils sont dans rapport de transgression ou d'enjambement—Ceci encore veut dire: mon corps n'est pas seulement un perçu parmi les perçus, il est mesurant de tous." *V.I.,* p. 302.

body is that sector of the accessible world by which the whole world becomes accessible.

We have briefly stated some applications of Merleau-Ponty's basic awareness, *en-être*. It is impossible to comment on all the consequences this has, simply because Merleau-Ponty himself had no time to fully develop it. These few examples, however, bring out the importance of this notion.

E. REFLECTION ON BEING

Merleau-Ponty's notion *en-être* expresses the fact that both our body and the world in which it is situated belong to Being. In another note of May, 1960,[145] Merleau-Ponty explains why the access to Being is difficult for us to see. He speaks of the "blind spot" of human consciousness. Our consciousness is necessarily blind to something. It does not see what makes possible its vision of everything else.[146] Consciousness does not see that which makes it see, viz., its involvement in Being. It is difficult for our consciousness to see that it is rooted in the body, and through the body in Being. Our consciousness is blind to its own existential characteristics which are the source of the visibility of the world and the existence of objects.

It seems almost inevitable that our consciousness should mystify itself by forgetting its own roots. We can hardly avoid preferring the object to Being.[147] What is the object? It is a being which has been set free of its context, of its connection with the subject. The position of the object, as an object, is the result of this rupture.[148] The positive character of the object depends upon its withdrawal from its birthplace. The positive character of the object makes us forget Being. We sacrifice

---

[145] *V.I.,* pp. 301-302.

[146] "Ce *qu'elle* ne voit pas, c'est pour des raisons de principe qu'elle ne le voit pas, c'est parce qu'elle est conscience qu'elle ne le voit pas. *Ce qu'*elle ne voit pas, c'est ce qui en elle prépare la vision du reste (comme la rétine est aveugle au point d'où se répandent en elle les fibres qui permettront la vision). *Ce qu'* elle ne voit pas, c'est ce qui fait qu'elle voit, c'est son attache à l'Être, c'est sa corporeité, ce sont les existentiaux par lesquels le monde devient visible, c'est la chair où naît l'*objet.*" *Ibid.*

[147] "Il est inévitable que la conscience soit mystifiée, inversée, indirecte, par principe elle voit les choses *par l'autre bout,* par principe elle méconnaît l'Être et lui préfère l'objet." *V.I.,* p. 302.

[148] ". . . l'objet, c'est-à-dire un Être avec lequel elle a rompu, et qu'elle pose par-delà cette négation, en niant cette négation." *Ibid.*

Being to have objects. Quite naturally, therefore, our consciousness thus becomes blind to Being.

What is Being? It is the common source of both subject and object. It co-appears in everything that appears, but in revealing itself it hides itself. It constitutes the accessibility of all that is accessible and yet is not directly accessible itself. A note dated January, 1959,[149] identifies Being with the perceptible world. Merleau-Ponty even says that Heidegger's *"das Sein"* should be understood as the perceptible world.[150] Merleau-Ponty's terminology is, however, confusing. We could understand perception as an act and then take the many successive perceptions as having a certain coherence. If we understand perception as an act, the perceptible world becomes the totality of perceived objects—a totality that is, of course, never completed. But when Merleau-Ponty in this context speaks of perception and of the perceptible world, he does not mean to speak of perception as an act nor of the perceptible world as a totality of objects. When we examined Merleau-Ponty's self-criticism, we saw that he does not like to speak of successive acts and that he even hesitates to speak of perception for this reason. In this note he uses the term "perceptive world" in a more fundamental sense. He indicates by this term not a totality of objects, but the source of all objects. The "perceptive world" is "savage Being" not yet ordered as a whole of objects by our isolated acts.

We order our world by ordering our activities. When we learn proper behavior we give a clear meaning to the things we handle. When we learn to see, we give rise to objects which stand out as figures in the worldly field. By speaking we transform aspects of the world into ideal meanings. Ordering our acts is equal to ordering our world. Our own "savage being" underlies our ordered life and the "savage world" underlies the ordered world. Our own "savage being" and the "savage world" together are "savage Being."[151]

"Savage Being" is accessible in everything that is accessible, but it is not directly accessible in itself. We are always in touch with it, and still we can never directly touch it. This is the "Being" of Merleau-Ponty

---

[149] *V.I.*, pp. 223-224.

[150] "Ce monde perceptif est au fond l'Être au sens de Heidegger." *V.I.*, p. 223.

[151] ". . . j'ouvre l'accès à un Être brut avec lequel je ne serai pas dans le rapport du *sujet et de l'objet,* et encore moins dans le rapport de l'effet avec la cause. *V.I.*, p. 276.

and, according to him, it is also Heidegger's *"das Sein."* We do not know whether Merleau-Ponty intends this to be an interpretation of what Heidegger himself actually says, or whether he only expresses what he thinks Heidegger should say. The note is not clear on this point.

We said that Merleau-Ponty's identification of "perceptive world" and "Being" is confusing because "perceptive world" could be understood as the totality of perceptible objects. His terminology is also confusing for another reason. One could think that Being, since it is identified with the perceptible world, is only the source of perception. This is certainly not the intention of Merleau-Ponty. Being is the source of all human activities, of perception and speech, of science and philosophy, of artistic expression and labor, of literature and music. Being is the perpetual source of our orderly life and of our orderly world. It is the source of all our innovations. Science, philosophy, art, work—they all renew themselves in this source. Merleau-Ponty calls Being the *logos endiathetos* (the pre-verbal logos) which provokes the *logos prophorikos* (the verbal logos). All our expressions manifest the latent richness of Being.[152] This richness, however, is accessible only in our expressions.

Being is active in our activity. A note of November, 1959,[153] criticizes philosophy for not sufficiently speaking of the passivity of our activity. It is true that we set about projects, and that we are active while doing so. The activity of our individual personality, however, does not entirely explain what we produce. Our projects are born in the heart of Being.[154] They are inserted into the current of time passing through us. They are based upon that fundamental orientation of our life which we usually ignore; yet their meaning, at the same time, gives direction.

Thinking and Being. These sentences of Merleau-Ponty express a real experience. On the one hand, our projects are new and they are ours. On the other, we feel, especially when our projects are really

---

[152] "Ce monde perceptif est au fond l'Être au sens de Heidegger qui est plus que toute peinture, que toute parole, que toute 'attitude', et qui, saisi par la philosophie dans son universalité, apparaît comme contenant tout ce qui sera jamais dit, et nous laissant pourtant, à le créer (Proust): c'est le logos endiathetos qui appelle le logos prophorikos." *V.I.,* pp. 223-224.

[153] *V.I.,* pp. 274-275.

[154] "Si neuves que soient nos initiatives, elles naissent au coeur de l'être." *V.I.,* p. 274.

valuable and when they are successful, that they are obvious and that we must take them.   How can they be obvious, since they imply a rupture with the situation which exists in fact?   Being works in us.   It makes us feel that its existing expressions are inadequate.   It brings about in us and through us a new expression of itself.

We are always thinking, says Merleau-Ponty.   We are a thinking existence.   Thinking is more a situation than an act.   We cannot stop thinking because we are open to a *field* of thought, and in this field things are present or absent.[155]   Thinking fundamentally is not an activity of our soul nor do we produce thoughts.   We do not bring about our own openness.   We do not make ourselves think any more than we make our heart beat.[156]   Creative scientists know this because solutions often come to mind, not at the moment when they are thinking intensely, but when they are not at all concentrating on their problem.   We activate our thought, but we do not constitute it.   We *find* ourselves thinking, just as we find ourselves seeing and perceiving.   We must give up, Merleau-Ponty believes, that philosophy which describes life as a succession of acts.   We are active, but our activity is the activation of what is already there.   Being thinks in us.   Being is active in our activity.   Our clarity is, consequently, not completely due to our own activity.

To say that we are an access to Being does not mean that we reproduce Being in our interior lives.   Merleau-Ponty rejects the idea that our knowledge is a reproduction.   Being is not an object, but the source of all objects.   This does not mean, however, that Being is a cause which produces effects in us.   Being is co-appearing in all that appears to us and it is active within our activity.   It does not produce something in us without us.

Being should not be conceived, Merleau-Ponty remarks, in a note of November, 1959, as the God of Leibniz.[157]   This God coordinates all monads in such a way that they do not coordinate themselves.   We coordinate ourselves because we are aware of Being.   However, several of Leibniz' points are quite applicable here.   We can say with Leibniz that each outlook on the world is a world in itself, that the private realm of

---

[155] "L'âme pense toujours: c'est en elle une propriété d'état, elle ne peut pas ne pas penser parce qu'un champ a été ouvert où s'inscrit toujours *quelque chose* ou l'*absence* de quelque chose.   Ce n'est pas là une activité de l'âme, ni une production de pensées au pluriel."   *V.I.*, pp. 274-275.

[156] "Ce n'est pas moi qui me fais penser pas plus que ce n'est pas moi qui fais battre mon coeur."   *V.I.*, p. 275.

[157] *V.I.*, p. 276.

each access to the world is of interest to all, that all the monads express one another and the world and yet that they are distinguished as different perspectives. But all these facts must be explained, not by the influence of an exterior God, but by the lateral accessibility of one and the same Being.

"Savage Being," Merleau-Ponty noted in September, 1959,[158] is our original realm of existence. It conditions the intelligibility of all that is intelligible.[159] It conditions our mutual accessibility. We can understand one another because we are rooted in the same Being. It assures the continuity of our own life, a continuity which we find and which we do not constitute. Merleau-Ponty speaks of the *"Vorhabe des Seins"*[160]*:* we are in contact with Being and we do not bring about this contact by our own activity. We activate this contact, but we always presuppose it. This *"Vorhabe des Seins"* is not a form of knowledge in the common sense of the word; we do not know Being as science knows its objects. But the intelligibility of scientific objects is conditioned by our access to Being. Science presupposes that of which philosophy speaks, but science itself cannot speak of it. Science, consequently, needs philosophy. But philosophy can never know its matter as science knows its objects.

Metaphysical Mysticism? Merleau-Ponty's reflections on Being bring us face to face with a fundamental question. He appeals to a fundamental reality, a final ground of all realities, which co-appears in everything which appears, but which does not directly appear itself. We cannot speak of it in clear words since our clear words are related to clear phenomena; Being, however, is not a clear phenomenon at all. The words which point to Being are always obscure. Does this way of speaking make sense? Is Merleau-Ponty's newest philosophy a form of metaphysical mysticism?

But this is not posing the question correctly. People who speak or write about music have always spoken, and will continue to speak, in an enigmatic style; they have used and will continue to use metaphors. We have no right to attack this, because the object itself demands this

---

[158] *V.I.,* pp. 256-258.

[159] "L'essentiel, décrire l'Être vertical ou sauvage comme ce milieu pré-spirituel sans lequel rien n'est pensable, pas même l'esprit." *V.I.,* p. 257.

[160] "La philosophie est l'étude de la *Vorhabe* de l'Être, *Vorhabe* qui n'est pas *connaissance,* certes, qui est en défaut envers la connaissance, l'opération, mais qui les enveloppe comme l'Être enveloppe les êtres." *Ibid.*

manner of speaking. We cannot speak of art with mathematical clarity.

The real question is this: Is it true that philosophical reflection compels us to assume an almost contradictory attitude, viz., to focus our attention on a realm of reality which cannot be directly observed because it only co-appears in all appearing reality? Merleau-Ponty, in fact, tries to do just that. He says, on the one hand, that the philosopher must concentrate on Being. As long as he does not view Being, he does not arrive at the ultimate realm of philosophical reflection. The philosopher is superficial until he speaks of Being. But, on the other hand, Merleau-Ponty says, Being is not directly accessible; it only co-appears; it is a field which can never become a figure.

Philosophy seems to be an almost impossible task. It must view what essentially withdraws itself from our view. It must speak of that which cannot be transformed into an ideal object. Merleau-Ponty tries to do what can hardly be done. Should we accept such a description of philosophy?

We have no right to determine *a priori* what philosophy is, nor to attempt to subject philosophy to such claims. Yet some thinkers, impressed by the clarity of mathematics and the exact sciences, formulate the conditions of clear knowledge and proclaim that philosophy must measure up to such conditions. If philosophy is conceived in this sense Merleau-Ponty is not a philosopher at all. But such claims cannot be *a priori* superimposed on philosophy. Philosophy is radical reflection on our lives, on our situation, on our world, on Being. If this radical reflection makes us aware of the fact that the ultimate realm of reality is obscure, that it is not directly accessible, that it does not directly appear but only co-appears, then Merleau-Ponty is right. Then the attitude of the philosopher is extremely difficult and almost contradictory. Then philosophy tries to say what can hardly be said.

Merleau-Ponty's philosophy is truly metaphysical because its last word is Being. In this sense he has a certain similarity to Heidegger. Like Heidegger, Merleau-Ponty finally asks the question of Being. Merleau-Ponty, too, stresses that man is involved in the question of Being; he, too, emphasizes that Being is obscure. There is, however, an immense difference between the two philosophers. Merleau-Ponty explains why Being is obscure, he explains why we cannot conceive it in a clear manner; he does not mystify anything at all. He only indicates a mysterious realm in which we are involved—this involvement is our human being. Both Heidegger and Merleau-Ponty are obscure, but Merleau-Ponty explains why his philosophy is obscure. Merleau-Ponty never gives the impression that he knows more than he actually expresses. He professes his own ignorance and explains why he does not know.

F. THE PROBLEM OF GOD

In our first book on Merleau-Ponty's philosophy, we wrote that he was an atheist and indicated why his philosophy had to be atheistic.[161] Close acquaintances know that he was no longer an atheist toward the end of his life. Sartre gives a simplified explanation of this change. Merleau-Ponty, Sartre says, enjoyed a happy youth because of his mother. He loved his mother, and when she died he could not believe that she no longer existed. This, according to Sartre, was why Merleau-Ponty could no longer be an atheist.[162] Such psychological explanations hardly account for fundamental changes of a writer's viewpoint.

There is a very clear reason why Merleau-Ponty's philosophy is no longer atheistic: the foundation of his atheism has disappeared. We do not say that Merleau-Ponty's new philosophy makes him positively accept the existence of God, but only that the former foundation of his atheism has disappeared.

Our earlier study indicated the fundamental reason for Merleau-Ponty's atheism. His philosophy was a philosophy of meaning. Meaning comes into existence, he thought, within the dialectical interchange between man and world. The encounter of man and world is the primary source of all meaning. Consequently, all meaning is conditioned by man's presence. But man's presence is a contingent fact. Contingency is therefore the final truth of philosophical reflection.

Merleau-Ponty considered it absolutely futile to seek a cause of man's contingent presence. To do so we would need a starting point for such a reflection. This starting point would always have to be some form of meaning. But all meaning presupposes man's presence. How could we explain man's presence itself? We cannot explain what is presupposed in every explanation. Contingency remains the final truth of philosophical reflection. Merleau-Ponty added that we destroy the contingency if

---

[161] Kwant, *The Phenomenological Philosophy of Merleau-Ponty*, pp. 128-149.
[162] Jean-Paul Sartre, *"Merleau-Ponty vivant,"* *Les Temps Modernes*, vol. 17, no. 184-185, October 1961, p. 360.

we assign a cause to it. The acceptance of God as the supreme cause of man's contingent presence would destroy the base of philosophy.

In his mature philosophy Merleau-Ponty no longer considers contingency the basic truth of philosophy. The intentional relationship, the dialectical interchange between man and world, is no longer the final source of all meaning. Merleau-Ponty does not deny the intentional relationship between man and world, but he affirms that this opposition is situated within a more fundamental unity, viz., the unity of Being. The unity of Being precedes, at least logically, the dialectical opposition. "The flesh of the world and my flesh," writes Merleau-Ponty," is not contingency, not chaos."[163] With contingency failing as the final truth of philosophy, the foundation of Merleau-Ponty's atheism disappears.

It would be wrong to say that Merleau-Ponty now poses the problem of God in a positive way. In a note of March, 1961, he writes that he will avoid every compromise with humanism, naturalism and theology.[164] Thus it is extremely improbable that he would have written on the problem of God.

There are only a few remarks concerning God in his last book. In February, 1959, he notes the deep crisis of philosophical reflection and adds that both classical philosophy—he does not explain this term—and "philosophies of the death of God" have become questionable.[165] This strengthens our statement that he abandons atheistic philosophy.

In a note of October, 1959,[166] he considers Leibniz' *Theodicea.* Leibniz summarized the efforts of Christians to reconcile their concept of the absolute necessity of Being with the contingent development of "savage Being." Leibniz proposed a compromise in which the latter was sacrificed to the former. This implies, according to Merleau-Ponty, that the "hidden God" is sacrificed to the *Ens realissimum,*[167] viz., that the "hidden God" is reduced to a rational construction. This text shows that Merleau-Ponty continues to reject the abstract God of rationalistic reflection. He can accept only a "hidden God," but he does not explain this biblical expression.

We find also an obscure text which could refer to the problem of God. We interrogate our experience, he says, in order to know how that

---

[163] *V.I.*, p. 192.
[164] *V.I.*, p. 328.
[165] *V.I.*, p. 236.
[166] *V.I.*, p. 264.
[167] "Le dieu caché étant sacrifié à l'Ens realissimum." *Ibid.*

experience opens us to what is distinguished from us. Then a remarkable sentence follows: "We cannot exclude the possibility that in our experience we will discover a movement toward that which in no case could be present to us itself; its irremediable absence could belong to the number of our original experiences."[168] This text is too broad and too isolated to allow any positive conclusion. But Merleau-Ponty does not rule out the possibility that our experience might compel us to accept the existence of a reality which is not present to us itself.[169]

---

[168] *"Il n'est pas même exclu par là que nous trouvions en elle un mouvement vers ce qui ne saurait en aucun cas nous être présent en original et dont l'absence irrémédiable compterait ainsi au nombre de nos expériences originaires."* V.I., p. 211.

[169] There has been some change in Merleau-Ponty's conception of Christianity. In his article "Faith and Good Faith" (*Sense and Non-Sense,* pp. 172-181), Merleau-Ponty objected that Christianity always vacillates between the Eternal Father who "surveys" history and the Son of God who entered into history. In his article "Indirect Language and the Voices of Silence" (*Signs,* pp. 39-83), Merleau-Ponty speaks of the distinction between "horizontal and vertical transcendence." Those who accept this distinction, he says, forget that "the Christian God wants nothing to do with a vertical relation of subordination," and that "God would not be fully God without becoming fully man." p. 71.

CONCLUSION

We have given a description of the latest development of Merleau-Ponty's philosophy, recognizing the limitation of our basis, i.e., an unfinished book and a number of notes. Still the available material allowed us to arrive at some interesting conclusions. Merleau-Ponty journied along the difficult path from phenomenology to metaphysics. This way was difficult because Husserl, the founder of Phenomenology, bracketed Being. Merleau-Ponty regained Being within the intentional relationship. Being is present in the intentional relationship itself, although not as an intentional object. Rather, the intentional relationship must be conceived as a relationship within Being.

Merleau-Ponty did not have to return to realism in order to regain Being. Being is not a reality reflected by us, since it is present in us and in the world to which we are related.

Merleau-Ponty could not develop all the consequences of his new philosophical view. But the long and difficult way he searched is both interesting and useful to all who are interested in phenomenology. They can be sure now that they need not be cut off from the metaphysical tradition of the West.

Merleau-Ponty did not develop clear metaphysical concepts and he has explained why he did not and could not give them. Metaphysicians have often sacrificed the genuine character of their research to the claims of clarity. The clear metaphysical system often stifled genuine metaphysical thought. In his philosophical fluctuations Merleau-Ponty has shown that metaphysical reflection is simply necessary for the genuine philosopher, but also that the access to metaphysical thought is difficult. It would be unjust for thinkers of a certain tradition to triumphantly say that they already knew what Merleau-Ponty has finally discovered. Merleau-Ponty would answer that metaphysics is not knowledge in the sense that these critics speak of knowledge. Metaphysics is an awareness of the sources of all knowledge. The awareness of these sources can never be transformed into knowledge in the most common sense of this word. We are aware of Being without ever knowing it as an object. This awareness cannot be taught in the way we teach other things. It has to be achieved by every genuine philosopher.   Merleau-Ponty did so.

It has been most interesting and useful to the writer of this book to follow the development of Merleau-Ponty's thought.[170]   And it is his hope that many others will have the same experience.

---

[170] The author of the present work published an earlier article on *The Visible and the Invisible:* "De ontwikkeling van Merleau-Ponty's denken," *Tijdschrift voor Filosofie,* vol. 26 (1964), pp. 627-669 (summary in French).

INDEX OF NAMES